The Illustrated Directory of
MODERN
AMERICAN
WEAPONS

Previously published as three separate volumes

The Illustrated Directory of
MODERN
AMERICAN
WEAPONS

Edited by
Ray Bonds

PRENTICE HALL PRESS
New York   London   Toronto   Sydney   Tokyo

An Arco Military Book

Published in 1986 by Prentice Hall Press,
A Division of Simon & Schuster, Inc.
Gulf + Western Building,
One Gulf + Western Plaza,
New York, NY 10023.

Originally published by Salamander Books Ltd., London.
Revised compilation of three separate volumes previously published in the United States by Arco Publishing, Inc.

This book may not be sold outside the United States of America and Canada

PRENTICE HALL PRESS is a trademark of Simon & Schuster, Inc.

Library of Congress Cataloging-in-Publication Data

Jordan, John.
    The illustrated directory of modern American weapons.

    Reprint (1st work). Originally published: An illustrated guide to the modern US Army / edited by Richard O'Neill. New York, N.Y. : Arco Pub., c1984.
    Reprint (2nd work). Originally published: An illustrated guide to the modern US Navy, the world's most advanced naval power / John Jordan. New York, N.Y. : Arco Pub., c1982.
    Reprint (3rd work). Originally published: An illustrated guide to USAF. New York, N.Y. : Arco, c1982.
    I. United States--Armed Forces--Weapons systems. I. Gunston, Bill.   II. O'Neill, Richard.   III. Illustrated guide to the modern US Army. 1986.   IV. Jordan, John. Illustrated guide to the modern US Navy, the world's most advanced naval power. 1986.   V. Illustrated guide to USAF. 1986.   VI. Title.
UF503.J67 1986   355.8'2'0973   86-12295
ISBN 0-13-938747-1 (pbk.)

10 9 8 7 6 5 4 3 2

Credits

Editor: Ray Bonds
Designer: Philip Gorton
Photographs: The publishers wish to thank all the organizations, in particular the US Department of Defense and the weapons systems manufacturers, for supplying the illustrations used in this book.
Printed in Belgium by Proost International Book Production, Turnhout.

Contents

Section One

LAND
WEAPONS
AND EQUIPMENT

Contents of Section One

Introduction

The beginning of 1986 found the US Army with global commitments on an almost unprecedented scale. In Central and Latin America and the Caribbean there are some 6,370 troops in Panama, Grenada and Nicaragua. In the Far East there are troops in Japan (2,400) and South Korea (29,750), while in the Middle East there are 1,200 in Egypt and 250 in Saudi Arabia. The major overseas concentration remains as always Western Europe with 217,100, leaving some 522,848 in the continental USA itself. Of these last 3⅓ divisions are "double-ear-marked" to both the Rapid Deployment Force (RDF) and to NATO. As the world's trouble-spots seem to increase in number, the 780,648 men and women of the US Army seem to be spread ever more thinly, and General John A. Whickham, Army Chief of Staff, has recently warned that the "current US commitments probably exceed the force capabilities".

Geopolitical factors pose considerations which affect Army structure and doctrine development, the most prominent being the problem of projecting military power abroad. Army planners need to be able to structure forces for possible deployment anywhere in the world, when the fundamental requirements of different areas, terrain, and types of warfare are quite dissimilar. Army assessments of possible military threats in the 1980s have led to two conclusions. One is that, given the technological and numerical realities, US forces cannot win by relying on attrition and a tactical doctrine based on defense. The second conclusion is that, while the Army must be organized and equipped to win on the conventional battlefield, it will also have to be prepared to respond to enemy-initiated use of chemical or nuclear weapons.

These conclusions prompted two new efforts which are having profound effects on the

AirLand Battle 2000

The US Army's most recent battle methodology is a totally new concept entitled AirLand Battle 2000. The central idea is a strategic defense of NATO's central region by aggressive tactics, which would include immediate, sustained and simultaneous attacks both in depth and on the line of contact.

Based on a 20-year Soviet threat projection, assessments conclude that the US Army, heavily outnumbered in both men and equipment, would be foolish to fight a war of attrition. Rather, the plan is for the Army to defend offensively, to strike quickly at Soviet assault echelons, while seeing subsequent echelons, in an attempt to finalize this stage of the battle before the enemy's follow-up armies join the fray. The intention is to attack the enemy throughout the depth of his formation with air, artillery and electronic means, and by use of high maneuverability. It is planned to confuse the enemy and cause him to fight in more than one direction, by deploying ground maneuver forces to the rear of his advance echelons. The Army will take advantage of the Soviet tactics which (as they exist today) mean there is an inevitable time-lag between follow-on echelons, such periods normally being lulls in the intense fighting. AirLand Battle tactics will upset the enemy's advance timetable, and force him to change his plans even to the

US Army. One is a tactical doc-
rine, the "AirLand Battle"; the
other an organizational change
to accommodate the new doc-
rine and weapons systems.

(continued on page 10)

▶

Above: The ideal military action
has a clearly demonstrable aim
and is quickly accomplished with
minimal casualties. These US
Army men in Grenada fulfilled
all of these requirements in 1983.

extent of altering routes or splitting forces, so that hopefully
subsequent defending forces will not have to face enemy forces too
strong for them to defeat.

A scenario would have a US Army brigade attack the enemy's first
echelon assault regiments while "seeing" the first echelon assault
divisions. These are attacked by a US Army division, which at
the same time "sees" the first echelon assault armies. These in turn
are attacked by the US Army corps which must also disrupt the
timetable of the second echelon divisions of the first echelon armies.

The depth attack, penetrating as much as 200 miles (321km),
would be by fully integrated air forces (hence the air-land aspect),
indirect fire systems, and by deep penetration ground units. The
concept will entail small combat units which will operate relatively
independently of each other. It also includes tactics for fighting
in 360 degrees to meet the threat posed by the Warsaw Pact tactics;
indeed, almost challenging them to attempt to surround the Army's
agile combat forces. The concept will depend heavily on new
technology, especially in communications, and in the rapid collection
and assessment of intelligence data. Brigade commanders must
know their superior commanders' intent, rather than have constant
dialogue, thus combining the strategic and tactical levels.

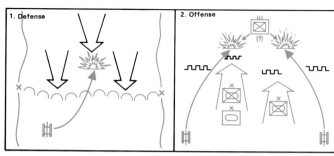

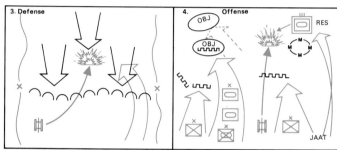

Basic Army Tactics

1—2: Delay of forces to prevent reinforcement
The first form of depth attack is used both when in defense (1) and in attack (2). The aim is to disrupt the enemy forces in depth, particularly the second echelon, to delay (or even prevent) their arrival in the battle area. This enables the enemy forces in contact to be isolated and then defeated in detail. Deception, offensive electronic warfare, artillery fire, counter-battery fire and air interdiction will all be used in this form of deep battle. The commander must decide when he needs particular enemy units isolated in this way.

3—4: Delay in enemy forces to allow maneuver completion
The second concept also involves attacking the enemy deep forces with fire. Its aim, however, is not so much to prevent the reinforcement of committed forces, as in (1) and (2) above, but rather to prevent them from interfering with own forces' attacks or counter attacks against the flanks or rear of enemy close-battle forces. Valuable targets in the deep battle may well prove to be different from those in the close-in battle; for example, bridges may be targets of higher value than tactical units when the aim is to prevent the arrival and deployment of the enemy's second echelon.

5—6: Decisive deep attack
The third form of tactical operation in this concept is both more complex and more difficult to achieve. It involves the engagement of the enemy follow-on echelon with both firepower and maneuver forces at the same time as the close-in battle continues. This is designed to stop the enemy from massing, to deprive him of momentum, and, most important of all, to destroy his force in its entirety. This will require the use of every combat and support element in close harmony. It will also require very close coordination between Army air and ground maneuver forces, artillery, electronic warfare, and Air Force battlefield interdiction.

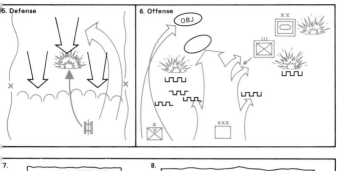

5. Defense

6. Offense

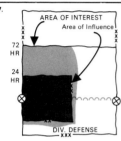

7.

AREA OF INTEREST
Area of Influence

72 HR

24 HR

DIV. DEFENSE

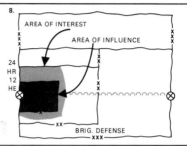

8.

AREA OF INTEREST

AREA OF INFLUENCE

24 HR

12 HE

BRIG. DEFENSE

7—8: Areas of influence and interest

The area of influence (7) is the operational area assigned to a commander within which he is capable of acquiring and fighting enemy units with assets organic to his command, plus any assigned to him in support of the particular operation. The size of the area will vary according to the prevailing conditions and the superior officer's plans. The latter also designates the front and flanking boundaries of the area. The area of interest (8) extends beyond the area of influence to include any enemy forces capable of affecting operations by the formation concerned.

9: Organization of the defense

The purpose of the defense is to provide an opportunity to gain the initiative, and commanders are expected to combine elements of static and dynamic tactical action. With this increased emphasis on offensive action and agility, reserve forces have become particularly important for counterattacks.

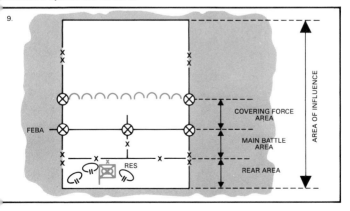

9.

COVERING FORCE AREA

FEBA

MAIN BATTLE AREA

RES

REAR AREA

AREA OF INFLUENCE

▶ US Army Tactical Doctrine

The principles of US Army tactical doctrine are influenced by economics, American attitudes, and the perceived threat. US and NATO strategists see the major threat as coming from the USSR and the Warsaw Pact and directed against Western Europe, and US land forces are structured to meet this. In an attack with little or no warning (the "cold-start" scenario) the Warsaw Pact has a numerical advantage in divisions, tanks, artillery, and aircraft. To counter this the US Army has developed qualitatively superior equipment and a tactical doctrine designed to defeat a numerically superior attacker. The new doctrine, promulgated in 1982, can be summarized as: to secure the initiative and exercise it aggressively to defeat the enemy. This inherently aggressive style is having far-reaching effects, and calls for greater use of maneuver and a greater recognition of human factors on the battlefield. There are four tenets derived from the operational concept: first, *Initiative,* ie, to cause the enemy to react to US forces rather than vice-versa; second, *Depth,* a three-dimensional combination of time, resources, and distance, which provides momentum in attack and elasticity in defense; third, *Agility,* which involves not only rapid mental and planning flexibility, but also acting faster than the enemy, described by one American general as "getting there firstest with the mostest"; fourth, *Synchronization,* a total unity of effort, with joint-Service and allied connotations. Implicit in this tenet is an awareness of higher commanders' intentions, so that all levels and activities are in pursuit of the same goals. ▶

Right: The essential raw material of any army is its soldiers. After Vietnam, there was some doubt about the quality and motivation of US soldiers, but their pride and self-confidence has been almost fully restored.

▶ Offensive Operations

Fundamental to the US Army's offensive operations are five principles—concentration, surprise, speed, flexibility, and audacity. *Concentration* to achieve local superiority followed by rapid dispersion to disrupt the enemy defensive efforts involves logistics as well as maneuver planning and execution. *Surprise* includes avoiding enemy strength and attacking his weaknesses. *Speed,* an element implicit in all of the concepts, is more than mere rapidity of movement, and includes any and all actions which promote the enemy's confusion as well as contributing to friendly maneuver. *Flexibility* in an environment where forces may cover 30 or more miles (50 or more km) a day, calls for the ability to exploit opportunities as they arise. *Audacity* recognizes risk but rejects tactical gamble.

Types of offensive operation describe the purpose rather than a method and have not changed from earlier listings: movement to contact—hasty attack—deliberate attack—exploitation—pursuit.

Movement to contact is intended to develop the situation while maintaining the commander's freedom of actions.

Hasty attacks are called for as a result of a meeting engagement or a successful defense.

Exploitation and *pursuit* follow successful attacks.

Right: US Army soldier (wearing the new helmet) aiming a Stinger missile. The gun versus missile argument has still not been settled in the air defense field.

Below: A Special Forces combat engineer about to blow a bridge. After a period of neglect, the Special Forces are now in great demand once again.

Defensive Operations

Changes in defense called for in the 1982 Operations Manual are more in spirit and operational style than mechanical or definitional. The defense is considered more a matter of purpose than form, with offensive combat characterizing operations. Commanders are expected to combine static and dynamic forms in light of their mission, terrain, relative strength, and mobility. In this context, "static" defense implies retention of particular terrain and tends to rely on fire power to destroy the enemy. "Dynamic" defense orients more on the enemy force than on retention of terrain objectives and tends to greater use of maneuver against attacking forces.

Heightened emphasis on rear area protection is a function of the increased demands on command and control systems as well as the high volume of fuel and ammunition consumption which the battlefield of the future will entail. Combat support and combat service support (logistics) units will be dispersed to avoid presenting lucrative targets but must be mutually supporting for possible rear area combat operations. Allocation of resources and placement takes into account the probabilities of enemy air mobile, nuclear, chemical and conventional air attack, along with such factors as sabotage and unconventional warfare.

The Corps

Organizational implications of the airland battle are extensive. All levels of operational forces must be modified to support the new doctrine and to accommodate the rapidly changing technology. The heavy corps design envisions operating with from 3⅔ divisions to 5 divisions. A type corps will have a minimum strength of some 60,000 personnel and be capable of expansion as needed. Design considerations include provisions for coordination with allied forces and the increased operational participation with US Tactical Air Forces.

▶

US Army Heavy Division

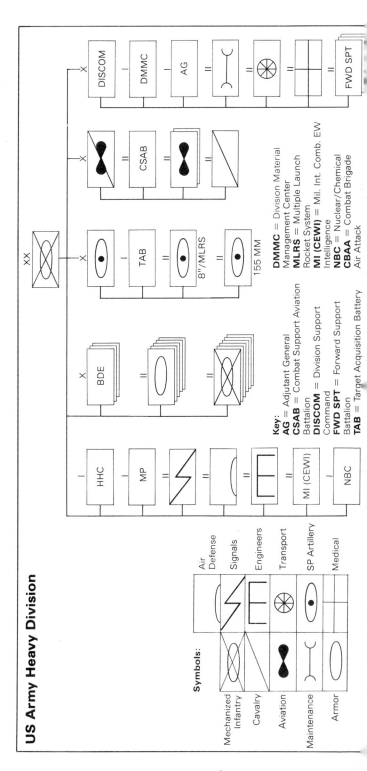

Key:
AG = Adjutant General
CSAB = Combat Support Aviation Battalion
DISCOM = Division Support Command
FWD SPT = Forward Support Battalion
TAB = Target Acquisition Battery
DMMC = Division Material Management Center
MLRS = Multiple Launch Rocket System
MI (CEWI) = Mil. Int. Comb. EW Intelligence
NBC = Nuclear/Chemical
CBAA = Combat Brigade Air Attack

Symbols:

Mechanized Infantry	Cavalry		Air Defense
Aviation	Maintenance		Signals
			Engineers
			Transport
Armor			SP Artillery
			Medical

The Division

A total of 16 divisions make up the active army ground combat force. The division is the largest force that trains and fights as a combined arms team. It is a balanced, self-sustaining force that normally conducts operations as part of a larger force, but is capable of conducting independent operations, especially when supplemented by additional combat support and combat service support elements. Normally, the division fights as part of a corps, with three to five divisions making up the corps force. The division is designed to fight conventional operations, or a mixture of conventional and chemical-nuclear operations, in any part of the world.

While the division is the basic combined arms formation, the battalion is the basic maneuver unit, with normally three to five battalions comprising a brigade. Each division has three brigade headquarters to which battalions are assigned as the commander sees fit. The HQ of the Cavalry Brigade Air Attack also has the capability of controlling ground maneuver units which, in effect, gives the division an additional brigade level headquarters. Heavy maneuver battalions—armor and mechanized

Current Major Maneuver Forces*		
Divisions	Active Army	Reserve Component
Armored Div	4	2
Infantry Div	6	5
Mechanized Div		2
Light Div	5	1
Air Assault Div	1	
Airborne Div	1	
High Tech Motor Inf Div	1	
Total	18	10
Nondivisional Maneuver Brigades/Regiments		
Armored Bde	1	3
Mechanized Bde		7
Infantry Bde	1	10
Air Cavalry Combat Bde	1	
Special Forces Group	4	4
Delta Force	1	
Army Avn Air Assault Bde	1	
Totals	9	19

*There are numerous other independent units and formations.
**Includes Army National Guard and Army Reserve.

infantry—fight best in open country operations, in any part of the world, using terrain to maximum advantage. The light maneuver forces—rifle infantry, air assault infantry, airborne infantry, and ranger infantry—are ideally suited to more restricted terrain where close-in fighting becomes the norm.

The maneuver elements of the division are grouped together under brigade control in accordance with the terrain, the ▶

Below: American soldiers must be prepared to fight anywhere in the world, from Arctic to desert.

▶ enemy they face, and the mission they must accomplish. Tank and mechanized infantry battalions rarely fight as pure organic units, but are cross-attached or task-organized by the brigade commanders to perform specific mission tasks to utilize more fully their capabilities and offset each other's vulnerabilities. The division commander allocates maneuver units to the brigade commanders, who in turn cross-attach these forces to optimize the weapon systems of each unit. The resultant battalion task forces are a combination of tank and mechanized infantry companies under the command of a battalion commander. A tank-heavy force would normally be structured to operate in open, rolling terrain, while the mechanized-infantry-heavy task force is better suited to operate in more restricted terrain and built-up areas. An even mix of tank and mechanized infantry results in a balanced task force that provides great flexibility to the commander. A balanced force would normally be structure when information about th enemy is vague or when th terrain is mixed and variable.

Because of global continger cies, US Army force structur provides for several types c divisions. In general terms, ligh divisions will have strength of approximately 17,000. Wit transportability as a major fac tor, these divisions will rely o armor-defeating systems othe than tanks, e.g. TOW missile Each division will have 9 or 1 infantry battalions and suppor ting units comparable to th heavy division but scaled to the lighter weaponry support re quirements. Currently, it is ant cipated that six divisions will b light (1 airborne, 1 air-mobile, infantry), the remaining te heavy.

Below: Post-storage proof firir of TOW missiles by soldiers of 1st Bn, 61st Infantry, at Fort Polk, La. TOW is one of the best anti-tank guided weapons (ATGWs) in the worle

Above: TOW missile is fired from the new M2 Bradley IFV; this is the vehicle upon which the US Army is pinning all its hopes.

Tank Battalion

The tank battalion has 565 officers and enlisted personnel organized into four tank companies and an HQ company. Each tank company has three platoons of four tanks each. Maintenance and support functions re consolidated in the battalion HQ company, as are a scout platoon and a six-tube mortar platoon. Current tank battalions have M60A3 or M1 Abrams tanks. The M60A3 has a 105mm gun which is highly effective at 2,190 yards (2,000m) and a cruising range of 310 miles (500km); the main gun is stabilized for firing on the move. The M1 Abrams tank is the newest system and will replace the M60 over the next few years. The new tank battalion is designed to employ 58 of the M1 tanks.

Tanks use their mobility and combat power to outflank the enemy or to penetrate the enemy defenses. Once armor has broken through to the enemy rear, it destroys or disrupts the enemy defenses in depth. Tanks are also well suited for rapid and dynamic exploitation and pursuit operations.

Mechanized Infantry Battalion

The mechanized infantry battalion has 880 officers and enlisted personnel organized into four mechanized rifle companies, an anti-armor company and an HQ company. The four-rifle-company configuration allows for cross-attachment with the similarly structured tank battalions. Each rifle company has three platoons of three squads each. Maintenance and support func- ▶

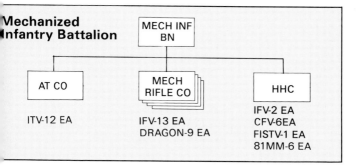

Mechanized Infantry Battalion

```
              MECH INF
                 BN
                  |
   _____
  |               |                   |
AT CO        MECH RIFLE CO          HHC
```

AT CO

ITV-12 EA

MECH RIFLE CO

IFV-13 EA
DRAGON-9 EA

HHC

IFV-2 EA
CFV-6EA
FISTV-1 EA
81MM-6 EA

▶ tions are consolidated in the battalion HQ company, along with a scout platoon and a mortar platoon. The anti-armor company has three platoons of two sections each, and contains a total of 12 Improved TOW Vehicles. (The TOW has a 3,280 yards/3,000m range.) Each rifle company has 9 Dragon (1,093 yards/1,000m range) man-portable anti-armor guided missiles. The M2 Infantry Fighting Vehicle (IFV) is designed to provide infantry with cross-country mobility comparable to the Abrams tank.

The mechanized infantry usually operates as part of a combined arms force. The infantrymen remain mounted in their carriers until they are required to assault or forced to dismount by the enemy. The carriers displace to protected positions to provide supporting fire. The new IFVs will greatly enhance the infantryman's ability to fight while mounted and protected.

Cavalry Brigade Air Attack (CBAA)

This organization of approximately 1,700 officers and enlisted personnel is designed to consolidate the aviation assets of the division as well as to provide an additional control headquarters. In addition to its headquarters troop, the CBAA has two attack helicopter battalions, a combat support aviation battalion, and the division's cavalry squadron. Principal weapons of the attack helicopter

battalions are their 21 AAH and 13 OH-58C (observation) aircraft. The cavalry squadron has two air cavalry troops which also have AAH and OH-58C aircraft (4 AAH, 6 OH-58C each). The two ground cavalry troops each have 19 cavalry fighting vehicles. Aerial movement of personnel and equipment, maintenance of aircraft, and aerial observer support for the division artillery is provided by the combat support aviation battalion.

The AAH uses speed as well as natural and manmade cover and concealment (hills, trees, buildings, etc) to avoid enemy air defenses. Equipped with sights and night vision sensors, the two-man crew can navigate and attack in darkness or poor visibility. Upon sighting a target, the AAH pops up from cover and fires one or more of its weapon systems. The weapons package for the AAH includes a 30mm chain gun, 2.75-inch rockets and the laser-homing Hellfire missile in various combinations.

The OH-58C, with its radar warning and heat suppression systems, provides a survivable observation capability which can operate at night.

Division Artillery

Some 3,000 strong, the division artillery organization follows traditional principles of direct support for the maneuver elements and a longer range capability to support the battle as a whole or general support. Each

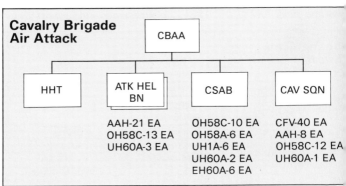

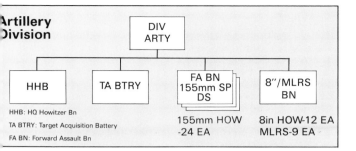

Artillery Division

```
              ┌──────────┐
              │   DIV    │
              │  ARTY    │
              └────┬─────┘
   ┌───────────┬───┴────────┬──────────────┐
┌──────┐  ┌─────────┐  ┌──────────┐  ┌──────────┐
│ HHB  │  │ TA BTRY │  │  FA BN   │  │ 8"/MLRS  │
│      │  │         │  │155mm SP  │  │   BN     │
│      │  │         │  │   DS     │  │          │
└──────┘  └─────────┘  └──────────┘  └──────────┘
```

HHB: HQ Howitzer Bn

TA BTRY: Target Acquisition Battery

FA BN: Forward Assault Bn

155mm HOW -24 EA

8in HOW-12 EA
MLRS-9 EA

55mm self-propelled howitzer attalion routinely supports one the division's brigades. These attalions are fully mobile and an split their component batteries into two sections capable of independent operation. The eneral support battalion with 8-inch howitzers and Multiple aunch Rocket Systems (MLRS) rovides the division with an rganic rocket capability as well longer range weapons to fight e Deep Battle envisioned in e new tactical doctrine.

While the division 86 artillery as more guns than previous organizations, it is the improved responsiveness and flexibility which contributes most to its battlefield potency. Additional ammunition resupply capacity, additional fire direction capability, and the integration of automated systems to speed key functions, all increase artillery accuracy, lethality, and responsiveness.
▶

Below: The Multiple Launch Rocket System (MLRS) will become a virtual NATO standard weapons system. It fires 12 rockets with an 18-mile range.

► Deployment Considerations

Recent Soviet demonstrations of the capability and willingness to project military power have caused some re-evaluation of deployment considerations for US forces. Heavier tanks and infantry fighting vehicles and a host of mechanized supporting systems will significantly enhance the fire power and mobility of deployed forces in Europe, but will also significantly increase the strategic airlift and sealift required to move reinforcing units across the Atlantic.

In case of conflict between NATO and the Warsaw Pact, several factors combine to alleviate deployment problems. The existence of a forward base and depot structure in place in Europe, coupled with recent agreements between the United States and its European NATO allies, will reduce initial requirements to deploy logistical support forces. The commitment of European civilian ships and aircraft to the deployment effort will further ease the burden on US capabilities. Finally, the advantage enjoyed by NATO forces in terms of familiarity with the terrain, established command and control systems, and exercise experience, combine to offer a high degree of assurance that timely reinforcement of Europe is feasible.

Similar circumstances, combined with reduced requirements for armor and mechanized forces, apply to Korea, although the distances involved are far greater.

No such advantages are currently found, however, whe[n] possible contingency require[e]ments for other potential are[as] of conflict are considered. Th[e] wide range of contingencies [is] reflected in the combat force[s] identified for employment wit[h] the Rapid Deployment Forc[e] (RDF), which include the 24[th] Mechanized Division, the 82n[d] Airborne Division, the 101st A[ir] Assault Division, the 6th Caval[ry] Brigade (Air Combat), plu[s] Ranger, Special Forces, an[d] support forces. This does n[ot] mean that all of these units wou[ld] be committed to all RDF conti[n]gencies, merely that a wide m[ix] of heavy and light forces is avai[l]able for tailoring packages [of] Army, Air Force, Navy, an[d] Marine elements to meet spec[i]fic circumstances, as happene[d] for example, in the Grenad[a] operation.

The Army National Guar[d] and the Army Reserve

There are two elements of th[e] Total Army which must not b[e] overlooked: the Army Nation[al] Guard (ARNG) and the Arm[y] Reserve. The ARNG reache[d a] paid strength of 417,019, whic[h] represents some 46 per cent [of] the Total Army, at the end of F[Y] 1983. In unit terms, the ARN[G] provides 33 per cent of the com[bat] divisions, almost 50 per ce[nt] of infantry, armor, and artiller[y] battalions, and nearly 30 p[er] cent of the combat support unit[s]. Although some ARNG equi[p]ment is old and difficult to mai[n]tain, recent changes in priori[ty] mean that the National Guar[d] will shortly receive such mode[rn] equipment as the UH-60 an[d]

US Ground Launched Tactical Nuclear Weapons Deployed in Europe

Name	No. of Launchers	Range miles (km)	Yield of Warhead	Year firs[t] deploye[d]
Pershing[1]	108	280 (450)	60-400 Kt	1962
Lance	36	43-68 (70-110)	1-100 Kt	1972
8in howitzer M110A2	56	19 (20)	sub-to-low Kt	1962
155mm howitzer M109A2	252	15 (24)	sub-to-low Kt	1964

Source: *The Military Balance 1982-83* (IISS).
1. Pershing II deployed 1983 has a 1,120-mile (1,800km) range.

AH-1S helicopters, M1 and M60A3 MBTs, and the squad automatic weapon (SAW).

The Army Reserve was 269,000 strong at the end of FY 1983. Its units are mainly in the combat support, combat service support, and general support roles, while there are also many officers and soldiers in the Individual Ready Reserve. Some 12,000 troops of the Army Reserve are an integral part of the RDF, providing transport, fuel, and civil affairs support. If mobilization was to be ordered, some 20 per cent of the Army Reserve would be committed within 30 days, a total of 57 per cent within 30 to 60 days, and virtually 100 per cent within 90 days.

Conclusion

The US Army is a large and complex military organization with extensive responsibilities. It bore the brunt of the Vietnam experience, but the recovery is now virtually complete. Like other Western military forces, the US Army has assumed that quantitative disadvantage

Above: These men of the US Army Reserve are an integral part of mobilization plans.

against the Warsaw Pact could be offset by Western technological superiority. There is, however, a growing realization that this can no longer be relied upon. Indeed, the US Army has suffered some major technical setbacks and difficulties. It has, for example, taken almost two decades to find successors to the M60 MBT and M113 APC, with many failures and much loss of time and waste of resources along the way. Some programs, such as the M60A2, M551 Sheridan, and Copperhead, have simply failed to fulfill the spectacular promises held out.

Despite all this, the US Army has some fine equipment and this book shows some of it. Inevitably, not all can be shown, and the selections have in some cases had to be a little arbitrary. Nevertheless, it is hoped that this book gives an overall picture of the equipment of a mighty fighting force.

Main Battle Tanks

The Main Battle Tank (MBT) is the linchpin of the US Army's plans for the land battle, although it could, of course, only be deployed as part of a combined arms force. It must certainly be at the core of the new and more aggressive tactics now promulgated in the AirLand Battle concept.

M1 Abrams

Type: Main battle tank.
Crew: 4.
Armament: One 105mm M68 gun; one 7·62mm machine gun co-axial with main armament; one 0·5in machine gun on commander's cupola; one M240 7·62mm machine gun on loader's hatch (see text).
Armor: Classified.
Dimensions: Length (gun forward) 32ft 0½in (9·766m); length (hull) 25ft 11¾in (7·918m); width 11ft 11¾in (3·655m); height 7ft 9½in (2·375m).
Weight: 120,000lb (54,432kg).
Engine: Avco Lycoming AGT-T 1500 HP-C turbine developing 1,500hp.
Performance: Road speed 45mph (72·4km/h); range 275 miles (443km); vertical obstacle 4ft 1in (1·244m); trench 9ft (2·743m); gradient 60 per cent.
History: First production vehicle completed in 1980.

In June 1973 contracts were awarded to both the Chrysler Corporation (which builds the M60 series) and the Detroit Diesel Allison Division of the General Motors Corporation (which built the MBT-70) to build prototypes of a new tank designated M1, and later named the Abrams tank. These tanks were handed over to the US Army for trials in February 1976. In November 1976 it was announced after a four-month delay that the Chrysler tanks would be placed in production. Production, which commenced at the Lima Army Tank Plant in Lima, Ohio, in 1979, with the first vehicles being completed the following year, is now also under way at the Detroit Arsenal Tank plant, which, like Lima, is now operated by the Land Systems Division

Development of the US MBT has proved time-consuming and costly, and only now are some 3,000 M1s in wide-scale service. With this tank the US Army has overtaken Soviet tank technology after at least a decade in which it has lagged badly behind. Despite the advent of the long-awaited M1, the M60 and M48 will remain in service in their improved versions for many years to come; indeed, production of the M60A3 has not yet ended. All US Army MBTs currently are armed with a 105mm gun, although the British and West Germans use 120mm and the USSR 125mm. The US will not be equipped with 120mm guns until the M1A1 with a West German gun, comes into service.

Above: The M1 Abrams main battle tank has taken many years to reach combat units but is now in service in very considerable numbers.

Far left: A prototype M1 fires its British-designed 105mm rifled main armament. From 1985 the M1E1 will be fitted with a German 120mm.

Left: An M1 lands after leaping an obstacle. The US Army intends that this MBT will set new standards in agility on the battlefield.

Above: The M1 has a 27 per cent lower silhouette than the M60A1 but with the same ground clearance of about 19 inches (48cm).

▶ of General Dynamics who took over Chrysler Defense Incorporated in 1982. By 1986 over 3,000 M1s had been built and the tank is now entering service at an increasingly rapid rate. The first units to field the M1 were the three armored battalions of 3rd Infantry Division (Mechanized) who proudly gave the tank its European debut in 'Exercise Reforger' in August 1982. The US Army has a requirement for some 7,058 M1s by the end of Fiscal year 1989. From 1987 it is expected that the 105mm M68 rifled tank gun will be replaced by the 120mm Rheinmetall smooth bore gun which is being produced under the designation XM256; this will fire both West German and American ammunition, although there have been more problems in adapting the turret to take the West German gun than had been anticipated.

The M1 has a hull and turret of the new British Chobham armor, which is claimed to make the tank immune to attack from all shaped-charge warheads and to give dramatically increased protection against other anti tank rounds, including kinetic energy (i.e., APDS and APFSDS). It has a crew of four; the driver at the front, the commander and gunner on the right of the turret, and the loader on the left. The main armament consists of a standard 105mm gun developed in Britain and produced under license in the United States and a 7·62mm machine-gun is mounted co-axially with the main armament. A 0·5in machine-gun is mounted at the commander's station and a 7·62mm machine-gun at the loader's station. Ammunition supply consists of 55 rounds of 105mm, 1,000 rounds of 12·7mm and 11,400 rounds of 7·62mm. Mounted each side of the turret is a bank of six

24

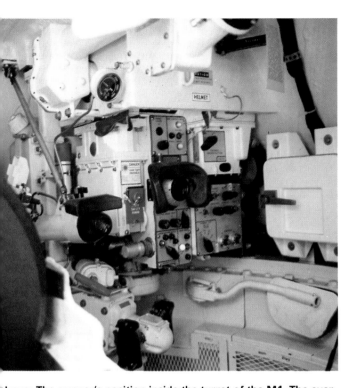

Above: The gunner's position inside the turret of the M1. The ever increasing sophistication of MBTs is leading to spiralling costs.

Below: An early-issue M1 Abrams moves through a village in West Germany. Current production is running at some 60 tanks per month.

▶ British-designed smoke dischargers. The main armament can be aimed and fired on the move. The gunner first selects the target, and then uses the laser rangefinder to get its range and then depresses the firing switch. The computer makes the calculations and adjustments required to ensure a hit

The fuel tanks are separated from the crew compartment by armored bulkheads and sliding doors are provided for the ammunition stowage areas. Blow-out panels in both ensure that an explosion is channeled outward. The suspension is of torsion-bar type with rotary shock absorbers. The tank can travel across country at a speed of 30mph (48km/h) and accelerate from 0 to 20mph (0 to 32km/h) in seven seconds, and this will make the M1 a difficult tank to engage on the battlefield. The M1 is powered by a turbine developed by Avco Lycoming, running on a variety of fuel including petrol, diesel and jet fuel. All the driver has to do is adjust a dial in his compartment. According to the manufacturers, the engine will not require an overhaul until the tank has traveled between 12,000 to 18,000 miles (19,312 to 28,968km), a great advance over existing tank engines. This engine is coupled to an Allison X-1100 transmission with four forward and two reverse gears. Great emphasis has been placed on reliability and maintenance, and it is claimed that the complete engine can be removed for replacement in under 30 minutes.

Right: Half the M1 production run will have the M68 105mm main gun seen here; the remainder will have a West German 120mm smoothbore

Below: The M1 represents a major addition to the US Army's combat strength; 7,058 are on order at a current cost of $1·84 million each

▶ The M1 is provided with an NBC system and a full range of night-visio equipment for the commander, gunner and driver.

It is not often realized that there are hundreds of sub contractors to major program such as a tank. On the Chrysler M1 there are eight majo subcontractors: the government for the armament, Avco Lycoming for th

Below: The M1 is powered by an Avco-Lycoming gas-turbine engir which develops 1,500hp. Fuel consumption has been criticized by some, but the tank has a range of 275 miles (443km) at a speed of 30mph (48km/h) on secondary roads, and can operate for a 24-hour combat day without needing to refuel.

ngine, Cadillac Gage for the turret drive and the stabilization system, the Control Data Corporation for the ballistic computer, the Detroit Diesel Allison Division of General Motors for the transmission and the final drive, the Hughes Aircraft Company for the laser rangefinder, the Kollmorgen Corporation for the gunner's auxiliary sight and the Singer Kearfott Division for the line-of-sight data link.

Those Europeans who criticize the Americans for failing to make the "two-way street" a reality need look no farther than the M1. This epitome of the US Army's might has British armor, main gun, and smoke dischargers, and a Belgian 7·62mm machine gun, while later versions will convert to a West German main gun.

M48

M48A5, M67, M67A1, M67A2, M48 AVLB

Type: Medium tank.
Crew: 4.
Armament: One 105mm M68; one 0·3in M1919A4E1 machine gun co
axial with the main armament (some have a 7·62mm M73 MG); one 0·5in
machine gun in commander's cupola.
Armor: 12·7mm-120mm (0·50-4·8in).
Dimensions: Length (including main armament) 28·3ft (8·686m); length
(hull) 22ft 7in (6·882m); width 11ft 11in (3·631m); height (including cupola)
10ft 3in (3·124m).
Weight: Combat 108,000lb (48,989kg).
Ground pressure: 11·80lb/in² (0·83kg/cm²).
Engine: Continental AVDS-1790-2A 12-cylinder air-cooled diesel devel
oping 750hp at 2,400rpm.
Performance: Road speed 30mph (48km/h); range 288 miles (463km);
vertical obstacle 3ft (0·915m); trench 8ft 6in (2·59m); gradient 60 per
cent.
History: Entered service with the US Army in 1953. Used by German,
Greece, Iran, Israel, Jordan, Lebanon, Morocco, Norway, Pakistan, Somalia,
South Korea, Spain, Taiwan, Thailand, Tunisia, Turkey, United States and
Vietnam. (*Specifications relate to M48A5 in US service.*)

Once the M47 was authorized for production, development started on a
new medium tank, as the M47 was only a stop-gap measure. So in October
1950 Detroit Arsenal started design work on a new medium tank armed
with a 90mm gun. This design study was completed two months later and
in December 1950 Chrysler was given a contract to complete the design
work and build six prototypes under the designation T48. The first of these
prototypes had to be completed by December 1951. Production started in
1952 and first deliveries were made to the US Army the following year. The
M48, as it was now called, was followed in production by the M60,
essentially an M48A3 with a 105mm gun and other detailed changes,
production of this model being undertaken at the Detroit Tank Plant.

The hull of the M48 is of cast armor construction, as is the turret. The
driver is seated at the front of the hull with the other three crew members
located in the turret, with the commander and gunner on the right and the
loader on the left. The engine and transmission are at the rear of the hull
and are separated from the fighting compartment by a fireproof bulkhead.

**Below: Armored Vehicle Launched Bridge (AVLB) based on the M48
chassis. The bridge is 63ft (19·2m) long and weighs some 32,000lb.**

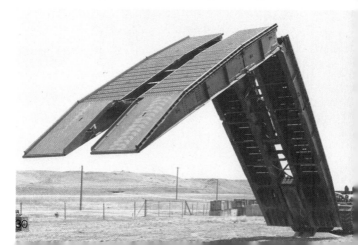

Above: M48 with an M68 105mm gun undergoing tests (but not flamethrowing). The basic design is well over 30 years old.

The suspension is of the torsion-bar type and consists of six road wheels, with the drive sprocket at the rear and the idler at the front. Depending on the model there are between three and five track-return rollers, and some models have a small track tensioning wheel between the sixth road wheel and the drive sprocket. The main armament consists of a 105mm gun with an elevation of +19° and a depression of −9°, traverse being 360°. A 0·3in M1919A4E1 machine-gun is mounted co-axially with the main armament. The cupola can be traversed through 360°, and the machine-gun can be elevated from −10° to +60°.

The M48 can be fitted with a dozer blade, if required, at the front of the hull. All M48s have infra-red driving lights and some an infra-red/white searchlight mounted over the main armament. The type can ford to a depth of 4ft (1·219m) without preparation or 8ft (2·438m) with the aid of a kit.

The first model to enter service was the M48, and this had a simple cupola for the commander, with the machine-gun mounted externally. The second model was the M48C, which was for training use only as it had a mild steel hull. The M48A1 was followed by the M48A2, which had many improvements including a fuel-injection system for the engine and larger capacity fuel tanks. The M48A2C was a slightly modified M48A2. The M48A3 was a significant improvement as this had a diesel engine, which increased the vehicle's operational range considerably, and a number of other modifications including a different fire-control system. Latest model is the M48A5, essentially an M48A1 or M48A2 with modifications including an M68 main 105mm gun, new tracks, a 7·62mm M60D co-axial machine-gun and a similar weapon on the loader's hatch, plus many other detail modifications. One interesting modification is the fitting of an Israeli-developed low-profile cupola.

Earlier M48A1, M48A2C and M48A3 in the US inventory (some 1,809 tanks) have been updated to M48A5 standard and serve with Army National Guard and reserve units. Some M48A1 and M48A2 chassis were to have been used for the Sergeant York DIVADS, but this is now defunct.

Three flamethrower tanks were developed: the M67 (using the M48A1 chassis), the M67A1 (using the M48A2 chassis) and the M67A2 (using the M48A3 chassis). Also in service is an M48 Armored Vehicle-Launched Bridge. This has a scissors bridge which can be laid over gaps up to 60ft (18·288m) in width.

M60

M60, M60A1, M60A3, M60 AVLB, M728 CEV

Type: Main battle tank.
Crew: 4.
Armament: One 105mm gun; one 7·62mm machine gun co-axial wi
main armament; one 0·5in anti-aircraft machine gun in commander
cupola.
Armor: 12·7mm-120mm (0·5-4·80in).
Dimensions: Length (gun forward) 30ft 11in (9·436m); length (hu
22ft 9½in (6·946m); width 11ft 11in (3·631m); height 10ft 8in (3·257m
Weight: Combat 114,600lb (51,982kg).
Ground pressure: 11·24lb/in² (0·79kg/cm²).
Engine: Continental AVDS-1790-2A 12-cylinder diesel developing 750bh
at 2,400rpm.
Performance: Road speed 30mph (48km/h); range 280 miles (450km
vertical obstacle 3ft (0·914m); trench 8ft 6in (2·59m); gradient 60 per cer
History: The M60 entered service with the US Army in 1960 and is als
used by Austria, Egypt, Ethiopia, Iran, Israel, Italy, Jordan, Morocco, Sau
Arabia, Somalia, South Korea, Tunisia, Turkey, US Marine Corps, Yeme
Arab Republic (North). (*Specifications relate to M60A3 model.*)

the 1950s the standard tank of the United States Army was the M48.
1957 an M48 series tank was fitted with a new engine for trials
rposes and this was followed by another three prototypes in 1958.
te in 1958 it was decided to arm the new tank with the British 105mm
series gun, to be built in the United States under the designation M68.
1959 the first production order for the new tank, now called the M60,
as placed with Chrysler, and the type entered production at Detroit Tank
senal in late 1959, with the first production tanks being completed the
lowing year.

From late in 1962, the M60 was replaced in production by the M60A1,
nich had a number of improvements, the most important being the
designed turret. The M60A1 had a turret and hull of all-cast construction.
e driver is seated at the front of the hull with the other three crew mem-
rs in the turret, commander and gunner on the right and the loader on
e left. The engine and transmission are at the rear, the latter having one
verse and two forward ranges. The M60 has torsion-bar suspension and
x road wheels, with the idler at the front and the drive sprocket at the rear;
ere are four track-return rollers. The 105mm gun has an elevation of ▶

**elow: A row of M60A3 MBTs with their turrets reversed. The gun
the M68 105mm. When production finally ended in 1985 some
0,600 M60s had been built, of which the US Army had 7,600.**

Above: An M60 on exercise. The device on the barrel is a simulat[e]
which emits smoke when activated by an "enemy" tank with a las[er]

Right: This shot of an M60A3 clearly shows the considerable hei[ght]
of the tank—10ft 8in (3·257m)—which is one of its main drawbac[ks].
The good ballistic shaping of the turret is also clearly shown.

▶ +20° and a depression of –10°, and traverse is 360°. Both elevation a[nd]
traverse are powered. A 7·62mm M73 machine-gun is mounted co-axia[l]
with the main armament and there is a 0·5in M85 machine-gun in t[he]
commander's cupola. The latter can be aimed and fired from within t[he]
turret, and has an elevation of +60° and a depression of –15°. So[me]
60 rounds of 105mm, 900 rounds of 0·5in and 5,950 rounds of 7·62m[m]
ammunition are carried. Infra-red driving lights are fitted as standa[rd]
and an infra-red/white light is mounted over the main armament. All M6[0]
have an NBC system. The tank can also be fitted with a dozer blade [at]
the front of the hull. The M60 can ford to a depth of 4ft (1·219[m])
without preparation or 8ft (2·438m) with the aid of a kit. For deep fordi[ng]
operations a schnorkel can be fitted, allowing the M60 to ford to a dep[th]
of 13ft 6in (4·14m).

Above: An M60 of the US Army in West Germany. "On-the-spot" training ensures maximum combat readiness.

▶ The M60A2 was a special model armed with a 152mm gun/launcher bu has now been phased out of service. Current production model is th M60A3 with numerous improvements including stabilization of mai armament, top loading air cleaner fitted, passive searchlight over mai armament, new tracks with removable pads, tube over bar suspension, RIS engine, thermal sleeve for main armament, laser rangefinder, passive nigh vision devices, new MAG 7·62mm MG, smoke dischargers each side c turret, muzzle reference system, engine smoke dischargers and improve personnel heater. Most M60A1s of the US Army are now being brought u to this new standard, with the aim of an M60A3 fleet totalling 7,35

Below: A total of 526 M60A2s was built at Detroit in the 1960s, bu due to many problems the tank did not enter service until 1975.

Above: M60 MBTs cross a floating bridge on exercise. Such sights will become rarer as M60 is replaced by M1.

1,691 from new production and 5,661 from conversion of M60A1s in rmy depots). Of these, 3,786 will be the M60A3 TTS version, which has ll the improvements listed above, plus a tank thermal sight. By 1981 otal production of the M60 series of MBTs had amounted to over 0,600 vehicles with the final vehicles being completed in 1985. pecialized versions of the M60 series include the M60 armored vehicle aunched bridge and the M728 Combat Engineer Vehicle which is fitted vith a bulldozer blade, 152mm demolition gun and an A-frame for lifting bstacles which is pivoted at the front of the hull. The basic vehicle an also be fitted with roller type mineclearing equipment or a dozer blade.

elow: One of the many specialized versions of the M60 is the M728 ombat Engineer Vehicle, with bulldozer blade and 6in (152mm) gun.

Armored Personne[
Carriers

With the M113 the US Army set the pattern for a simple, tracked, armored box (a "battle taxi") which has been followed by most Free World armies for two decades. After many years of indecision and confusion—and some costly

M2/M3

Type: (M2) Infantry fighting vehicle; (M3) Cavalry fighting vehicle.
Crew: 3 plus 6.
Armament: One 25mm Hughes "chain-gun"; one 7·62mm machine-gun co-axial with main armament; twin launcher for Hughes TOW ATGW.
Armor: Classified.
Dimensions: Length 21ft 2in (6·45m); width 10ft 6in (3·20m); height 9ft 9in (2·97m).
Weight: 50,000lb (22,680kg).
Ground pressure: 7·7lb/in² (0·54kg/cm²).
Engine: Cummins (VTA-903T water-cooled 4-cycle diesel developing 506bhp.
Performance: Road speed 41mph (66km/h); water speed 4·5mph; range 300 miles (384km); vertical obstacle 3ft (0·91m); trench 8ft 4in (2·54m) gradient 60 per cent.
History: Entered US Army service in 1983.

Below: An M2 Bradley Infantry Fighting Vehicle (IFV) at speed, showing its excellent agility, which equates with that of the M1 MBT.

mistakes—the M2 Infantry Combat Vehicle is at last entering service. It is fast, well protected, heavily armed, and enables the mounted infantry to fire weapons (albeit over a limited arc) from inside the vehicle. It is also heavy (over 22 tons), very expensive, and has reduced the effective size of the infantry squad to six men. Indeed, the tactical use of the M2 and of its dismounted squad do not seem to have been fully defined as yet, some crucial decisions having been left until the new vehicle is actually in service. Even when the M2 is in full service many thousands of M113s will remain in front-line units as weapons carriers and as communications and headquarters vehicles.

The United States Army has had a requirement for an MICV for well over 15 years. The first American MICV was the XM701, developed in the early 1960s on the M107/M110 self-propelled gun chassis. This proved unsatisfactory during trials. The Americans then tried to modify the current M113 to meet the MICV role: a variety of different models was built and tested, but again these vehicles failed to meet the army requirement. As a result of a competition held in 1972, the FMC Corporation, which still builds the M113A2, was awarded a contract to design an MICV designated the XM723. The XM723 did not meet the requirements of the US Army and further development, based on the same chassis, resulted in the Fighting Vehicle System (FVS) which comprised two vehicles, the XM2 Infantry Fighting Vehicle and the XM3 Cavalry Fighting Vehicle. These were eventually accepted for service as the M2 and M3 Bradley Fighting Vehicles. The US Army has a requirement for some 6,882 M2/M3 vehicles, and three battalions of M2s were formed in 1983, the first at Ford Hood, Texas.

The primary task of the M2 in the eyes of the US Army is to enable infantry to fight from under armor whenever practicable, and to be able both to observe and to use their weapons from inside the vehicle. The M2 ▶

Below: An infantry squad "debussing" from its M2. The small size of the crew compartment has reduced the dismounting squad to six.

Above: M2 IFV with twin launcher for TOW ATGWs in the traveling position alongside the two-man turret. M231 rifles are not fitted.

Left: M2 on a road-test. Note the splash-board resting on the glacis plate and the steel armor on the vehicle side for added protection.

will replace some, but not all, of the current M113 APCs, as the latter are more than adequate for many roles on the battlefield. The M2 has three major advances over the existing M113 APC. First, the IFV has greater mobility and better cross-country speed, enabling it to keep up with the M1 MBT when acting as part of the tank/infantry team. Second, it has much greater firepower. Third, it has superior armor protection. The tank provides long-range firepower whilst the IFV provides firepower against softer, close-in targets. The M2's infantry also assist tanks by locating and destroying enemy anti-tank weapons.

The hull of the M2 is of all-welded aluminum construction with an applique layer of steel armor welded to the hull front, upper sides and rear for added protection. The hull sides also have a thin layer of steel armor, the ▶

Above: M2 Bradley IFV on the firing range. Note the box on the near-side of the turret which is a twin TOW anti-tank missile launcher.

Above: An M2 on a cross-country driving course. Main gun is a Hughes 25mm "Chain-Gun"; to its right is 7·62mm coaxial MG.

Left: An M2 launches a TOW missile. The armament on the M2 IFV will add substantially to the firepower available to infantry battalions.

space between the aluminum and steel being filled with foam to increase the buoyancy of the vehicle. The armored protection of the IFV is claimed to be effective against Soviet 14·5mm armor-piercing rounds and 155mm air-burst shell splinters.

The driver is seated at the front of the vehicle on the left, with the engine to his right. The two-man turret is in the center of the hull and the personnel compartment is at the rear. Personnel entry is effected through a large power-operated ramp in the hull rear. The two-man power operated turret is fully stabilized and is armed with a 25mm Hughes Chain Gun and a co-axial 7·62mm machine gun. The weapons can be elevated to +60° and depressed to −10°, turret traverse being 360°. Mounted on the left side of the turret is a twin launcher for the Hughes TOW ATGW. A total of 900 rounds of 25mm, 2,340 rounds of 7·62mm and seven TOW missiles are carried. The troop compartment is provided with six firing ports (two in each side and two at the rear) for the 5·56mm M231 weapon. The M231 is a specially developed version of the M16, cut-down and sealed in a ball mount. It is somewhat ironic that the outcome of a requirement for the infantry to be able to use their weapons from inside the vehicle should be an additional and specialized rifle. Three M72A2 light anti-tank weapons are also carried. The M2 is fully amphibious, although a flotation screen is required, and is propelled in the water by its tracks. An NBC system is fitted, as is a full range of night vision equipment.

Some 3,300 M3 Cavalry Fighting Vehicles are to be purchased to replace M60s and M113s in armored cavalry units and in the scout platoons of mechanized infantry and tank battalions. The M3 is outwardly identical with the M2: the major differences lie in the internal stowage and the layout of the crew compartment. The M3 carries twice the number of stowed 25mm rounds and ten stored TOW missiles. Only two cavalrymen are housed in the rear compartment and the firing ports are not used.

The chassis of the M2/M3 is also used as the basis for the Vought Multiple Launch Rocket System and the Armored, Forward-Area, Rearm Vehicle (AFARV) which has been designed to supply MBTs with ammunition when they are in the battlefield area.

M113A2

M113, M113A1, M113A2, M106, M132, M163 and variants.

Type: Armored personnel carrier.
Crew: 2 plus 11.
Armament: One Browning 0·5in (12·7mm) machine-gun.
Armor: 12mm-38mm (0·47-1·58in).
Dimensions: Length 15ft 11in (4·863m); width 8ft 10in (2·686m); height 8ft 2in (2·5m).
Weight: Combat 24,600lbs (11,156kg).
Ground Pressure: 7·82lb/in^2 (0·55kg/cm^2).
Engine: General Motors Model 6V53 six-cylinder water-cooled diesel developing 215bhp at 2,800rpm.
Performance: Road speed 42mph (67·6km/h); water speed 3·6mph (5·8km/h); range 300 miles (483km); vertical obstacle 2ft (0·61m); trench 5ft 6in (1·68m); gradient 60 per cent.
History: Entered service with the United States Army in 1960. Also used by 50 other countries.

In the early 1950s the standard United States Army APC was the M75 followed in 1954 by the M59. Neither of these was satisfactory and in 1954 foundations were laid for a new series of vehicles. In 1958 prototypes of the T113 (aluminum hull) and T117 (steel hull) armored personnel carriers were built. A modified version of the T113, the T113E1, was cleared for production in mid-1959 and production commenced at the FMC plant at San Jose, California, in 1960. The vehicle is still in production today and some 70,000 have been built in the USA. It is also built in Italy by Oto Melara, which has produced a further 4,000 for the Italian Army and for export. In 1964 the M113 was replaced in production by the M113A1, identical with the earlier model but for a diesel rather than a petrol engine.

The M113A1 had a larger radius of action than the earlier vehicle. The M113 had the distinction of being the first armored fighting vehicle of

Below: The squat shape of the M113 is distinctive even amidst the snows of Alaska, as a squad from Company A, 1st BG, 23rd Infantry, goes through a tactical demonstration at the Fort Richardson training aids area.

Above: More M113 chassis have been built than any other since 1945. This is the M557 unarmed command post version.

Below: M113s in convoy through a German town during "Autumn Reforger" NATO exercises in 1982. It is the standard personnel carrier in mechanized infantry units but, unable to keep pace with the M1 tank, will be replaced by the M2 IFV.

luminum construction to enter production. The driver is seated at the front
of the hull on the left, with the engine to his right. The commander's hatch is
in the center of the roof and the personnel compartment is at the rear of the
hull. The infantry enter and leave via a large ramp in the hull rear, although
there is also a roof hatch over the troop compartment. The basic vehicle is
normally armed with a pintle-mounted Browning 0·5in machine-gun, which
has 2,000 rounds of ammunition. The M113 is fully amphibious and is
propelled in the water by its tracks. Infra-red driving lights are fitted as
standard. FMC has developed a wide variety of kits for the basic vehicle
including an ambulance kit, NBC kit, heater kit, dozer-blade kit, various
shields for machine-guns and so on.

The current production model is the M113A2 which is essentially an
M113A1 with improved engine cooling and improved suspension. Most US
Army M113 and M113A1 vehicles are now being brought up to M113A2
standard.

There are more variants of the M113 family than any other fighting
vehicle in service today, and there is room here to mention only some of the ▶

**Left: The M901 Improved TOW Vehicle (ITV), whose missile components
can be removed for ground-launching if tactically necessary.**

**Below: The M730 Chaparral launcher is a variant of the M548,
based on the M113 chassis.**

Above: One of the many derivatives of the basic M113 is this XM981 Fire-Support Team Vehicle (FIST-V) for artillery forward observers

Right: M548A1 cargo carrier is based on the M113 and is widely used in the US Army for a variety of load-carrying tasks.

▶ more important models. The M577 is the command model, with a much higher roof and no armament. There are two mortar carriers: the M125 with an 81mm mortar, and the M106 with a 107mm mortar. The flame thrower model is known as the M132A1, and is not used outside the United States Army. The M806 is the recovery model, and this is provided with winch in the rear of the vehicle and spades at the rear. The anti-aircraft model is known as the Vulcan Air Defense System or M163; this is armed with a six-barrelled 20mm General Electric cannon. The M548 tracked cargo carrier is based on an M113 chassis, can carry 5 tons (5,080kg) of cargo and is fully amphibious. There are many models of the M54 including the M727, which carries three HAWK surface-to-air missiles, and the M730, which carries four Chaparral short-range surface-to-air missiles. Yet another version, the M752, carries the Lance tactical missile system whilst the M688 carries two spare missiles.

One recent model is the M901 Improved TOW Vehicle (ITV), with retractable launcher that carries two Hughes TOW ATGWs in the ready-to-launch position. Almost 2,000 of these vehicles have been ordered by the US Army. The latest model to be ordered is the Surface-Launched Unit Fuel-Air Explosive (SLUFAE) launcher, which is an unguided rocket system based on the M548 chassis.

The M113 series and its derivatives will remain in service with the US and foreign armies for many years to come. Like the "Jeep" of World War II, it cheap, simple to manufacture, easy to maintain, and effective in use. The US Army may well one day wish that the same applied to the M2/M3 series

Above: An infantry squad debussing from an M113, virtually the standard APC in Western-oriented armies since the 1960s.

Reconnaissance Vehicles

The US Army has put more emphasis than most other armies on the helicopter as a reconnaissance vehicle, although the M551 Sheridan was intended to be the primary ground role system. Unfortunately, the Sheridan has proved to be a relative failure, due mainly to an over-ambitious

LAV-25

Type: Light armored vehicle.
Crew: 3.
Armament: M242 25mm Bushmaster automatic cannon; M240 7·62mm co-axial MG.
Armor: Steel, sufficient to withstand 7·62mm AP in front, 7·62mm elsewhere.
Dimensions: Length 21ft (6·4m); width 7ft 2½in (2·2m) height 8ft 2½in (2·5m).
Weights: Empty 19,850lb (9,004kg); combat loaded 27,559lb (12,501kg).
Engine: Detroit Diesel 6V-53T, 6-cylinder turbocharged diesel; 275hp at 2,800rpm.
Performance: Maximum road speed 63mph (101km/h); road range 485 miles (781km); swimming speed 6mph (9·65km/h); gradient 70 per cent side slope 35 per cent.

In 1981-82 the US Army's Tank-Automotive Command (TACom) carried out a series of tests for a light armored vehicle (LAV) to be procured for the US Army and US Marine Corps. Four vehicles were tested: the British Alvis Scorpion-Stormer, the Swiss-designed but Canadian-produced MOWAG "Piranha", and the Cadillac-Gage V-150 and V-300. The Scorpion-Stormer

operational requirement which tried to put too much into too small a vehicle and also stretched technology to breaking point. The situation became so bad that the somewhat unsuitable M60 Main Battle Tank had to be pressed into service for a short period. The new reconnaissance vehicle—the M3—is now entering service, much to the relief of the cavalry. For non-European scenarios the Army is looking to the Light Armored Vehicle (LAV), its first wheeled combat vehicle since the Stag armored car of World War II. Unfortunately, like so many programs, the LAV has hit political snags in the Congress, even though the Marine Corps requirement has been approved.

Above: The Light Armored Vehicle (LAV) started life in Switzerland as the MOWAG "Piranha". In 1983 it won the competition for an LAV for the US Army and USMC.

Left: This side shot of the LAV clearly shows its low silhouette. The main gun is the M242 Bushmaster automatic cannon. All eight wheels are driven by the 275hp diesel engine. In 1983 the US Congress denied the Army the funds for purchasing LAV.

series is tracked; the remainder are wheeled. Both the Army and Marine Corps required these vehicles for employment with the Rapid Deployment Force (RDF), although the Army's original requirement was reduced from 1,315 to 680 in 1982, and is now totally in doubt. Indeed, in mid-1983 the Congress denied funds for Army procurement of the LAV because it was considered that the requirement had not been properly justified. This is not to say, however, that the Army will not get its LAV in the long run.

The US Army's basic requirement is for a Mobile Protected Gun-Near Term (MPG-N), which differs substantially from the LAV required by the USMC. The Army plans to equip its light divisions with two MPG battalions, each with 41 LAVs and 40 HMMWVs (Hummer), for reconnaissance, fire support, and anti-tank defense. These battalions appear—on paper, at least—to be too lightly equipped, even for the RDF.

M551 Sheridan

Type: Light tank.
Crew: 4.
Armament: One 152mm gun/missile launcher; one 7·62mm machine-gun co-axial with main armament; one 0·5in anti-aircraft machine-gun; four smoke dischargers on each side of turret.
Armor: Classified.
Dimensions: Length 20ft 8in (6·299m); width 9ft 3in (2·819m); height (overall) 9ft 8in (2·946m).
Weight: Combat 34,898lbs (15,830kg).
Ground pressure: 6·96lb/in² (0·49kg/cm²).
Engine: Detroit Diesel 6V53T six-cylinder diesel developing 300bhp at 2,800rpm.
Performance: Road speed 45mph (70km/h); water speed 3·6mph (5·8km/h); range 373 miles (600km); vertical obstacle 2ft 9in (0·838m); trench 8ft 4in (2·54m); gradient 60 per cent.
History: Entered service with United States Army in 1966 and still in service.

In August 1959 the United States Army established a requirement for "new armored vehicle with increased capabilities over any other weapon its own inventory and that of any adversary". The following year the Allison Division of General Motors was awarded a contract to design a vehicle called the Armored Reconnaissance Airborne Assault Vehicle (ARAAV) to meet the requirement. The first prototype, designated XM551, was completed in 1962, and this was followed by a further 11 prototypes. Late in 1965 a production contract was awarded to Allison, and the first production vehicles were completed in 1966, these being known as the M551 or Sheridan. Production was completed in 1970 after 1,700 vehicles had been built.

The hull of the Sheridan is of all-aluminum construction whilst the turret is of welded steel. The driver is seated at the front of the hull and the other three crew members are in the turret, with the loader on the left and the gunner and commander on the right. The engine and transmission are at the rear of the hull. The suspension is of the torsion-bar type and consists of five road wheels, with the drive sprocket at the rear and the idler at the front. There are no track-return rollers. The most interesting feature of the

Sheridan is its armament system. This consists of a 152mm gun/launcher which has an elevation of +19° and a depression of −8°, traverse being 360°. A 7·62mm machine-gun is mounted co-axially with the main armament, and there is a 0·5in Browning machine-gun on the commander's cupola. The latter cannot be aimed and fired from within the turret, and as a result of combat experience in Vietnam many vehicles have now been fitted with a shield for this weapon. The 152mm gun/launcher, later fitted to the M60A2 and MBT-70 tanks, can fire either a Shillelagh missile or a variety of conventional ammunition including HEAT-T-MP, WP and canister, all of them having a combustible cartridge case. The Shillelagh missile was developed by the United States Army Missile Command and the Philco-Ford Corporation, and has a maximum range of about 3,281 yards (3,000m). The missile is controlled by the gunner, who simply has to keep the crosshairs of his sight on the target to ensure a hit; however, severe problems exist in "capturing" the missile, making it of little value at ranges under 1,300 yards (1,200m). The missile itself weighs 59lbs (26·7kg) and has a single-stage solid-propellant motor which has a burn time of 1·18 seconds. Once the missile leaves the gun/missile-launcher, four fins at the rear of the missile unfold and it is guided to the target by a two-way infra-red command link which eliminates the need for the gunner to estimate the lead and range of the target. A Sheridan normally carries ten missiles and 20 rounds of ammunition, but this mix can be adjusted as required. In addition, 1,000 rounds of 0·5in and 3,080 rounds of 7·62mm ammunition are carried. The Sheridan is provided with a flotation screen, and when erected this enables the vehicle to propel itself across rivers and streams by its tracks. Night-vision equipment is provided as is an NBC system.

The M551 has not been a success. Its development was long and expensive, and a further in-service product-improvement program has failed to bring it up to an acceptable standard. As a result, it has long since been replaced by the M60 in reconnaissance units of the US Army in Europe. It remains in active use only at the National Training Center, Fort Irwin, where it is used to stimulate Soviet Army vehicles, but some redundant chassis may be used as interim self-propelled anti-tank guns for 9th Infantry Division.

Below: M551 Sheridan demonstrating its amphibious capability—an essential element for its reconnaissance role.

Below left: M551s show 152mm gun/launcher barrels. Combining the best aspects of gun and missile was fine only on paper.

Self-propelled Artillery

Since the end of World War II the US Army has led the increasingly rapid conversion from towed to self-propelled artillery. The M109 and M110 have become the standard weapons of most NATO armies and are reliable and effective

M109A2

Type: Self-propelled howitzer.
Crew: 6.
Armament: One 155mm howitzer; one ·5in (12·7mm) Browning anti aircraft machine-gun.
Armor: 20mm (0·79in) maximum, estimated.
Dimensions: Length (including armament) 21ft 8in (6·612m); length (hull) 20ft 6in (6·256m); width 10ft 10in (3·295m); height (including anti-aircraft machine-gun) 10ft 10in (3·295m).
Weight: Combat 55,000lb (24,948kg).
Ground Pressure: 10·95lb/in² (0·77kg/cm²).
Engine: Detroit Diesel Model 8V71T eight-cylinder turbocharged diesel developing 405bhp at 2,300rpm.
Performance: Road speed 35mph (56km/h); range 242 miles (390km vertical obstacle 1ft 9in (0·533m); trench 6ft (1·828m); gradient 60 per cent.
History: Entered service with the United States Army in 1963. Also used by Austria, Belgium, Canada, Denmark, Germany, Great Britain, Ethiopi Greece, Iran, Israel, Italy, Jordan, Kampuchea, Kuwait, Libya, Morocco the Netherlands, Norway, Oman, Pakistan, Saudi Arabia, Spain, South Korea, Switzerland, Taiwan, Tunisia and Turkey. Still in production.

The first production models of the M109 were completed in 1962, and some 3,700 examples have now been built (of which about 1,800 are in US Army service), making the M109 the most widely used self-propelled howitzer in the world. It has a hull of all-welded aluminum construction, providing the crew with protection from small arms fire. The driver is seated at the front of the hull on the left, with the engine to his right. The other five crew members are the commander, gunner and three ammunition members, al located in the turret at the rear of the hull. There is a large door in the rear of the hull for ammunition resupply purposes. Hatches are also provided in the sides and rear of the turret. There are two hatches in the roof of the turret, the commander's hatch being on the right. A 0·5in (12·7mm Browning machine-gun is mounted on this for anti-aircraft defense. The suspension is of the torsion-bar type and consists of seven road wheels, with the drive sprockets at the front and the idler at the rear, and there are no track-return rollers.

The 155mm howitzer has an elevation of +75° and a depression of −3° and the turret can be traversed through 360°. Elevation and traverse are powered, with manual controls for emergency use. The weapon can fire a variety of ammunition, including HE, tactical nuclear, illuminating, smoke and chemical rounds. Rate of fire is four rounds per minute for three minutes followed by one round per minute for the next hour. A total of 28 rounds of separate-loading ammunition is carried, as well as 500 rounds of machine

though their range is not as good as that of comparable
oviet equipments. One major complication is that rates of
re are now so high that special arrangements are having
o be made to ensure that the logistic system will be able
o cope with the resupply requirement. Artillery has always
een somewhat ineffective against armored vehicles—the
ajor contemporary threat to the US Army in Europe—and
reat efforts are being made to overcome this. One attempt,
he laser-guided Copperhead artillery shell, has failed
o live up to expectations, but artillery shells are being
eveloped which can deliver minelets, capable of attacking
rmored vehicles from above.

**bove: The business end of the 155mm howitzer of the 2nd Field
rtillery during a Reforger exercise in West Germany. Range of this
asic M109 is 16,070 yards (14,700m); nuclear shells can be fired.**

un ammunition.

The second model to enter service was the M109A1, identical with the
1109 apart from a much longer barrel, provided with a fume extractor
s well as a muzzle-brake. The fume extractor removes propellant gases
om the barrel after a round has been fired and thus prevents fumes from
ntering the fighting compartment. The M109A2 has an improved shell
ammer and recoil mechanism, the M178 modified gun mount, and other
ore minor improvements. The M109A3 is the M109A1 fitted with the
1178 gun mount.　　　　　　　　　　　　　　　　　　　　　　▶

▶   The M109 fires a round to a maximum range of 16,070 yards (14,700m the M109A1 fires to a maximum range of 19,685 yards (18,000m). Rocke assisted projectiles (M549A1) increase the maximum range to 26,250 yard (24,000m). A new nuclear round (M785) is now under development: it ballistically compatible with the M549A1 RAP and will utilize the sam protective container as the M758 eight-inch round (*see M110A2 entry*).

The M109 can ford streams to a maximum depth of 6ft (1·828m). special amphibious kit has been developed for the vehicle but this is no widely used. It consists of nine inflatable airbags, normally carried by truck. Four of these are fitted to each side of the hull and the last to the fror of the hull. The vehicle is then propelled in the water by its tracks at a max mum speed of 4mph (6·4km/h). The M109 is provided with infra-red drivin lights and some vehicles also have an NBC system.

To keep the M109 supplied with ammunition in the field Bowen-McLaug lin-York have recently developed the M992 Field Artillery Ammunitio Support Vehicle which is expected to enter production in the near futur

Right: M109A1 155mm SP howitzer fresh from the production line the Cleveland Ordnance Plant, run by Cadillac Motor Car Division

Below: An M109A2 of the US Army. This fine weapons system is i service with at least 28 armies and has proved a great success.

M110A2

M110, M110A1, M110A2

Type: Self-propelled howitzer.
Crew: 5 plus 8 (see text).
Armament: One 8in (203mm) howitzer.
Armor: 20mm (0·79in) maximum (estimated).
Dimensions: Length (including gun and spade in traveling position) 35ft 2½in (10·731m); length (hull) 18ft 9in (5·72m); width 10ft 4in (3·149m) height 10ft 4in (3·143m).
Weight: Combat 62,500lb (28,350kg).
Ground pressure: 10·80lb/in² (0·76kg/cm²).
Engine: Detroit Diesel Model 8V-7T eight-cylinder turbo-charged diese developing 405bhp at 2,300rpm.
Performance: Road speed 34mph (54·7km/h); range 325 miles (523km) vertical obstacle 3ft 4in (1·016m); trench 7ft 9in (2·362m); gradient 60 per cent.
History: Original version, M110, entered service with the United States Army in 1963. Now used by Belgium, West Germany, Greece, Iran, Israel Japan, Jordan, Saudi Arabia, South Korea, Netherlands, Pakistan, Spain Turkey, United Kingdom and United States.

In 1956 the United States Army issued a requirement for a range of self-propelled artillery which would be air-transportable. The Pacific Car and Foundry Company of Washington were awarded the development contract and from 1958 built three different self-propelled weapons on the same chassis. These were the T235 (175mm gun), which became the

M107, the T236 (203mm howitzer), which became the M110, and the T245 (155mm gun), which was subsequently dropped from the range. These prototypes were powered by a petrol engine, but it was soon decided to replace this by a diesel engine as this could give the vehicles a much greater range of action. The M107 is no longer in service with the US Army; all have been rebuilt to M110A2 configuration. The M110A2 is also in production by Bowen-McLaughlin-York Company, and when present orders have been completed the US Army wil have a total inventory of over 1,000.

The hull is of all-welded-steel construction with the driver at the front on the left with the engine to his right. The gun is mounted towards the rear of the hull. The suspension is of the torsion-bar type and consists of five road wheels, with the fifth road wheel acting as the idler, the drive sprocket is at the front. Five crew are carried on the gun (driver, commander and three gun crew), the other eight crew members following in an M548 tracked vehicle (this is based on the M113 APC chassis), which also carries the ammunition, as only two ready rounds are carried on the M110 itself. The 203mm howitzer has an elevation of $+65°$ and a depression of $-2°$, traverse being $30°$ left and $30°$ right. Elevation and traverse are both hydraulic, although there are manual controls for use in an emergency. The M110 fires an HE projectile to a maximum range of 26,575 yards (24,300m), and other types of projectile that can be fired include HE carrying 104 HE grenades, HE carrying 195 grenades, Agent GB or VX and tactical nuclear. A large hydraulically-operated spade is mounted at the rear of the hull and is lowered into position before the gun opens fire, and the suspension can also ▶

Below: M110A2 of the US Army. This version has the new M201 cannon which is 8ft (2·44m) longer than that mounted on the M110. The major shortcoming is the lack of a protective gun housing.

▶ be locked when the gun is fired to provide a more stable firing platform. The gun can officially fire one round per two minutes, but a well trained crew can fire one round per minute for short periods. As the projectile is very heavy, an hydraulic hoist is provided to position the projectile on the ramming tray; the round is then pushed into the breech hydraulically before the charge is pushed home, the breechlock closed and the weapon is then fired. The M110 can ford streams to a maximum depth of 3ft 6in (1·066m) but has no amphibious capability. Infra-red driving lights are fitted as standard but the type does not have an NBC system.

All M110s in US Army service, and in an increasing number of NATO countries as well, have been brought up to M110A2 configuration. The M110A1 has a new and longer barrel, while the M110A2 is identical to the M110A1 but has a double baffle muzzle brake. The M110A1 can fire up to charge eight while the M110A2 can fire up to charge nine. The M110A1 M110A2 can fire all of the rounds of the M110 but in addition binary high-explosive Rocket Assisted Projectile (M650), and the improved con

Below: Loading the M110A2, improved version of the Army's heaviest cannon artillery weapon. It has conventional and nuclear capability

entional munition which contains 195 M42 grenades. The latter two have maximum range, with charge nine, of 32,800 yards (30,000m).

The M110A2 also fires the M753 rocket-assisted tactical nuclear round, hich entered production in FY 1981. The M753 will be available in two rsions: the first as a normal nuclear round; the second as an "Enhanced adiation" version. These nuclear rounds are packed in very sophisticated ntainers to prevent unauthorized use and are subject to very stringent ntrols. The ER rounds will not be deployed outside the USA except in an nergency.

One major shortcoming of the M110 design has always been its lack of otection for the gun crew: it is virtually the only modern self-propelled ın to suffer such a deficiency. The US Army plans to rectify this by fitting a rew Ballistic Shelter (CBS), a high, square gun housing that will improve ırvivability against small arms and shell fragments by some 33 per cent ıd will also provide collective NBC protection.

One of the problems with heavy artillery of this type is keeping the guns ıpplied with sufficient ammunition. As noted above the weapon is sup- ɔrted by an M548 tracked vehicle, and this in turn is kept supplied by 5- or)-ton trucks.

Towed Artillery

The requirement for increased crew protection and greater mobility has led to the virtual total replacement of towed artillery pieces in the European theater by self-propelled guns and howitzers. As a result, towed artillery has been "relegated" to less taxing environments with airborne forces and

M102

Type: Light howitzer.
Caliber: 105mm.
Crew: 8.
Weight: 3,298lb (1,496kg).
Length firing: 22ft (6·718m).
Length traveling: 17ft (5·182m).
Height firing: 4·29ft (1·308m).
Height traveling: 5·22ft (1·594m).
Width: 6·44ft (1·964m).
Ground clearance: 1·08ft (0·33m).
Elevation: −5° to +75°.
Traverse: 360°.
Range: 12,576 yards (11,500m), standard ammunition; 16,513 yards (15,100m) with RAP.

The 105mm M102 was developed at Rock Island Arsenal to replace the standard 105mm M101 howitzer in both airborne and airmobile divisions. The first prototype was completed in 1962 and the weapon entered service in 1966. It was widely used in Vietnam. Improvements over the M101 include a reduction in weight, longer range, and it can be quickly traversed through 360°. Both the M101 and M102 were to have been replaced by

Below: The M102 has served for many years in 82nd Airborne Division, for which its light weight and compact dimensions, combined with good stability and all-round traverse made it an ideal weapon. All-up weight of 3,298lb (1,496kg) has been achieved by extensive use of aluminum.

he Rapid Deployment Force (RDF). Thus, towed equipments re still in production and under development, and there s, of course, still a lucrative export market. Like other Western armies, the US Army still finds it difficult to obtain s much range for its shells for a given caliber as do the Soviets, unless recourse is made to esoteric devices such as Rocket Assisted Projectiles (RAP). The M198, however, s a very promising weapon and should become the standard US Army towed howitzer, replacing both the current 105mm nd 155mm weapons. Its performance characteristics, however, are in most cases little better than the Soviet D30 howitzer of 122mm caliber.

bove: An M102 in action under a somewhat sparsely scrimmed amouflage net. The gun is resting on a firing turntable; a roller at he rear of the trail enables the gun to be traversed quickly.

ew 105mm howitzer called the XM204, but this was cancelled by Congress 1977 owing to both tactical and technical problems.

The M102 is normally deployed in battalions of 18 guns (each of these aving three batteries, each with 6 guns), and both the 82nd Airborne and 01st Airmobile/Air Assault Divisions each have three battalions of M102s, ut these are now being replaced by the 155mm M198. It is normally towed y the M561 (6×6) Gama Goat vehicle or a 2½ ton 6×6 truck, and can be arried slung underneath a Boeing Chinook CH-47 helicopter.

When in the firing position the wheels are raised off the ground and the weapon rests on a turntable under the front of the carriage; a roller tire is mounted at the rear of the trail and this enables the weapon to be quickly raversed through 360° to be laid onto a new target. The M102 has an nusual bow shape box type trail which is of aluminum construction to educe weight. Its breechblock is of the vertical sliding wedge type and its ecoil system is of the hydropneumatic type. The barrel is not provided with muzzle brake, although this was fitted to the prototype weapons. A wide ange of ammunition can be fitted including high explosive, high explosive nti-tank, anti-personnel, illuminating, smoke, chemical, HEP-T, and leaflet. en rounds per minute can be fired for the first three minutes, and 3 rounds er minute in the sustained fire role.

M114A2

Type: Howitzer.
Caliber: 155mm.
Crew: 11.
Weight: 12,700lb (5,761kg).
Length traveling: 23·9ft (7·315mm).
Width traveling: 7·99ft (2·438m).
Height traveling: 5·9ft (1·8m).
Elevation: −2° to +63°.
Traverse: 25° right and 24° left.
Range: 21,106 yards (19,300m).

In 1939, Rock Island Arsenal started the development of a new 155mm towed howitzer to replace the 155mm M1918 howitzer which at that time was the standard 155mm howitzer of the US Army (this was basically a modified French 155mm weapon built in the United States). This new 155mm weapon was designated the M1 and first production weapons were completed in 1942. Production continued until after the end of the war by which time over 6,000 weapons had been built. After the war the M1 was redesignated the M114. The 4·5 inch M1 used the same carriage as the M114 but none of these remain in service today. A self-propelled model called the M41 was also built, but again, none of these remain in service with the US Army.

When the weapon is in the firing position, it is supported on its trails and a firing jack which is mounted under the carriage. When in the traveling position, the trails are locked together and attached to the prime mover which is generally a 6x6 truck. The M114 can also be carried slung under a Boeing CH-47 Chinook helicopter.

Its recoil system is of the hydropneumatic variable type and its breech block is of the stepped thread/interrupted screw type. The M114 can fire a variety of ammunition of separate loading type (eg, the projectile and charge) including an HE round weighing 95lb (43kg), tactical nuclear

uminating and chemical. Sustained rate of fire is one round per minute. It annot however fire the new Rocket Assisted Round which has a longer ange than the standard 155mm round.

The US Marine Corps developed a new tube for the M114 which has een adopted by the US Army as the M114A2. This tube is a ballistic match or that on the M109A2 (qv), and the M114A2 can thus fire all ammunition red by its self-propelled counterpart. The M114A2 is used by general-upport artillery units of the US Army Reserve and the National Guard.

M198

Type: Towed howitzer.
Caliber: 155mm.
Crew: 10.
Weight: 15,795lb (7,165kg).
Length firing: 37ft 1in (11·302m).
Length traveling: 23ft 3in (7·086m).
Width firing: 28ft (8·534m).
Width traveling: 9ft 2in (2·79m).
Height firing (minimum): 5·91ft (1·803m).
Height traveling: 9·92ft (3·023m).
Ground clearance: 13in (0·33m).
Elevation: −4·2° to +72°.
Traverse: 22½° left and right; 360° with speed traverse.
Range: 32,808 yards (30,000m) with RAP; 24,060 yards (22,000m) with conventional round.

In the late 1960s, Rock Island Arsenal started work on a new 155mm howitzer to replace the M114, and this was given the development designation of the XM198. The first two prototypes were followed by eight further prototypes, and during extensive trials these weapons fired over 45,000 rounds of ammunition. The M198 is now in production at Rock Island; the Army has a requirement for 435 M198s while the Marine Corps requires 282. It has also been adopted by a number of other countries including Australia, India, Greece, Pakistan, Thailand and Saudi Arabia. The M198 is used by airborne, airmobile and infantry divisions. Other divisions will continue to use self-propelled artillery. The weapon will be developed in battalions of 18 guns, each battery having 6 weapons. The M198 is normally towed by a 6×6 5-ton truck or a tracked M548 cargo carrier, the latter being a member of the M113 family of tracked vehicles. It can also be carried under a Boeing CH-47 Chinook, but (and this is a most important drawback) its 5-ton prime mover cannot. A further problem is that the carriage is some 5in (127mm) too wide to fit into the Low-Attitude Parachute Extraction System (LAPES) rails in USAF C-130 aircraft.

When in the traveling position, the barrel is swung through 180° so that it rests over the trails. This reduces the overall length of the weapon. When in the firing position the trails are opened out and the suspension system is raised so that the weapon rests on a non-anchored firing platform. A hydraulic ram cylinder and a 24in (0·609m) diameter float mounted in the bottom carriage at the on-carriage traverse centerline provides for rapid shift of the carriage to ensure 360° traverse. This enables the weapon to be quickly laid onto a new target.

The weapon has a recoil system of the hydropneumatic type and the barrel is provided with a double baffle muzzle brake. The M198 uses separate loading ammunition (e.g. a projectile and a separate propelling charge) and can fire an HE round to a maximum range of 22,000m, or out to 30,000m with a Rocket Assisted Projectile. The latter is basically a conventional HE shell with a small rocket motor fitted at the rear to increase the range of the shell. The weapon will also be the primary user of the new Cannon Launched Guided Projectile (or Copperhead) round. Nuclear and Improved Conventional Munitions, as well as rounds at present used with the M114, can also be fired. It will also be able to fire the range of ammunition developed for the FH70. The latter is a joint development between Britain, Germany and Italy, and is now in production. Maximum rate of fire is four rounds per minute for the first three minutes, followed by two rounds per minute thereafter. A thermal warning device is provided so that the gun crew know when the barrel is becoming too hot.

Although a great improvement on its predecessors, the M198 has suffered from a number of problems. The desired range and accuracy requirements

Above: An M198 howitzer firing at its maximum elevation of 72°, a capability necessary to clear crests or to fire out of a jungle clearing. M198 will serve with artillery units in the US RDF.

ave been achieved at the expense of mobility and size. Further, unit price as increased from an original estimate of $184,000 to $421,000— lthough the M198 is by no means the only weapon system to suffer such roblems.

Aviation

The US Army possesses some 550 fixed-wing and 8,000 rotary-wing front-line aircraft; a larger air component than many air forces. These are, in the main, an integral part of the combat components of the Army, especially the Cavalry Brigades Air Attack. The helicopter force ranges in size

Beechcraft C-12
C-12, RC-12D, RU-21J

Type: Fixed-wing utility aircraft.

Engines: Two 850shp Pratt and Whitney of Canada PT6A-38 (C-12A turboprops.

Dimensions: Overall length 43·75ft (13·34m); height 15ft (4·57m); wing span 54·5ft (16·61m); wing area 303ft² (28·15m²).

Weights: Gross weight (C-12) 12,500lb (5,670kg), (RC-12D) 14,000lb (6,350kg).

Performance: Cruising speed 242 knots (448km/h); range with full pay load 1,681 nautical miles (3,115km); mission ceiling (C-12) 31,000f (9,450m), (RC-12D) 27,000ft (8,230m).

Armament: Nil.

History: First flight (Super King Air 200) 27 October 1972; entered service (C-12A) July 1975.

Development: The C1-12, a military version of the Super King Air 200, is latest in a long line of small, fixed-wing utility aircraft used by the US Army Its primary tasks are the transportation of priority cargo and passengers

rom the diminutive (but highly effective) Hughes OH-6 to the win-rotor Boeing Vertol CH-47, and is being substantially mproved by the UH-60 utility helicopter and the AH-64 attack helicopter. Large numbers of the older OH-58, UH-1, and AH-1 will, however, remain in service for many years o come. The size of the fixed-wing aircraft is limited to a specific weight by an inter-Service agreement with the USAF, but the Army still operates many OV-1 and RU-21/C-12 aircraft. For the future, the Army has been involved in the VX program—a development of the Bell XV-15 technology— but like many previous joint-Service undertakings this has un into severe problems.

Above: Beechcraft RC-12D aircraft of the US Army, with an impressive array of antennas. A recent analysis of this aircraft suggests that its role is missile suppression in support of airborne operations.

Left: Beechcraft U-21 aircraft of the US Army, loading freight. The Army maintains a small fleet of U-21 and C-12 aircraft for flying urgent freight and passengers, but lost its heavier fixed-wing aircraft such as the de Havilland Canada C-7) to the USAF in a politically nspired inter-Service transfer in 1967. The larger C-12 supplements the U-21 and is the basic version of the RC-12D. Some 98 C-12 transports are in service worldwide. With close monitoring by the USAF, larger Army aircraft will not be allowed.

and it has an all-weather day and night capability. Special equipment fits suit the basic airframe for intelligence gathering, airborne command post, or flying ambulance duties. The US Army has taken delivery of 60 C-12As, 14 C-12Cs (identical with the C-12A except for PT6A-41 engines), and 24 C-12Ds. The latter differs from the C-12C only in the fitting of a cargo door and wing-tip tanks.

The US Army has recently devoted a great deal of attention to airborne Electronic Warfare (EW) platforms. One such is the EH-60A Quick Fix (see UH-60A entry), but fixed-wing aircraft offer significant advantages over helicopters in this field. The most recent project is Guardrail V, which is designed to intercept and locate enemy ground transmissions in certain frequency bands. The original aircraft in Guardrail V was the RU-21H, the US Army version of the earlier Beech King Air, but under the Improved Guardrail V program, eight C-12s are being fitted out under the designation RC-12D, with antennas above and below the wing and ECM pods.

Bell AH-IS HueyCobra

Type: Attack helicopter.
Engine: 1,800shp Lycoming T53-L-703 turboshaft.
Dimensions: Main-rotor diameter 44ft (13·4m); overall length (rotor turning) 52ft 11½in (16·14m); length of fuselage 44ft 5in (13·54m); height 13ft 5½in (4·1m).
Weights: Empty 6,598lb (2,993kg); maximum 10,000lb (4,536kg).
Performance: Maximum speed (TOW configuration) 141mph (227km/h); max rate of climb (SL, rated power) 1,620ft (494m)/min; service ceiling (rated power) 12,200ft (3,719m); hovering ceiling in ground effect, same; range (max fuel, SL, 8% reserve) 315 miles (507km).
Armament: M65 system with nose telescope sight and crew helmet sights for cueing and guiding eight TOW missiles on outboard under-wing pylons; chin turret (to 100th AH-1S) M28 with 7·62mm Minigun and 40mm M129 grenade launcher with 300 bombs, (from No 101) GE Universal turret with 20mm M197 three-barrel gun (or alternative 30mm); also wide range of cluster/fuel-air explosive and other weapons or five types of rocket fired from 7 or 19-tube launchers.
History: First flight 7 September 1965; combat service June 1967 (TOW Cobra January 1973, AH-1S March 1977).

Development: First flown in 1965 after only six months of development, the HueyCobra is a combat development of the UH-1 Iroquois family. It combines the dynamic parts—engine, transmission, and rotor system—of the original Huey with a new streamlined fuselage providing for a gunner in the front and pilot above and behind him and for a wide range of fixed and power-aimed armament systems. The first version was the US Army AH-1G, with 1,100hp T53 engine, of which 1,124 were delivered, including eight to the Spanish Navy for anti-ship strike and 38 as trainers to the US Marine Corps. The AH-1Q is an anti-armor version often called TOWCobra because it carries eight TOW missile pods as well as the appropriate sighting system. Latest versions are the -1Q, -1R, and -1S with more power and new equipment.

The US Army plans to upgrade many earlier models to -1S standard which, with 324 new production aircraft, will give a total fleet of 982. Several hundred are already in service. Thus, the HueyCobra, developed in just six months in 1965, will remain in front-line service with the US Army well into the 1990s and probably beyond the year 2000.

Above: Bell AH-1S at the moment of firing one of its TOW anti-tank guided missiles. The US Army plans to have a fleet of 982 AH-1s.

Above: The pilot's cockpit of an AH-1Q. The multiplicity of analog indicators clearly shows the 1960/70s origins of this ubiquitous aircraft, which will continue to serve the US Army into the next century.

Left: An AH-1S, showing one of the many weapons permutations possible. Note the nose sights and 7·62mm Minigun in the chin turret.

Bell OH-58C Kiowa

Type: Light observation helicopter/Army Helicopter Improvement Program (AHIP).

Engine: (OH-58A, TH-57A) one 317shp Allison T63-700 turboshaft (OH-58C) 420shp T63-720.

Dimensions: Diameter of two-blade main rotor 35ft 4in (10·77m); length overall (rotors turning) 40ft 11¾in (12·49m); height 9ft 6½in (2·91m).

Weights: Empty (C) 1,585lb (719kg), (D) 2,825lb (1,281kg); maximum (C) 3,200lb (1,451kg).

Performance: Maximum speed 139mph (224km/h); service ceiling (C) 19,000ft (5,791m); range (SL, no weapons, 10% reserve) 299 miles (481km).

Armament: Usually none (see text).

History: First flight (OH-4A) 8 December 1962, (206A) 10 January 1966 (production OH-58C) 1978, (AHIP) 1983.

Development: The loser in the US Army Light Observation Helicopter contest of 1962, the 206 was marketed as the civil JetRanger, this family growing to encompass the more powerful 206B and more capacious 206L LongRanger. In 1968 the US Army re-opened the LOH competition, naming Bell now winner and buying 2,200 OH-58A Kiowas similar to the 206A but

ith larger main rotor. Since 1976 Bell has been rebuilding 585 OH-58A Kiowas to OH-58C standard with uprated engine, flat-plate canopy to reduce glint, new instrument panel, improved avionics, and many minor improvements. Standard armament kit, not always fitted, is the M27 with a 7·62mm Minigun firing ahead.

In 1981 Bell was named winner of the AHIP (Army Helicopter Improvement Program) for a "near-term scout". The first of five prototype Model 406 AHIP machines flew in 1983. Features include a new rotor with four composite blades driven by a much more powerful T63-type (Model 250) engine, very comprehensive protection systems, and a mast-mounted ball with TV and FLIR (forward-looking infra-red), laser ranger/designator, inertial navigation, and one or two pairs of MLMS missiles.

The AHIP will serve in air cavalry, attack helicopter, and field artillery units. One of its main tasks will be target acquisition and laser designation for Hellfire missiles, Copperhead, and other US Army/USAF laser-guided munitions. The number of OH-58As and -58Cs to be converted to AHIP standard has yet to be decided, but the first 16 were delivered in FY85. Yet another version, the Model 406CS (Combat Scout) is now flying.

Below: The Bell OH-58C Kiowa is a modified version of the earlier OH-58A with a more powerful engine, uprated transmission and an anti-glare flat-glass canopy. More minor improvements have also been fitted, like the infra-red suppressed exhaust stacks seen here.

Bell UH-1H Iroquois (Huey)

Type: Utility helicopter.

Engine: Originally, one Lycoming T53 free-turbine turboshaft rated at 600-640shp, later rising in stages to 825,930, 1,100 and 1,400shp; (212) 1,800shp P&WC PT6T-3 (T400) coupled turboshafts, flat-rated at 1,250shp and with 900shp immediately available from either following failure of the other.

Dimensions: Diameter of twin-blade main rotor (204, UH-1B, C) 44ft 0in (13·41m), (205,2 12) 48ft 0in (14·63m) (tracking tips, 48ft 2¼in, 14·69m); (214) 50ft 0in (15·24m); overall length (rotors turning) (early) 53ft 0in (16·15m), (virtually all modern versions) 57ft 3¼in (17·46m); height overall (modern, typical) 14ft 4¾in (4·39m).

Weights: Empty (XH-40) about 4,000lb (1,814kg), (typical 205) 4,667lb (2,110kg), (typical 212) 5,549lb (2,517kg); maximum loaded (XH-40) 5,800lb (2,631kg), (typical 205) 9,500lb (4,309kg), (212/UH-1N) 10,500lb (4,762kg).

Performance: Maximum speed (all) typically 127mph (204km/h); econ cruise speed, usually same; max range with useful payload, typically 248 miles (400km).

Armament: See text.

History: First flight (XH-40) 22 October 1956, (production UH-1) 1958 (205) August 1961, (212) 1969.

Development: Used by more air forces, and built in greater numbers, than any other military aircraft since World War II, the "Huey" family of helicopters grew from a single prototype, the XH-40, for the US Army. Over 20 years the gross weight has been almost multiplied by three, though the size has changed only slightly. Early versions seat eight to ten, carried the occasional machine-gun, and included the TH-1L Seawolf trainer for the US Navy. Prior to 1962 the Army/Navy designation was basically HU-1, which gave rise to the name Huey, though the (rarely used) official name is Iroquois. Since 1962 the basic designation has been UH-1 (utility helicopter type 1).

In August 1961 Bell flew the first Model 205 with many changes of which

the greatest was a longer fuselage giving room for up to 14 passengers or troops, or six litters (stretchers) and an attendant, or up to 3,880lb (1,759kg) of cargo. All versions have blind-flying instruments, night lighting, AM/VHF/UHF radios, IFF transponder, DF/VOR, powered controls, and searchlight. Options include a hook for a slung load, rescue hoist, and various fits of simple weapons or armor. Newest and most important of the Model 205 helicopters in US military service is the UH-1H, which remained in production until 1980. Ten have been converted as EH-1H Quick Fix EW (electronic-warfare) machines, but this role has been taken over by the more powerful EH-60A. Two were given augmented avionics and special equipment as UH-1V medevac transports.

Some 3,900 UH-1s are currently in US Army service; about 3,500 are the UH-1H model, which was introduced in 1967. Some 2,700 of the -1Hs are scheduled to remain in service beyond the year 2000 for a wide range of duties, and apart from fitting glassfiber composite blades they will be completely upgraded with over 220 new items or improvements including a radar-warning receiver, chaff/flare dispenser, IR jammer, exhaust IR suppressor, radar altimeter, DME, and secure communications even in NOE (nap of the Earth) flying.

Left: Troopers of 1st Cavalry (Airmobile) doing a "hoverjump" from a UH-1D during Operation Oregon (August 1967) in the Vietnam War.

Below: The Vietnam War saw an unprecedented advance in the use of the helicopter on the battlefield: UH-1H delivers troops at a LP.

Boeing Vertol
CH-47D Chinook

Type: Medium transport helicopter.
Engines: Two 3,750shp Lycoming T55-L-11A free-turbine turboshafts.
Dimensions: Diameter of main rotors 60ft (18·29m); length, rotors turnin
99ft (30·2m); length of fuselage 51ft (15.54m); height 18ft 7in (5·67m)
Weights: Empty 20,616lb (9,351kg); loaded (condition 1) 33,000l
(14,969kg); (overload condition II) 46,000lb (20,865kg).
Performance: Maximum speed (condition I) 189mph (304km/h); (I
142mph (229km/h); initial climb (I) 2,880ft (878m)/min; (II) 1,320
(402m)/min; service ceiling (I) 15,000ft (4,570m); (II) 8,000ft (2,440m
mission radius, cruising speed and payload (I) 115 miles (185km) at 158mp
(254km/h) with 7,262lb (3,294kg); (II) 23 miles (37km) at 131mp
(211km/h) with 23,212lb (10,528kg).
Armament: Normally none.
History: First flight (YCH-47A) 21 September 1961, (CH-47C) 14 Octobe
1967, (D) 11 May 1979.

Above: US Army troops wait to board a prototype CH-47D, the test model of this versatile and extremely capable aircraft.

Left: An early model CH-47 delivers a water trailer to a forward position, its downdraught demolishing troops' "hootchies"!

Below: A CH-47C delivers an M102 105mm light howitzer, a load well within its capabilities. The -D model has three cargo hooks.

▶ **Development:** Development of the Vertol 114 began in 1956 to meet th
need of the US Army for a turbine-engined all-weather cargo helicopt
able to operate effectively in the most adverse conditions of altitude ar
temperature. Retaining the tandem-rotor configuration, the first YCH-47
flew on the power of two 2,200shp Lycoming T55 turboshaft engines ar
led directly to the production CH-47A. With an unobstructed cabin 7½ft
(2·29m) wide, 6½ft (1·98m) high and over 30ft (9·2m) long, the Chinoc
proved a valuable vehicle, soon standardized as US Army medium helicopt
and deployed all over the world. By 1972 more than 550 had served
Vietnam, mainly in the battlefield airlift of troops and weapons but als
rescuing civilians (on one occasion 147 refugees and their belongings we
carried to safety in one Chinook) and lifting back for salvage or repa
11,500 disabled aircraft valued at more than $3,000 million. The A mod
gave way to the CH-47B, with 2,850hp engines and numerous improv
ments. Since 1967 the standard basic version has been the CH-47C, wi
much greater power and increased internal fuel capacity. Most exports ▶
BV are of this model, which in 1973 began to receive a crashworthy fu
system and integral spar inspection system.

In the late 1970s there was a resurgence of orders, and by 1981 th

Above: These two non-standard Chinooks were modified CH-47Bs with additional sensors fitted in the nose for night observation and attack trials. They have since been rebuilt to the CH-47D standard.

were nearing 1,000, with many new customers. Argentina's Type 308 is an Antarctic logistic/rescue machine with radar, duplex inertial navigation and range of 1,265 miles (2,036km). Canada's CH-147s have many advanced features, but the 33 Chinook HC.1 transports of the RAF are to an even later standard with 44 seats or 24 stretcher casualties, triple cargo hooks (front and rear, 20,000lb, 9,072kg, center at 28,000lb, 12,700kg), Decca TacNav, Doppler and area navigation, new cockpit lighting, L-11E engines driving folding glass/carbon-fiber blades and amphibious capability in Sea State 3.

Development work on the RAF Chinook has led to the CH-47D for the US Army. The first 436 D models will be converted from older machines, but these will be followed by 91 new-builds, for a total inventory of 527. These feature 3,750shp L-712 long-life engines, 7,500shp transmission, redundant and uprated electrics, glassfiber blades, modular hydraulics, triple cargo hook, advanced light control system, new avionics, single-point fueling, survivability gear, and T62 APU.

Grumman OV-1 Mohawk

OV-1A to -1D, EV-1, JOV, RV

Type: (OV) multi-sensor tactical observation and reconnaissance; (EV) electronic warfare; (JOV) armed reconnaissance; (RV) electronic reconnaissance.

Engines: Two 1,005shp Lycoming T53-7 or -15 free-turbine turboprops (OV-1D) two, 1,160shp T53-701.

Dimensions: Span (-1A, -C) 42ft (12·8m); (-1, -D) 48ft (14·63m); length 41ft (12·5m); (-1D with SLAR, 44ft 11in); height 12ft 8in (3·86m).

Weights: Empty (-1A) 9,937lb (4,507kg); (-1B) 11,067lb (5,020kg); (-1C 10,400lb (4,717kg); (-1D) 12,054lb (5,467kg); maximum loaded (-1A 15,031lb (6,818kg); (11B, C) 19,230lb (8,722kg); (-1D) 18,109lb (8,214kg)

Performance: Maximum speed (all) 297-310mph (480-500km/h); initial climb (-1A) 2,950ft (900m)/min; (-1B) 2,250ft (716m)/min; (-1C), 2,670f (814m)/min; (-1D) 3,618ft (1,103m)/min; service ceiling (all) 28,800 31,000ft (8,534-9,449m); range with external fuel (-1A) 1,410 mile (2,270km); (-1B) 1,230 miles (1,980km); (-1C) 1,330 miles (2,140km' (-1D), 1,011 miles (1,627km).

Armament: Not normally fitted, but can include a wide variety of air-to ground weapons including grenade launchers, Minigun pods and sma guided missiles.

History: First flight (YOV-1A) 14 April, 1959; service delivery, Februar 1961; final delivery (new aircraft) December 1970.

Development: Representing a unique class of military aircraft, the OV- Mohawk is a specially designed battlefield surveillance machine wit characteristics roughly midway between lightplanes and jet fighters. On of its requirements was to operate from rough forward airstrips and it ha exceptional STOL (short takeoff and landing) qualities and good low-spee control with full-span slats and triple fans and rudders. Pilot and observe sit in side-by-side Martin Baker J5 seats and all versions have extremel good all-round view and very comprehensive navigation and communica tions equipment. All versions carry cameras and upward-firing flares fo night photography. Most variants carry UAS-4 infra-red surveillance equip ment and the -1B carries APS-94 SLAR (side-looking airborne radar) in long pod under the right side of the fuselage, with automatic film processin giving, within seconds of exposure, a permanent film record of rada image on either side of the flight path. The -1D combined the functions o the two previous versions in being quickly convertible to either IR o SLAR missions. Underwing pylons can carry 150 US gal drop tank

Above: OV-1D with Sideways-Looking Airborne Radar (SLAR) and Infra-Red (IR) sensors monitors Mount St Helens eruption.

ECM (electronic countermeasures) pods, flare/chaff dispensers, or, in the OV-1A such weapons as FFAR pods, 0.50in gun pods or 500lb (227kg) bombs—though a 1965 Department of Defense rule forbids the US Army to arm its fixed-wing aircraft! The EV-1 is the OV-1B converted to electronic surveillance with an ALQ-133 target locator system in centerline and tip pods. The RV-1C and -1D are conversions of the OV-1C and -1D for permanent use in the electronic reconnaissance role. Total production of all versions was 371, and since the mid-1970s the USA has maintained a continuing modernization programme involving (by 1983) 91 earlier models to OV-1D standard, and four to RV-1D, to maintain a force of 110 OV-1Ds and 36 RV-1Ds into the 1990s.

Below left: An OV-1D painted in overall "low-contrast" grey, which is not in reality as light as it appears from this photograph.

Below: An early model OV-1 coming in to land at a forward airstrip.

Hughes AH-64 Apache

Model 77, AH-64

Type: Armed helicopter.

Engines: Two 1,536shp General Electric T700-700 free-turbine turbo shafts.

Dimensions: Diameter of four-blade main rotor 48ft 0in (14·63m); length overall (rotors turning) 57ft ½in (17·39m); length of fuselage 49ft 1½in (14·97m); height to top of hub 13ft 10in (4·22m).

Weights: Empty 10,268lb (4,657kg); maximum loaded 17,650lb (8,006kg)

Performance: Maximum speed (13,925lb/6,316kg) 192mph (309km/h) maximum cruising speed 182mph (293km/h); max vertical climb 2,880ft (878m)/min; max range on internal fuel 380 miles (611km); ferry range 1,121 miles (1,804km).

Armament: Four wing hardpoints can carry 16 Hellfire missiles or 76 rockets (or mix of these weapons); turret under fuselage (designed to collapse harmlessly upwards in crash landing) houses 30mm Chain Gun with 1,200 rounds of varied types of ammunition.

History: First flight (YAH-64) 30 September 1975; entry into service scheduled 1984.

Development: A generation later than the cancelled Lockheed AH-56A Cheyenne (the world's first dedicated armed escort and attack helicopter the AH-64 was selected as the US Army's standard future attack helicopter in December 1976. This followed competitive evaluation with the rival Bell YAH-63, which had tricycle landing gear and the pilot seated in front

Right: The AH-64 Apache is visually one of the least attractive of modern helicopters, but is also the most potent combat machine of a

Below: A development aircraft showing its heavy armament and "black hole" engine exhausts to defeat heat-seeking missiles.

▶ of the co-pilot/gunner. The basic development contract also included the Chain Gun, a lightweight gun (in 30mm calibre in this application) with a rotating lockless bolt. In 1977 development began of the advanced avionics, electro-optics and weapon-control systems, progressively fitted to three more prototypes, followed by a further three—designated Total Systems Aircraft—flown by early 1980. The 56-month development ended in mid-1981 and limited production began at the end of that year. Total US Army requirement is for 572 machines, but actual procurement may be rather less, because of rapid cost escalation.

McDonnell Douglas (formerly Hughes) is responsible for dynamic components, while Teledyne Ryan produces the bulk of the rest of the airframe (fuselage, wings, engine nacelles, avionic bays, canopy and tail unit). The entire structure is designed to withstand hits with any type of ammunition up to 23mm calibre. The main blades, for example, each have five stainless-steel spars, with structural glassfiber tube linings, a laminated stainless steel skin and composite rear section, all bonded together. The main sensors are PNVS (pilot's night vision system) and TADS (target acquisition and designation sight) jointly developed by Martin Marietta and Northrop.

Both crew members are equipped with the Honeywell IHADSS (integrated helmet and display sight system) and each can in emergency fly the helicopter and control its weapons. The helicopter's nose sight incorporates day/night FLIR (forward-looking infra-red) laser ranger/designator and laser tracker. The AH-64 carries an ordnance load of some 2,650lb (1,202kg), which can include up to 16 Hellfire anti-tank missiles, 76 2·75in (6·98cm) rockets, up to 1,200 rounds for its 30mm cannon, or lesser combinations of these.

Below: An AH-64 armed with 2·75in (7cm) rockets and Hellfire anti-tank missiles. Under the nose is a Hughes 30mm cannon.

Above: An AH-64 demonstrating its ability to carry a maximum of 16 Hellfire anti-tank missiles. Typical mission weight is 13,920lb (6,314kg).

Hughes OH-6A Cayuse

Type: Light observation helicopter.
Engine: One Allison turboshaft T63-5A flat-rated at 252·5shp.
Dimensions: Diameter of four-blade main rotor 26ft 4in (8·03m); length overall (rotors turning) 30ft 3¼in (9·24m); height overall 8ft 1½in (2·48m).
Weights: Empty 1,229lb (557kg), maximum loaded 2,700lb (1,225kg).
Performance: Max cruise at S/L 150mph (241km/h); typical range on normal fuel 380 miles (611km).
Armament: See text.
History: First flight (OH-6A) 27 February 1963.

Development: Original winner of the controversial LOH (Light Observation Helicopter) competition of the US Army in 1961, the OH-6A Cayuse is one of the most compact flying machines in history, relative to its capability. The standard machine carries two crew and four equipped troops, or up to 1,000lb (454kg) of electronics and weapons including the XM-27 gun or XM-75 grenade launcher plus a wide range of other infantry weapons. The US Army bought 1,413 and several hundred other military or para-military examples have been built by Hughes or licencees. In 1986 the Model 500 was in production with, or offering, nine military helicopters all significantly uprated compared with the Cayuse, and bristling with advanced avionics sensors, weapons and protective features, but the only sale to the US

Sikorsky CH-54A Tarhe

Type: Crane helicopter.
Engines: (CH-54A) two 4,500shp Pratt & Whitney T73-1 turboshaft (CH-54B) two 4,800shp T73-700.
Dimensions: Diameter of six-blade main rotor 72ft 0in (21·95m); length overall (rotors turning) 88ft 6in (26·97m); height overall 18ft 7in (5·67m).
Weights: Empty (A) 19,234lb (8,724kg); maximum loaded (A) 42,000lb (19,050kg), (B) 47,000lb (21,318kg).
Performance: Maximum cruise 105mph (169km/h); hovering ceiling out of ground effect 6,900ft (2,100m); range with max fuel and 10 per cent reserve (typical) 230 miles (370km).
Armament: Normally none.
History: First flight (S-64) 9 May 1962; service delivery (CH-54A) late 1964, (B) late 1969.

Development: Developed from the first large US Army helicopter, the S-56, via the piston-engined S-60, the S-64 is an efficient weight-lifter which in Vietnam carried loads weighing up to 20,000lb (9,072kg). The CH-54A Tarhes used in that campaign retrieved more than 380 shot-down aircraft, saving an estimated $210 million, and carried special vans housing up to 87 combat-equipped troops. The improved CH-54B, distinguished externally by twin main wheels, has lifted loads up to 40,780lb (18,497kg) and reached a height of 36,122ft (11,010m). There is no fuselage, just a structural beam joining the tail rotor to the cockpit in which seats are provided for three pilots, one facing to the rear for maneuvering with loads. The dynamic components (rotor, gearboxes, shafting) were used as the basis for those of the S-65. With cancellation of the HLH (Heavy-Lift Helicopter) the S-64 remains the only large crane helicopter in the West. A total of just over 100 was built, of which the US Army took delivery of 89; 72 of these currently survive.

By 1983 the CH-54 could be outperformed by the CH-47D and had been phased out of regular Army service. It remains in service with aviation units of the Army National Guard.

Above: OH-6D AHIP contender. Hughes, taken over by McDonnell Douglas in 1984, was retitled McDonnell Douglas Helicopter

military has been USA funding of a single research Notar (NO TAil Rotor) helicopter modified from an OH-6A.

Virtually all OH-6As in the US Army inventory are now with National Guard or Army Reserve units.

Above: The CH-54 has for many years been the only large crane helicopter in the Army, but is now only in service with the National Guard.

Sikorsky UH-60A Black Hawk

UH-60A, EH-60A

Type: (UH) combat assault transport, (EH) electronic warfare and target acquisition.

Engines: (UH, EH) two 1,560shp General Electric T700-700 free-turbine turboshafts.

Dimensions: Diameter of four-blade rotor 53ft 8in (16·36m); length overall (rotors turning) 64ft 10in (19·76m); length (rotors/tail folded) 41ft 4in (12·6m); height overall 16ft 10in (5·13m).

Weights: Empty 10,624lb (4,819kg); maximum loaded 20,250lb (9,185kg) (normal mission weight 16,260lb, 7,375kg).

Performance: Maximum speed, 184mph (296km/h); cruising speed 167mph (269km/h); range at max wt, 30 min reserves, 373 miles (600km).

Armament: (UH) provision for two M60 LMGs firing from side of cabin plus chaff/flare dispensers; (EH) electronic only.

History: First flight (YUH) 17 October 1974, (production UH) October 1978, service delivery (UH) June 1979.

Development: The UH-60 was picked in December 1976 after four years of competition with Boeing Vertol for a UTTAS (utility tactical transport aircraft system) for the US Army. Designed to carry a squad of 11 equipped troops and a crew of three, the Black Hawk can have eight troop seats replaced by four litters (stretchers), and an 8,000lb (3,628kg) cargo load can be slung externally. The titanium/glassfibre/Nomex honeycomb rotor is electrically de-iced, as are the pilot windscreens, and equipment includes comprehensive navaids, communications and radar warning. Deliveries to the 101st Airborne Division took place in 1979-81, followed by a further

Right: A UH-60A Black Hawk is off-loaded from a C-5 at Cairo West airport after flying in from the USA on a RDF exercise.

Below: In their true element a group of UH-60s collecting troops from an ad hoc landing zone in scrubland, during an exercise in the USA.

89

▶ block of 100 to the 82nd Division in 1981. It is now also in service with 9⏀ and 24th Infantry Divisions in CONUS, and with US Army Europe. Becaus⏀ it is much more capable than the UH-1 it is replacing the older machine in⏀ ratio of 15:23 in combat support companies and 7:8 in air cavalry unit⏀ The current aim is to field a total of 1,107 UH-60As at a cost of $6·58 billic⏀ (of which R&D accounts for $481 million).

The EH-60A is an ECM (electronic countermeasures) version with Quic⏀ Fix II (as used in the Bell EH-1H) radar warning augmentation, chaff/fla⏀ dispenser, and infra-red jammer. The EH-60B SOTAS (stand-off targe⏀ acquisition system) was to have been a dedicated platform for detectir⏀ and classifying moving battlefield targets under all weather conditions, wi⏀ a data terminal in the cabin fed from a large rotating surveillance radar aeri⏀ under the fuselage (the main wheels retracting to avoid it), but it wa⏀ canceled in 1981.

Right: One of the YUH-60 prototypes during trials with a squad of⏀ equipped troops. The Army has ordered 1,107 of these machines.

Below: The ability to allow four soldiers to descend by rope at the⏀ same time greatly reduces the vulnerable period in the hover.

Remotely Piloted Vehicles (RPV)

Following the great strides made in RPV technology during the Vietnam War (mainly in an Air Force context) and the recent Israeli successes, the US Army is now heavily involved in RPV development. The program, currently funded at some $395 million over the Fiscal Years 1982-85, is

Aquila (Army RPV)

Type: Remotely piloted vehicle.
Engine: One McCulloch MC101 M/C, 10hp.
Dimensions: Wingspan 12·33ft (3·76m); length 5·41ft (1·65m).
Weights: Maximum takeoff 119·1lb (54.4kg); payload 35·93lb (16·3kg).
Performance: Maximum speed 140mph (222km/h); maximum endurance 3 hours; ceiling 11,800ft (3,600m) plus.
Armament: None.
History: First flight December 1975. *(Specifications relate to Aquila.)*

Most modern armies are now faced with a problem of possessing artillery systems that far outperform the current target acquisition means. These new artillery systems have much increased range and markedly shorter response times; thus, the ground commander needs long-range, responsive reconnaissance systems transmitting data in real or near-real time. This

Below and right: Launch and recovery of the Army's RPV test vehicle, based on the Lockheed Aquila. Control is with the ground commander throughout. The RPV is difficult to detect and hit and can transmit or record battlefield images and information. It is unlikely that service operation will commence before 1988.

intended to produce a system which will improve the Army's ability to locate targets, adjust artillery fire, and designate targets for laser-guided weapons. Such RPVs are very difficult to detect and, unlike manned aircraft, a hit does not involve the loss of a valuable, highly trained pilot. Further, they offer to ground commanders—always slightly suspicious of aircraft not under their direct command—an airborne reconnaissance system under their total control. Unfortunately, even though the RPV looks like a straight and simple military adaptation of a model airplane, the program has proved to be very expensive and also far more complex than had originally been anticipated.

▶ almost inevitably means a system under his own direct control. The Israelis have demonstrated the effectiveness of such systems with their Scout Mini-RPV. Another requirement is for an airborne laser designator system cheaper and tougher than a fixed-wing aircraft or helicopter.

The US Army's first venture into this field was the XMQM-105 Lockheed Aquila Mini-RPV, which was basically a limited "technology demonstrator" program. Four launch/control stations were produced, together with 30 Mini-RPVs. The payload comprises a stabilized TV camera and a laser.

Experience gained with the Aquila has been fed into the Army RPV program which has been under development since 1979. The requirement is for 80 launch/control stations and 548 RPVs, much reduced on the initial quantities, due to escalating costs. Present estimates are that the total system costs will be in the region of $1·6 billion. There have been considerable problems, mainly arising from the requirement for a very small airframe to avoid detection by the enemy. As a result, it has proved very difficult to fit in all the components: TV, laser, data down-link, up-link receiver, and vehicle control systems.

The present RPV, made of Kevlar, is some 6ft (1·83m) long, has a wingspan of just under 13ft (3·96m), and weighs some 220lb (99·8kg). It is powered by a 24hp twin-cylinder engine driving a pusher propeller giving a speed range of 56-113mph (90-182km/h). Endurance is some three hours. The RPV has proved very difficult to detect and, when found, has escaped damage even when under heavy fire.

Despite the apparent simplicity of the requirement the program is proving to be both lengthy and very expensive. The US Army has also had a look at the Canadair CL-289 re-usable drone, a new development of the CL-89 which has been used with the great success by various other NATO armies since 1972.

Above: Canadair's CL-289 re-usable drone, which has been the subject of US Army evaluation, including troop trials.

Below: Difficulties with Aquila include keeping the guidance, optical and transmission systems within stringent size and weight restrictions. There is a 43lb (19·5kg) unit under the nose, with surveillance camera, target tracker and laser designator/rangefinder.

95

Theater Rockets and Missiles

Nowhere is American technological excellence more clearly seen than in the US Army's rocket and missile systems. The Pershing II system has now become one of the few Army weapons to have a truly strategic significance, for this new missile possesses a range sufficient to reach well into

Lance, MGM-52C

Type: Battlefield support missile.
Dimensions: Length 20ft 3in (6·17m); body diameter 22in (56cm)
Launch weight: 2,833 to 3,367lb (1,285-1,527kg) depending on warhead
Propulsion: Rocketdyne P8E-9 storable-liquid two-part motor with infinitely throttleable sustainer portion.
Guidance: Simplified inertial.
Range: 45 to 75 miles (70-1120km) depending on warhead.
Flight speed: Mach 3.
Warhead: M234 nuclear 468lb (212kg, 10kT), W-70-4 ER/RB (neutron or Honeywell M251, 1,000lb (454kg) HE cluster.

In service since 1972, this neat rocket replaced the earlier Honest John rocket and Sergeant ballistic missile, with very great gains in reduced system weight, cost and bulk and increases in accuracy and mobility. Usual vehicle is the M752 (M113 family) amphibious tracked launcher, with the M688 carrying two extra missiles and a loading hoist. For air-dropped operations a lightweight towed launcher can be used. In-flight guidance accuracy, with the precisely controlled sustainer and spin-stabilization, is already highly satisfactory, but a future missile could have DME (Distance Measuring Equipment) command guidance. The US Army has eight battalions, six of which are deployed in Europe with six launchers each; the two remaining

Below: US Army soldiers transferring a Lance missile from the loader transporter vehicle (on the left) to the launcher vehicle. This very compact missile can carry nuclear, neutron, or high-explosive warhead

he western military districts of the Soviet Union. In addition,
s warhead is capable of attacking buried headquarters.
onsequently, the fielding of Pershing II has become a major
olitical issue, especially in Western Europe, as well as a
argaining counter in arms limitation talks. The most
nportant rocket system in NATO's armies will soon be the
Aultiple Launcher Rocket System (MLRS), which will almost
ertainly become a standard NATO weapons system. Capable
f high rates of fire, the MLRS is specifically intended to
reak up massed Warsaw Pact armor attacks. Unfortunately,
ke the latest self-propelled artillery, it is likely to impose
evere strains on the resupply system.

**bove: A Lance launch: flames and white smoke come from the
ocket motor; black smoke from the front end comes from the spin
iotors. The Warsaw Pact has a whole series of battlefield missiles;
ie West has only two—US Lance and French Pluton.**

attalions are at Fort Sill, Okla. Lance production lasted from 1971 to
980, during which time 2,133 missiles were built.
 Lance is the most powerful long-range missile currently under the direct
ontrol of the tactical ground commander. Its importance lies in its potential
r breaking up Warsaw Pact second and third echelon forces before they
an be committed. A successor in this vital mission is under development
 the Corps Support Weapon System (CSWS). This is intended to carry
 even wider variety of payloads over ranges up to 124 miles (200km),
sing simpler support equipment and requiring fewer men. Possible war-
eads include tactical nuclear, chemical, terminally-guided sub-munitions,
d scatterable mines.

MLRS

Type: Multiple-launch rocket system.
Dimensions: (Rocket) length 13ft (3·96m); diameter 8·94in (227mm).
Launch weight: (Rocket) 600lb (272kg).
Propulsion: Atlantic Research solid rocket motor.
Range: Over 18·6 miles (30km).
Flight speed: Just supersonic.
Warhead: Dispenses payload of sub-munitions, initially 644 standard M42 bomblets.

Known from 1972 until 1979 as the GSRS (General Support Rocket System), the MLRS (Multiple Launch Rocket System) entered service with 1st Infantry Division (Mechanized) at Fort Riley, Kansas, in 1983. It has the same battlefield mobility as armored formations, being carried on a tracked vehicle which carries a trainable and elevating launcher; this can be rapidly loaded with two six-round containers without the crew of three leaving their cab. Each box houses six preloaded tubes with a 10-year shelf life. The crew can ripple-fire from two to 12 rounds in less than one minute, the fire control re-aiming after each shot. The rocket is highly accurate and is intended to carry any of three types of submunition, M42 shaped-charge grenade-size, scatterable anti-armor mines, or guided sub-missiles. In the

Below: An MLRS rocket at the moment of launch. The rocket is 13ft (3·96m) long and 9in (230mm) in diameter; it weighs 600lb (272kg)

Above: MLRS vehicle with launch platform in the traveling position. Note the two rocket containers, each with six pre-loaded tubes.

▶ future a binary chemical warhead may also be developed. Each launcher load of 12 missiles is said to "place almost 8,000 submunitions in an area the size of four (US) football fields". The first production system was delivered to the Army in early 1982, by which time $317 million had been voted for the first 112 vehicles and 6,210 rockets. Production is intended to rise to 5,000 rounds per month, in a program costing an estimated $4·2 billion.

The carrying vehicle is designated a Self-Propelled Launcher Loader (SPLL) and is based on the M2 IFV (*qv*). The SPLL weighs some 50,000l (22,680kg) fully loaded and is air portable in a C-141 Starlifter. It can travel at 40mph (64km/h) and can ford a depth of 40in (1·02m), but is not amphibious.

One of the major problems with high rate-of-fire rocket systems is that

**Above: MLRS ready to fire. The tracked, self-propelled launcher
vehicle is derived from the M2/M3 IFV/CFV, and has the same
cross-country capability.**

of resupply, and MLRS is no exception. Each battery of nine launchers
will have its own ammunition platoon of 18 resupply vehicles and trailers,
and there will be many more farther back in the logistic system.

In mechanized and armored divisions there will be one MLRS battery in
the general support battalion (with two batteries of M110A2), while light
divisions will have an independent battery. There will be an MLRS battalion
of three batteries with each corps.

The MLRS is also the subject of a major NATO program involving
France, Italy, the Federal Republic of Germany, and the United Kingdom.

Pershing, MGM-31

Type: Battlefield support missile.
Dimensions: Length 34ft 6in (10·51m); body diameter 40in (1·01m); fin span about 80in (2·02m).
Launch weight: About 10,150lb (4,600kg).
Propulsion: Two Thiokol solid motors in tandem, first stage XM105 second stage XM106.
Guidance: Army-developed inertial made by Eclipse-Pioneer (Bendix).
Range: 100 to 460 miles (160-740km).
Flight speed: Mach 8 at burnout.
Warhead: Nuclear, usually W-50 of approximately 400kT.

Originally deployed in 1962 on XM474 tracked vehicles as Pershing 1, the standard US Army long-range missile system has now been modified to 1a standard, carried on four vehicles based on the M656 five-ton truck. All are transportable in a C-130. In 1976 the three battalions with the US 7th Army in Europe were updated with the ARS (Azimuth Reference System) allowing them quickly to use unsurveyed launch sites, and the SLA (Sequential Launch Adapter) allowing one launch control center easily to fire three missiles. To replenish inventory losses caused by practice firings, 66 additional Pershing 1a missiles were manufactured in 1978-80.

Deployment of Pershing 1a in mid-1986 totalled 54 launchers with US Army Europe and 72 with West German forces (these latter being operated by the Luftwaffe, not the Army). The US intends to replace its Pershing 1as with Pershing IIs on a one-for-one basis, but the intentions of the West German government are not yet known.

Right and below: Pershing II prototype is launched during the test program. This missile, although designated a battlefield support weapon, has a range which takes it well beyond the combat zone.

► Pershing II has been studied since 1969 and has been in full development since 1974. It mates the existing vehicle with Goodyear Radag (Radar area-correlation guidance) in the new nose of the missile. As the forebody plunges down towards its target the small active radar scans the ground at 120rpm and correlates the returns with stored target imagery. The terminal guidance corrects the trajectory by means of new delta control surfaces giving c.e.p. expected to be within 120ft (36m). As a result a lighter and less-destructive warhead (reported to be based on the B61 bomb of some 15kT) can be used, which extends maximum range. The Pershing II is fitted with an "earth-penetrator" device which enables the nuclear warhead to "burrow" deep underground before exploding. This is clearly intended for use against buried facilities such as headquarters and communications centers.

Development of Pershing II was envisaged as being relatively simple and cheap, but it has, in the event, proved both complicated and expensive. One problem has been with the rocket motors, which are entirely new to obtain the greatly increased range. A further complication was the sudden

elevation of the Pershing II program into a major international issue, with the fielding of the missiles becoming a test of US determination. The problems were further compounded by repeated failures in the test program, but the final test was a success and full production has gone ahead. First fielding took place in December 1984 and all 108 were due to be deployed by mid-1985.

The reason for the furore over Pershing II stems from its quite exceptional accuracy. The "hard-target kill potential" of a nuclear warhead is derived from the formula: $(\text{Raw Yield})^{2/3} \div (\text{c.e.p.})^2$. This means that the effect can be increased by two methods. In the first, the raw yield is increased, but this not only leads to a larger warhead, and thus a larger missile, but also the rate of increase in effect decreases as the raw yield is increased, ie, there is a law of diminishing returns. The other method of achieving a greater effect is to increase the accuracy (ie, decrease the c.e.p.), and as the effect increases by the square of the c.e.p. this is far more efficacious. Hence, the c.e.p. of 120ft (36m) has led to a warhead of much less raw yield, but very much greater effect than that fitted to the Pershing 1a.

Left: A Pershing II battlefield support missile ready for launch from its mobile platform. The new re-entry vehicle has four triangular fins and contains a 15kT nuclear warhead, with an exceptional degree of accuracy—the circular error probable (c.e.p.) is a mere 120ft (36m).

Below: A West German Luftwaffe crewman raising a Pershing 1a missile to the vertical in preparation for a launch simulation. There are now 54 Pershing 1a in Western Europe with US forces and a further 72 with the Luftwaffe. All US missiles will eventually be replaced by Pershing II by the late 1980s.

Mortars

Mortars are known in most armies as "the battalion commander's artillery", since they are the major fire support asset under his direct command. Mortars provide a very effective means of bringing heavy fire to bear both speedily and accurately, while their light weight and simplicity of operation make them ideal weapons for the infantry. Unlike

M29A1

Type: Mortar.
Caliber: 81mm.
Weight of barrel: 27·99lb (12·7kg).
Weight of baseplate: 24·91lb (11·3kg).
Weight of bipod: 40lb (18·15kg).
Total weight with sight: 115lb (52·2kg).
Elevation: +40° to +85°.
Traverse: 4° left and 4° right.
Maximum range: 5,140 yards (4,700km).
Rate of fire: 30rpm for 1 minute; 4-12rpm sustained.

In service with US Army and some Allied countries, the 81mm M29 mortar is the standard medium mortar of the US Army and is in service in two basic models, infantry and self-propelled. The standard infantry model can be disassembled into three components, each of which can be carried by one man—baseplate, barrel, mount and sight. The exterior of the barrel is helically grooved both to reduce weight and to dissipate heat when a high rate of fire is being achieved.

The mortar is also mounted in the rear of a modified member of the M113 APC family called the M125A1. In this vehicle the mortar is mounted on a turntable and this enables it to be traversed quickly through 360° to be laid onto a new target. A total of 114 81mm mortar bombs are carried in the vehicle.

The mortar can fire a variety of mortar bombs including HE (the M374 bomb has a maximum range of 5,025 yards (4,595m)), white phosphorus (the M375 bomb has a maximum range of 5,180 yards (4,737m)) and illuminating (the M301 bomb has a maximum range of 3,444 yards (3,150m)). The 81mm M29 has been replaced in certain units by the new M224 60mm Lightweight Company Mortar.

M224

Type: Lightweight company mortar.
Caliber: 60mm.
Total weight: 46lb (20·9kg); (hand-held with M8 baseplate) 17lb (7·7kg).
Maximum range: 3,828 yards (3,500m).

During the Vietnam campaign, it was found that the standard 81mm M29 mortar was too heavy for the infantry to transport in rough terrain, even when disassembled into its three main components. In its place the old 60mm M19 mortar was used, but this had a short range. The M224 has been developed to replace the 81mm M29 mortar in non-mechanized

he Soviet Army, however, the US Army has done away
with the larger caliber mortars and when the M252 81mm
replaces the 4·2in (106mm) in a few years time it will be
the largest in US service. This mortar is of British design
(the ML L16, with a Canadian-designed baseplate of forged
aluminum and the Canadian C2 sight) and was very
successfully combat tested in the British campaign in the
Falklands in 1982. Its total weight is some 78lb (35·4kg) and
it can be broken down into three man-portable loads of
about equal weight. Technology is unlikely to produce any
major breakthroughs in mortars, although work on the
ammunition has led to significant increases in range.

---

infantry, airmobile and airborne units at company level, and is also issued to
the US Marine Corps. The weapon comprises a lightweight finned barrel,
sight, M7 baseplate and bipod, although if required it can also be used with
the lightweight M8 baseplate, in which case it is hand-held. The complete
mortar weighs only 46lb (20·9kg) compared to the 81mm mortar which
weighs 115 (52kg). The M224 fires an HE bomb which provides a substantial
portion of the lethality of the 81mm mortar with a waterproof "horseshoe"
snap-off, propellant increments, and the M734 multi-option fuze. This new
fuze is set by hand and gives delayed detonation, impact, near-surface burst
0-3ft, 0-0·9m), or proximity burst (3-13ft, 0·9-3·96m).

The mortar can be used in conjunction with the AN/GVS-5 hand held
laser rangefinder, this can range up to 10,936 yards (10,000m) to an
accuracy of ±10·936 yards (±10m). This enables the mortar to engage a
direct-fire target without firing a ranging bomb first. The M224 fires a
variety of mortar bombs to a maximum range of 3,828 yards (3,500m) and
is currently in production at Watervliet Arsenal. The Army has ordered
,590 of these mortars while the Marine Corps has ordered 698.

Below: The thirty-year-old M29 mortar is gradually being replaced
by the M224 60mm mortar in dismounted infantry units.

Air Defense Weapons

The full scale and severity of the potential threat by the Warsaw Pact air forces to NATO ground forces is only now beginning to be fully appreciated. The US Army is trying to cope with this threat through a "layered" approach. At

Chaparral, M48

Type: Forward area air-defense missile system.
Dimensions: Length 114·5in (2·91m); body diameter 5·0in (12·7cm); span 25in (64cm).
Launch weight: 185lb (84kg).
Propulsion: Rocketdyne Mk 36 Mod 5 single-stage solid motor.
Guidance: Initial optical aiming, IR homing to target heat emitter.
Maximum range: About 5,250 yards (4,800m).
Maximum effective altitude: About 8,200ft (2,500m).
Flight speed: About Mach 2·5.
Warhead: (MIM-72C missile) 28lb (12·7kg) continuous rod HE.

When the purpose-designed Mauler missile was abandoned this weapon was substituted as a makeshift stop-gap, the missile being the original Sidewinder 1C modified for ground launch. A fire unit has four missiles on a manually tracked launcher, carried on an M730 (modified M548) tracked vehicle, with a further eight rounds on board ready to be loaded by hand.
    Chaparral is widely used by the Army and Marine Corps, usually with an equal number of Vulcan air-defense gun systems. The missile now in production is MIM-72C, which not only carries a better warhead than the earlier version, but also has improved DAW-1 all-aspect guidance and the Harry Diamond Labs M-817 proximity fuze.

he lower end is the hand-held missile system, such as
Stinger and Redeye. The next level was to have been the
Euromissile Roland on a self-propelled launcher, but this has
been reduced to a single battalion's worth mounted on a
wheeled chassis, a humiliating end to a once proudly flaunted
example of the "two-way street". At the divisional level
here is a mix of the Sergeant York and Patriot systems,
illustrating the still unresolved argument between the gun
and missile lobbies. The US Army also operates the Improved
Hawk and Nike Hercules missile systems, and at the very
upper end of the spectrum will be responsible for any
ballistic missile defense system which the USA may deploy.

Though totally inadequate, Chaparral is having to remain the USA's
forward-area low-altitude SAM system for at least the next decade, instead
of being replaced by Roland (*qv*) as originally planned. As a result, the
US Army has begun an improvement program that includes fitting the
launchers with a thermal-imaging (TI) sight to give the system a night and
(albeit limited) bad-weather capability. A smokeless motor to reduce the
battlefield signature is also being fitted.

The Chaparral system is now likely to have to remain in service until
the mid-1990s.

**Above and left: Chaparral fires
four ready rounds (with eight
reloads) of MIM-72C missiles.
The gunner acquires targets
visually or is cued by
AN/MPQ-49 forward-area
alerting radar, and tracks them
optically until the missile's heat-
seeking guidance takes over.
The Army is having to make
expensive modifications to
maintain Chaparral's
effectiveness, including
retrofitting its launchers with
FLIR to permit night and (some)
bad-weather operations (since
it would operate mostly in
central Europe), and an
improved guidance system with
better resistance to aircraft
infrared ECM.**

Improved Hawk, MIM-23B

Type: Air-defense missile.
Dimensions: Length 16ft 6in (5·03m); body diameter 14in (360mm),
span 48·85in (1,190mm).
Launch weight: 1,383lb (627·3kg).
Propulsion: Aerojet M112 boost/sustain solid rocket motor.
Guidance: CW radar SARH.
Range: 25 miles (40km).
Flight speed: Mach 2·5.
Warhead: HE blast/frag. 165lb (74·8kg).

Hawk (Homing All-the-Way Killer) was the world's first missile with CW
guidance. When developed in the 1950s it looked a good system, but by
modern standards it is cumbersome, each battery having a pulse acquisitio
radar, a CW illuminating radar, a range-only radar, two illuminator radar
battery control center, six three-missile launchers and a tracked loader, th
whole weighing many tons. An SP version has ground-support items o
wheels and towed by tracked launchers or loaders. Hawk became opera
tional in August 1960 and is deployed widely throughout the Army an
Marine Corps and 17 other nations.

Improved Hawk (MIM-23B) has a better guidance system, larger wa
head, improved motor and semi-automatic ground systems ("certifie
rounds" are loaded in launchers without the need for further attention
Further development is attempting to improve CW radar reliability an
improve pulse-acquisition speed by allowing automated threat-orderin
of all targets that could be of importance.

It was originally intended that Improved Hawk would be replaced b
Patriot by about 1987, but this changeover has now been postpone
probably until the early 1990s.

Nike Hercules, MIM-14B

Type: Large surface to air missile system for fixed emplacement.
Dimensions: Length 500in (41ft 8in, 1,270cm); body diameter 34·6i
(88cm); span 105in (266cm).
Launch weight: 10,712lb (4,858kg).
Propulsion: Tandem boost motor, quad cluster with solid propellan
sustainer, internal solid motor.
Guidance: Radar command.
Range: Out to 93 miles (150km).
Flight speed: Mach 3·5.
Warhead: Blast/preformed-splinter frag (usual) or nuclear, with comman
detonation.

An outgrowth of the Nike Ajax, Nike Hercules became operational with th
US Army in 1958. It uses a large high-performance missile and an extensiv
array of ground installations which detect, interrogate and track the targe
track the launched missile, drive the two into coincidence and detonate th
large warhead. US Army batteries were deactivated by 1974 except for
few in Alaska, southern Florida and Fort Sill (for training US and man
foreign operating personnel). The replacement has for ten years bee
planned to be Patriot.

**Right: The US Army still operates a few Nike Hercules batteries
overseas, though none has served in the US since the 1970s.
Though some NATO Nike Hercules installations are being updated
generally US installations are to be replaced by Patriot.**

Above: Three Improved Hawks are prepared for test launch in Butzbach, West Germany. These missiles can engage aircraft at altitudes from below 100ft to over 38,000ft (30.5 to 11,582m) in all weathers and up to 25 miles (40km) range.

Patriot, MIM-104

Type: Advanced mobile battlefield SAM system.
Dimensions: Length 209in (5·31m); body diameter 16in (40·6cm); span 36in (92cm).
Launch weight: 2,200lb (998kg).
Propulsion: Thiokol TX-486 single-thrust solid motor.
Guidance: Phased-array radar command and semi-active homing.
Range: About 37 nautical miles (68·6km).
Flight speed: About Mach 3.
Warhead: Choice of nuclear or conventional blast/frag.

Originally known as SAM-D, this planned successor to both Nike Hercules and Hawk has had an extremely lengthy gestation. Key element in the Patriot system is a phased-array radar which performs all the functions of surveillance, acquisition, track/engage and missile guidance. The launcher carries four missiles each in its shipping container, from which it blasts upon launch. Launchers, spare missile boxes, radars, computer, power supplies and other items can be towed or self-propelled. Patriot is claimed to be effective against all aircraft or attack missiles even in the presence of clutter or intense jamming or other ECM. Fundamental reason for the serious delay and cost-escalation have been the complexity of the system, the 1974 slowdown to demonstrate TVM (track via missile) radar guidance, and inflation. Unquestionably the system is impressive, but often its complication and cost impresses in the wrong way and the number of systems to be procured has been repeatedly revised downwards. The authorized development program was officially completed in 1980 when low-rate production was authorized. In 1983 production was cautiously stepped up and the first operational units were formed in late 1984. The US Army plans to have 81 Patriot batteries, but current authority is limited to 48 fire units and 2,165 missiles.

Right and below: Test launches of Patriot missiles. This system is being procured by the West Germans as well as the US Army and will play a significant role in NATO battlefield and air defense operations.

Redeye, FIM-43A

Type: Shoulder-fired infantry surface-to-air misisle.
Dimensions: Length 48in (122cm); body diameter 2·75in (7cm); span 5·5in (14cm).
Launch weight: 18lb (8·2kg); whole package weighs 29lb (13kg).
Propulsion: Atlantic Research dual-thrust solid.
Guidance: Initial optical aiming, IR homing.
Range: Up to about 2 miles (3·3km).
Flight speed: Mach 2·5.
Warhead: Smooth-case frag.

The first infantry SAM in the world, Redeye entered US Army service in 1964 and probably 100,000 had been delivered to the Army and Marine Corps by 1970. It has severe limitations. It has to wait until aircraft have attacked and then fire at their departing tailpipes; there is no IFF. Flight speed is only just enough to catch modern attack aircraft and the guidance is vulnerable to IRCM. Engagement depends on correct identification by the operator of the nature of the target aircraft. He has to wait until the aircraft has passed, aim on a pursuit course, listen for the IR lock-on buzzer, fire the missile, and then select a fresh tube. The seeker cell needs a cooling unit, three of which are packed with each missile tube.

Right: Each combat-arms battalion in Europe has a Redeye section with four to six teams, now being re-equipped with Stinger.

Stinger, FIM-92A

Type: Portable air-defense missile.
Dimensions: (Missile) length 60in (152cm); body diameter 2·75in (7cm); span 5·5in (14cm).
Launch weight: 24lb (10·9kg); whole package 35lb (15·8kg).
Propulsion: Atlantic Research dual-thrust solid.
Guidance: Passive IR homing (see text).
Range: In excess of 3·1 miles (5km).
Flight speed: About Mach 2.
Warhead: Smooth-case frag.

Developed since the mid-1960s as a much-needed replacement for Redeye, Stinger has had a long and troubled development but is at last in service. An improved IR seeker gives all-aspect guidance, the wavelength of less than 4·4 microns being matched to an exhaust plume rather than hot metal and IFF is incorporated (so that the operator does not have to rely on correct visual identification of oncoming supersonic aircraft).

To rescue something from the Roland program, Boeing has developed a container for four Stinger missiles which fits the Roland launch tube, though this had not entered production by 1983. In FY 1981 the first 1,144 missiles for the inventory were delivered at $70·1m, and totals for 1982 and 1983 were respectively 2,544 at $193·4m and 2,256 at $214·6m. Total requirements for the US Army and Marine Corps are currently some 17,000 fire units and 31,848 missiles.

An improvement program entitled Stinger-POST (Passive Optical Seeker Technique) is now in hand. This operates in both the ultra-violet and infra-red spectra, the combination of the two frequency bands giving improved discrimination, longer detection range, and greater ECCM options.

Right: Whereas Redeye is limited to stern chase, Stinger permits effective attack from all angles, and is more resistant to ECM.

Sergeant York, M998

Type: Divisional air-defense gun (DIVAD).
Crew: 3.
Armor: Hull, as for M48A5; turret, rolled homogenous armor steel.
Dimensions: Length (hull) 22ft 7in (6·882m); width 11ft 11in (3·631m);
height (turret roof) 8·15ft (2·484m); height (antenna) 11·28ft (3·439m).
Combat weight: Approximately 60 tons.
Armament: Twin 40mm L/70 Bofors automatic guns.
Performance: As for M48A5.

For many years NATO armies have envied the Soviet ZSU-23-4 self-propelled
air-defense gun, in which a proven 23mm quad MG was married to a
valve-technology radar and mounted on an existing chassis to produce one
of the most effective current air-defence systems. The US Army seemed
at least to have heeded this object lesson in cost-effectiveness with the
Sergeant York DIVAD, but the programme has now collapsed.

Right: The M998 Sergeant York DIVAD, showing M48 chassis.

**Below: An existing tank chassis, the Bofors L70 gun, and the F-16
fighter radar combined to give a promising AD gun system.**

▶ The US Army's main problem lay in deciding just what kind of forward air-defense system it needed: gun, missile, or a mix? Once it was decided that a gun was required, there followed many studies on caliber, type and number of tubes per chassis. The process began in 1962 and it was not until 1977 that the Army asked industry to submit proposals, using the M48A5 chassis and as much "mature, off-the-shelf" equipment as possible. The resulting competition was won in 1981 by Ford, who combined a twin Bofors L/70 installation with a radar developed from that used on the F-16 fighter, on the M48 chassis. First delivery should have taken place in 1983 and first fielding in 1985, but this was not to be.

The Bofors L/70 gun, in wide service throughout NATO, is both effective and extremely reliable. Two combat rounds will be used: a pre-fragmented proximity-fuzed HE round for use against aircraft; a point-detonating round for use against ground targets. Maximum slant range against aircraft is about 9,843ft (3,000m) and maximum ground range is some 4,370 yards

Above: The Sergeant York system is produced by Ford and the total Army requirement is 618 fire units; first fielding scheduled for 1985.

(4,000m). 502 rounds are carried for each gun and combined rate of fire is some 620 rounds per minute.

The radar automatically determines target type, assigns priorities and updates the fire control unit which automatically aligns the turret and guns. The Identification Friend-or-Foe (IFF) fitted has 90 per cent commonality with that fitted to the Stinger SAM (*qv*). Air defense engagements on the move are possible, although accuracy in this case is open to question.

The program was, however, dogged by ill-fortune, and a series of tests led to the cancellation of the entire project in 1985, leaving a critical gap in the US Army's air defenses at divisional level which will be very hard to fill. Work continues on Improved Chapparal and on Stinger POST as interim solutions, while a team is examining every feasible alternative.

US Roland

Type: Forward area air-defense missile.
Dimensions: Length 94·5in (240cm); body diameter 6·3in (16cm); span 19·7in (50cm).
Launch weight: 143lb (65kg).
Propulsion: Internal boost and sustain solid motors.
Guidance: Initial IR gathering followed by semi-active radar command to line-of-sight.
Range 3·73 miles (6km).
Flight speed: Burnout velocity Mach 1·6.
Warhead: 14·3lb (6·5kg), contains 65 shaped charges each with lethal radius of 20ft (6m); prox fuze.

Below: A US Roland air-defense missile is fired from its tracked launcher, discarding sabots as it leaves the launch-tube. After a prodigiously expensive conversion program the US Army has decided to procure only one battalion's worth, mounted on a wheeled launcher

Originally developed as a mobile battlefield system with plain optical (clear-weather) guidance, Roland has from 1969 onwards been further developed as Roland 2 with blindfire radar guidance. The missile has folding wings and is fired from a launch tube on a tracked vehicle, the US Army carrier being the M109. Decision to buy Roland was taken in 1974, but the introduction to Army service has been affected by prolonged technical difficulties and cost overruns, and no American Roland was fired until the end of 1977. The cost of developing the US system escalated by several hundred per cent, and after prolonged delays the decision was taken to cancel the program, even though production had already begun. The 27 fire units and 595 missiles will therefore be utilized by a light air defense battalion of the New Mexico National Guard, with a combat mission in the third echelon of the Rapid Deployment Force. Further, the fire units, instead of being mounted on the M975 tracked carrier, will now be mounted on an M812 5-ton truck chassis.

It is a somewhat humiliating end to a program which was once hailed as a great European breakthrough into the American weapons market. It also leaves a major deficiency in the US Army's low-level air defense capability.

Vulcan, M163/M167

Type: 20mm Vulcan air defense system.
Crew: 1 (on gun).
Weight (firing and traveling): 3,500lb (1,588kg).
Length traveling: 16ft (4·9m).
Width traveling: 6·49ft (1·98m).
Height traveling: 6·68ft (2·03m).
Elevation: −5° to +80°.
Traverse: 360°.
Effective range: 1,750 yards (1,600m).
(*Note: specification refers to the towed version.*)

The 20mm Vulcan is the standard light anti-aircraft gun of the US Army
and has been in service since 1968. There are two versions of the Vulcan
system in service, one towed and the other self-propelled; both are fair
weather, daylight only systems. The towed version is known as the M167
and this is mounted on a two wheeled carriage and is normally towed by an
M715 or M37 truck. When in the firing position the weapon rests on three
outriggers to provide a more stable firing platform. The self-propelled
model is known as the M163 and this is mounted on a modified M113A1
APC chassis, the chassis itself being the M741. The latter will be replaced
by the twin 40mm Sergeant York DIVAD (*qv*).

The 20mm cannon used in the system is a modified version of the air-
cooled six-barrel M61 Vulcan cannon developed by General Electric. It
is also the standard air-to-air cannon of the US Air Force. The Vulcan
cannon has two rates of fire, 1,000 or 3,000 rounds per minute, and the
gunner can select either 10, 30, 60 or 100 round bursts. The M163 has 500
rounds of linked ready-use ammunition while the self-propelled model has
1,100 rounds of ready-use ammunition.

The fire control system consists of an M61 gyro lead-computing gun
sight, a range-only radar mounted on the right side of the turret (developed
by Lockheed Electronics), and a sight current generator. The gunner
normally visually acquires and tracks the target while the radar supplies
range and range rate data to the sight current generator. These inputs are
converted to proper current for use in the sight. With this current the sight
computes the correct lead angle and adds the required super elevation.

The turret has full power traverse and elevation, slewing rate being
60°/second, and elevation rate being 45°/second. Power is provided by an
auxiliary generator.

The Vulcan air defense system is normally used in conjunction with the
Chaparral SAM. Each Vulcan/Chaparral battalion has 24 Chaparral units
and 24 self-propelled Vulcan systems. Airborne and Airmobile divisions

Above: M167A1 is the towed version of Vulcan; this uses linked ammunition whereas SP version fires electrically primed linkless.

have a total of 48 towed Vulcan systems. The Vulcan system is normally used in conjunction with the Saunders TPQ-32 or MPQ-49 Forward Area Alerting Radar, which provides the weapons with basic information such as from which direction the targets are approaching.

The 20mm cannon has a maximum effective slant range in the anti-aircraft role of 1,750 yards (1,600m). It can also be used in the ground role, and was deployed to Vietnam for this purpose; in this role it has a maximum range of 4,920 yards (4,500m). A variety of different types of ammunition can be fired, including armor piercing, armor piercing incendiary, and high-explosive incendiary. The weapon is also produced for export without the range-only radar. All American M167 VADS now have dual road wheels for improved stability.

Below: Range and lethality of the six-barreled gun are considered inadequate, and the Army planned to replace Vulcans with the twin twin 40mm Sergeant York DIVAD from 1985. There are 380 M163s and 220 M167s in service and these will now remain for some years.

Below left: Tracked version of the Vulcan is M163A1 on converted M113 chassis. Combat loaded its cruising range is some 275 miles (440km).

Anti-Tank Weapon

The great tank versus anti-tank battle continues to be waged, with the advantage swinging from one side to another every few years. With the advent of new types of protection such as the British "Chobham armor", the traditional hollow-charge warhead must inevitably become of ever-decreasing value, although it will remain effective against

Copperhead, M712

Type: Cannon-launched guided projectile (CLGP).
Dimensions: Length 54in (1·37m); diameter 155mm.
Launch weight: 140lb (63·5kg).
Propulsion: Fired from gun.
Guidance: Laser homing.
Range: 1·9-10 miles (3-16km).
Flight speed: Supersonic.
Warhead: Shaped charge, 49·6lb (22·5kg).

Conventional artillery, when used in the indirect fire role, has a 1-in-2,500 chance of killing a tank. The US Army started a high-risk program to develop a projectile which could be fired from a standard 155mm weapon (for example, the M109A1 self-propelled gun or the M198 towed howitzer) and hit targets over 7·5 miles (12km) away.

Basic research proved that the project was possible and contracts were awarded to Texas Instruments and Martin Marietta. Each company built a small number of projectiles (designated Cannon-Launched Guided Projectiles) which were tested at the White Sands Missile Range. The Martin Marietta CLGP scored direct hits on both stationary and moving tanks at ranges of 5-7·5 miles (8-12km). The projectile hit the target despite deliberate aiming errors of several hundred metres. In September 1975 a CLGP hit a stationary M48 tank 5 miles (8km) away while the target was being illuminated by a laser carried in a Praeire IIA RPV. The RPV located the target with a TV camera, focusing on the target, and signalled the artillery to

Right: Tripod-mounted version of AN/TVQ-2 laser locater designator which could be used with Copperhead AT missiles.

Below: The extremely accurate and highly destructive Copperhead AT missile demonstrates its killing capabilities on an M47 on test.

older types of tanks for as long as they remain in service. The new armors must, however, pose a serious problem for the infantry, for whom the hollow-charge rocket-propelled missile provides an excellent lightweight and accurate short-range anti-tank weapon. For heavier anti-tank weapons, the immediate future seems to lie with top-attack and the penetration of the currently less well protected upper surfaces—to which the tank designers' reply will doubtless be thicker armor. A first attempt at such a weapon— Copperhead—has not been a total success, and it may be some years before second-generation top-attack weapons are proved to be really viable weapons systems.

---

fire a CLGP. As a result of these trials, Martin Marietta was awarded a contract for full scale development of the CLGP.

The basic idea is that a forward observer sees an enemy tank approaching. He then radios its approximate position to the artillery and one weapon fires a CLGP in the general direction of the target. Once the CLGP is on its way the forward observer illuminates the target with his Ground Laser Locator Designator (or GLLD), the CLGP senses the reflected laser energy and, by applying commands to its control fins, flies into the laser spot on the target. It can be steered into the target provided the nominal gun-aiming point is

within about 0·7 miles (1·1km) of it. Copperhead is treated like any other gun ammunition.

There has been exceptional cost escalation in the Copperhead program, rising from an estimated $5,500 per round in FY 1975 to $37,632 in FY 1982. This, coupled with the realization that the M712 is not so wonderful a weapon as once was thought, has led to a drastic curtailment of the program. Production ceased in 1982 when 8,750 rounds had been made, and these will serve only in artillery units assigned to the RDF. Copperhead will not be used by the US Army in Europe, nor will the once-planned European production consortium be formed. The program that was once claimed to herald an artillery "revolution" is thus coming to an expensive and somewhat ignominious end.

Dragon, M47, FGM-77A

Type: Infantry anti-tank/assault missile.
Dimensions: Length 29·3in (74cm); body diameter 4·5in (11·4cm); fin span 13in (33cm).
Launch weight: 24·4lb (11·1kg.
Propulsion: Recoilless gas-generator thruster in launch tube; sustain propulsion by 60 small side thrusters fired in pairs upon tracker demand.
Guidance: See text.
Range: 200 to 3,300ft (60-1,000m).
Flight speed: About 230mph (370km/h).
Warhead: Linear shaped charge, 5·4lb (2·45kg).

Dragon was designed as a medium-range complement to TOW (*qv*). In service since 1971, Dragon comes sealed in a glass-fiber launch tube with a fat rear end containing the launch charge. The operator attaches this to his tracker comprising telescopic sight, IR sensor and electronics box. When the missile is fired its three curved fins flick open and start the missile spinning. The operator holds the sight on the target and the tracker automatically commands the missile to the line of sight by firing appropriate pairs of side thrusters. The launch tube is thrown away and a fresh one attached to the tracker. The Army and Marine Corps use the basic Dragon while developments involve night sights and laser guidance.

The Dragon system is not without its problems. Perhaps the most important is that the missile body diameter of 4·5in (11·4cm) sets the limit on the size of the warhead. The effectiveness of a shaped charge warhead is a function of its diameter, and at least 6in (15cm) is likely to be needed to counter the new armors coming into service on the latest Soviet tanks. In addition, the missile is slow; this aggravates the difficulties of the operator who must hold his breath throughout the flight of the missile. The operator is also adjured to grasp the launch-tube tightly, for if he does not his shoulder may rise at the moment of launch, thus sending the missile into the ground. Finally, the rocket thrusters have been found to deteriorate in storage, and many need replacement.

Initial plans for a Dragon replacement centered on a program designated IMAAWS, but this was halted in 1980. Another program called Rattler was stopped in 1983 and a new program called AAWS started in 1984.

Tank Breaker

Type: Fire-and-forget anti-tank missile.
Dimensions: Length 43in (1·09m); body diameter 3·94in (100mm).
Launch weight: Complete system under 35lb (15·8kg); missile 20lb (9·1kg).
Propulsion: Boost/sustain solid motors.
Guidance: Staring focal-plane array IR.
Range: About 2,187 yards (2,000m).
Flight speed: Transonic.
Warhead: Shaped charge.

One of the first weapons to use a focal-plane array, an advanced imaging IR seeker, Tank Breaker is a one-man portable missile which can be locked-on to a tank, helicopter, low-performance fixed-wing aircraft, or other target and fired. It will thereafter home by itself, the operator having previously programmed it either to fly a direct course or (against armor) plunge down from above. This overhead attack technique has become necessary because the frontal and side armor on modern tanks will defeat a shaped-charge warhead carried by a missile of this size.

Above: Dragon is useful, if limited: it seems the gunner must avoid blinking while aiming; the missile is considered slow, short of range and not particularly effective against "new armor".

Above: Tank Breaker could allow the gunner to fire the missile and then either take cover immediately or engage another target.

TOW, BGM-71

Type: Heavy anti-tank missile.
Propulsion: Hercules K41 boost (0·05s) and sustain (1s) motors.
Dimensions: Length 45·75in (1,162mm); body diameter 6in (152mm); span (wings extended) 13·5in (343mm).
Launch weight: (BGM-71A) 46·1lb (20·9kg).
Range: 1,640 to 12,300ft (500 to 3,750m).
Flight speed: 625mph (1,003km/h).
Warhead: (BGM-71A) Picatinny Arsenal 8·6lb (3·9kg) shaped-charge with 5·3lb (2·4kg) explosive. See text for later.

The TOW (Tube-launched, Optically-tracked, Wire-guided) missile is likely to set an all-time record in the field of guided-missile production. Prime contractor Hughes Aircraft began work in 1965 to replace the 106mm recoilless rifle. The missile's basic infantry form is supplied in a sealed tube which is clipped to the launcher. The missile tube is attached to the rear of the launch tube, the target sighted and the round fired. The boost charge pops the missile from the tube, firing through lateral nozzles amidships. The four wings indexed at 45° spring open forwards, and the four tail controls flip open rearwards. Guidance commands are generated by the optical sensor in the sight, which continuously measures the position of a light source in the missile relative to the LOS and sends steering commands along twin wires. These drive the helium-pressure actuators working the four tail controls in pairs for pitch and yaw. In 1976 production switched to ER (Extended-Range) TOW with the guidance wires lengthened from

Right: From left, the three main members of the family—TOW, I-TOW (Improved) and the larger TOW-2 now in production.

Below: The TOW gunner needs only to keep the sight cross hairs on target to score a hit at up to 12,300ft (3,750m). Thermal imaging infrared night sights are also included.

▶ 9,842ft (3,000m) to the figure given. Sight field of view reduces from 6°
for gathering to 1·5° for smoothing and 0·25° for tracking. The miss
electronics pack is between the motor and the warhead.

TOW reached IOC in 1970, was used in Vietnam and the 1973 Mid
East war, and has since been produced at a higher rate than any other know
missile. The M65 airborne TOW system equips the standard America
attack helicopter, the AH-1S TowCobra and the Marines' twin-engine AH-
and -1T Improved SeaCobra, each with a TSU (Telescopic Sight Unit) ar
two quad launchers. Other countries use TOW systems on the BO 105, Lyn
A109, A129, 500MD and other attack helicopters.

In late 1981 production began of the Improved TOW, with a new warhea
triggered by a long probe, extended after launch to give 15in (381mr

stand-off distance for greater armor penetration. The shaped-chargehead, with LX-14 filling and a dual-angle deformable liner, is also being retrofitted to many existing rounds.

Hughes is now producing TOW 2, which has several I-TOW improvements, plus a new warhead with the same diameter as the rest of the missile with a mass of 13lb (5·9kg) and an even longer (21·25in, 540mm) extensible probe, calculated to defeat all tanks of the 1990s. Flight performance is maintained by a new double-base motor giving about 30 per cent greater total impulse, and the command guidance link has been hardened.

Below: TOW has been used on a wide range of mounts, including Jeep, tripod, armored vehicles, and many helicopter types.

Small Arms

US Army small arms have been repeatedly dragged into the domestic political arena, since they represent a comprehensible part of the American frontier ethos. Having forced its NATO allies first to 7·62mm and then to 5·56mm caliber, the US Army now finds itself with the M16 unable to make optimum use of the actual 5·56mm round adopted by NATO. Repeated efforts to find a replacement for the

M16A1

Type: Rifle.
Caliber: 5·56mm.
Length overall (with flash suppressor): 38·9in (99cm).
Length of barrel: 19·9in (50·8cm).
Weight (including 30-round loaded magazine): 8·2lb (3·72kg).
Range (maximum effective): 300 yards (274m).
Rate of fire: 700-950rpm (cyclic); 150-200rpm (automatic); 45-65rpm (semi-automatic).
Muzzle velocity: 3,280ft/s (1,000m/s).

The M16 (previously the AR-15) was designed by Eugene Stoner and was a development of the earlier 7·62mm AR-10 assault rifle. It was first adopted by the US Air Force, and at a later date the US Army adopted the weapon for use in Vietnam. When first used in combat numerous faults became apparent and most of these were traced to a lack of training and poor maintenance. Since then the M16 has replaced the 7·62mm M14 as the standard rifle of the United States forces. To date over 5,000,000 have been manufactured, most by Colt Firearms and the weapon was also made under licence in Singapore, South Korea and the Philippines. Twenty-one

Below: An M16 being used during training with the Multiple Integrated Laser Engagement System (MILE).

Below right: An M16 fitted with the M203 40mm grenade launcher which has a range of up to 382 yards (350m).

venerable M1911A1 0·45in pistol have been frustrated by the US Congress; this elderly (to put it kindly!) handgun fires a round which is not NATO standardized, although the US Special Forces, and especially Delta, think highly of its stopping power at short ranges. The M60 is widely used but is being progressively replaced by a Belgian light machine gun—an excellent example of the "two-way street", but regarded as something of an affront by some elements of the US "establishment". One factor still to be addressed is the infantry's predilection for "prophylactic" fire, which is expensive in ammunition and logistic resources, and unlikely to be effective in European conditions.

---

armies use the M16. The weapon is gas-operated and the user can select either full automatic or semi-automatic. Both 20- and 30-round magazines can be fitted, as can a bipod, bayonet, telescope and night sight. The weapon can also be fitted with the M203 40mm grenade launcher, and this fires a variety of 40mm grenades to a maximum range of 382 yards (350m). The M203 has now replaced the M79 grenade launcher on a one-for-one basis. The Colt Commando is a special version of the M16 and this has a shorter barrel, flash supressor and a telescopic sight, reducing the overall length of the weapon to 27·9in (71cm). The M231 is a special model which can be fired from within the M2 Bradley Infantry Fighting Vehicle.

There has been consistent dissatisfaction with the M16A1 in the US Army, and even more so in the other main user—the US Marine Corps. One of the major complaints is its lack of effectiveness at ranges above 340 yards (300m), which has come to a head with the increased emphasis on desert warfare with the RDF. This, combined with the high average age of current stocks, led to a major review in 1981.

As a result, a "product improved" weapon (M16A2) is now under consideration. A major feature would be a stiffer and heavier barrel, utilizing one-turn-in-seven-inches (17·8cm) rifling—as opposed to one-turn-in-twelve-inches (30·5cm)—to enable the new standard NATO 5·56mm (0·218in) round to be fired. Other features under consideration are a three-round burst capability to replace the current full-automatic, an adjustable rearsight, and a modified flash eliminator. The opportunity would also be taken to introduce tougher "furniture", ie, butt-stock, pistol grip, and handguard.

A program is in hand to examine new technologies for incorporation in a possible future weapon. These include controlled-burst fire and multiple projectiles (eg, flechettes).

M1911A1

Type: Pistol.
Caliber: 0·45in (11.43mm).
Length: 8·63in (21·93cm).
Length of barrel: 5·03in (12·78cm).
Weight loaded: 2·99lb (1·36kg).
Weight empty: 2·49lb (1·13kg).
Effective range: 65ft (20m).
Muzzle velocity: 826ft/s (252m/s).

The 0·45 caliber M1911 pistol was the standard American sidearm of World War I. In 1923, work on an improved model commenced at Springfield Armory, and this was standardized as the M1911A1 in 1926, and since then the weapon has been the standard sidearm of the US Army. The Army does however, use other pistols for special missions, as the M1911A1 is rather heavy and has quite a recoil. Between 1937 and 1945, over 19 million M1911A1 pistols were manufactured by Colt, Ithaca and Remington. The weapon is semi-automatic, and all the user has to do is to pull the trigger each time he wants to fire. The magazine, which is in the grip, holds a total of seven rounds. The fore sight is of the fixed blade type and the rear sight consists of a U notch on dovetail slide. The weapon has three safety devices: the grip safety on the handle, the safety lock, and the half cock position on the hammer.

Manufacture of the M1911A1 ceased in 1945 and the cost of spare parts especially barrels and slides, is becoming very high. This, combined with a number of operational shortcomings (such as the heavy recoil), and the lack of commonality with the standard NATO 9mm round, has led to a long search for a replacement. This resulted in a 1982 shoot-off between four competing designs: the US Smith & Wesson 459M, the Swiss-German SIG-Sauer P226, the German Heckler & Koch P7A13, and the Italian

M60

Type: General purpose machine gun.
Caliber: 7·62mm.
Length: 43·3in (110cm).
Length of barrel: 22in (56cm).
Weight: 23lb (10·48kg) with bipod; 39·6lb (18kg) with tripod.
Maximum effective range (bipod): 984 yards (900m).
Maximum effective range (tripod): 1,968 yards (1,800m).
Rate of fire: 550rpm (cyclic); 200rpm (automatic).

The M60 is the standard GPMG of the US Army and has now replaced the older 0·30 Browning machine gun. The weapon was developed by the Bridge Tool and Die Works and the Inland Division of General Motors Corporation, under the direction of Springfield Armory. Production of the M60 commenced in 1959 by the Maremont Corporation of Saco, Maine.

The M60 is gas-operated, air-cooled and is normally used with a 100 round belt of ammunition. To avoid overheating the barrel is normally changed after 500 rounds have been fired. Its fore sight is of the fixed blade type and its rear sight is of the U-notch type and is graduated from about 656ft to 3,937ft (200 to 1200m) in about 328ft (100m) steps. The weapon is provided with a stock, carrying handle and a built in bipod. The M60 can also be used on an M122 tripod mount, M4 pedestal mount and M142 gun

Right: The M60 can be fired from the hip, shoulder, bipod or a variety of mounts for use on aircraft and vehicles.

Above: There are well over 400,000 M1911A1s in US service, each of them overhauled an average of three times. An unusually accurate marksman could make this elderly self-loading pistol effective up to 160 yards (50+m).

Beretta 92SB. All four failed the test in one way or another and, as a result, in February 1982 Congress prohibited the use of any further funds in projects involving a 9mm handgun. It would, therefore, appear that the famous "45" will soldier on for many years to come.

---

mount for vehicles. Other versions include the M60C remote for helicopters, M60D pintle mount for vehicles and helicopters and the M60E2 internal model for AFVs.

The M60 will remain in service with the US Army for many years. It is sturdy, reliable, and highly effective.

M2 HB

Type: Heavy machine gun.
Caliber: 0·50in (12·7mm).
Length overall: 65·07in (165·3cm).
Length of barrel: 44·99in (114·3cm).
Weight (gun only): 83·33lb (37·8kg); 127·8lb (57·98kg) with tripod.
Range: 1,996 yards (1,825m) effective in ground role; 7,470 yards (6,830m) maximum; 820 yards (750m) anti-aircraft role.
Rate of fire: 450/575rpm.

The 0·50 caliber M2 machine gun was developed for the US Army in the early 1930s, as the replacement for the 0·50 M1921A1 MG. The weapon was developed by John Browning (who designed many other famous weapons including the Browning Automatic Rifle and the Browning 0·30 machine gun), and the Colt Firearms company of Hartford, Connecticut.

The M2 is air-cooled and recoil operated, and is fed from a disintegrating metallic link belt. The weapon can fire either single shot or full automatic and various types of ammunition can be fired including ball, tracer, armor piercing and armor-piercing incendiary. For ground targets the weapon is mounted on the M3 tripod while for the anti-aircraft role the M63 mount is used. It is also mounted on many armored fighting vehicles including the M113A1 series of APC (and variants), the M109/M108 SPH and the M578 and M88 ARV. The M55 anti-aircraft system (no longer in service with the US Army) has four M2s, and the M2 is also mounted in helicopters and in some commanders' turrets as the M85. The M2 HB MG is still being produced in the United States by Ramo Incorporated and the Maremont

---

M72A2

Type: Light anti-tank weapon (LAW).
Caliber: 66mm.
Length of rocket: 20in (50·8cm).
Weight of rocket: 2·2lb (1kg).
Muzzle velocity: 476ft/s (145m/s).
Maximum effective range: 355 yards (325m).
Length of launcher closed: 25·7in (65·5cm).
Length of launcher extended: 35in (89·3cm).
Weight complete: 4·75lb (2·15kg).

The M72 is the standard Light Anti-Tank Weapon (LAW) of the US Army and is also used by many other armies around the world. Development of weapon started in 1958 with the first production LAWs being completed by the Hesse Eastern Company of Brockton, Massachusetts, in 1962. It is also manufactured under licence in Norway by Raufoss. The LAW is a lightweight, shoulder-fired rocket launcher and its rocket has a HEAT warhead which will penetrate over 11·8in (300mm) of armor. It can also be used against bunkers, pillboxes and other battlefield fortifications.

When the M72 is required for action, the infantryman removes the safety pins, which open the end covers, and the inner tube is telescoped outwards cocking the firing mechanism. The launcher tube is then held over the shoulder, aimed and the weapon fired. The launcher is then discarded. Improved models are known as the M72A1 and the more recent M72A2.

The successor to the M72A2 was to be the Viper, which was supposed to be so cheap and effective that it was planned to issue it to virtually every man in the front line. Weighing a little under 9lb (4·1kg), Viper has a 2·75in (70mm) diameter warhead with a performance against modern Soviet armor that is marginal, to say the least. Following strong criticism by the

**Above: The M2 HB on M3 tripod. It is fed from a 100-round dis-
integrating-link belt at a cyclic rate of fire of 450-575 rounds a minute.**

Corporation, and it remains in service in some 20 countries.

The M2 HB went out of production shortly after World War II, but the line
was recently re-opened, mainly, but not entirely, for export sales. The letters
"HB" in the designation stand for "hydraulic buffer", a modification introduced in the late 1930s.

**Above: Effective range of LAW against stationary "soft" targets is
355 yards (325m), and less than half that against moving targets.**

General Accounting Office (GAO), the US Congress ordered a shoot-off
between Viper and three European weapons: the British LAW 80, the
Norwegian M72-750, and the Swedish AT4. A further complication arose
when General Dynamics refused to sign a fixed-price contract for Viper.
The US Army is thus faced with either buying a European LAW system
off-the-shelf or soldiering on with the M72A2 until a better US-designed
successor is available.

M79

Type: Grenade launcher.
Caliber: 40mm.
Weight of grenade: 0·610lb (0·277kg).
Length of launcher: 29in (73·7cm).
Length of barrel: 14in (35·6cm).
Weight of launcher: (empty) 5·99lb (2·72kg); loaded, 6·5lb (2·95kg).
Muzzle velocity: 249ft/s (76m/s).
Range: 437·4 yards (400m) maximum; 383 yards (350m) effective, area targets; 164 yards (150m) effective, point targets.
Effective casualty radius: 5·46 yards (5m).
Rate of fire: 5 rounds per minute.

The 40mm M79 Grenade Launcher was developed to give the infantryman the capability to deliver accurate firepower to a greater range than could be achieved with a conventional rifle grenade. The M79 is a single shot, break-open weapon and is fired from the shoulder. It is breech loaded and fires a variety of different types of ammunition including high explosive, high explosive air burst, CS gas and smoke. Its fore sight is of the blade type and its rear sight is of the folding leaf adjustable type. The latter is graduated from 82 yards (75m) to 410 yards (375m) in about 27 yards (25m) increments. When the rear sight is in the horizontal position, the fixed sight may be used to engage targets up to 109·3 yards (100m). The M79 has been replaced in front line units by the M203 grenade launcher which is fitted to the standard M16A1 rifle.

M249

Type: Squad automatic weapon (SAW).
Caliber: 5·56mm.
Lengths: Overall 39·4in (100cm); barrel 18·5in (47cm).
Weights: Empty 15·5lb (7·03kg); with 200-round magazine 22lb (9·97kg).
Effective range: 1,421 yards (1,300m).
Rate of fire: 750rpm.
Muzzle velocity: 3,033ft/s (924m/s).

The SAW idea was conceived in 1966, but it has taken a long time to reach service. When the M16 was issued to infantry squads, all infantrymen had an automatic weapon, but with a maximum effective range of some 330 yards (300m) only. It was considered that each fire team in the squad needed a weapon of greater all-round capability than the M16, but obviously not a weapon as heavy or as sophisticated as the M60. The SAW meets this requirement, and will be issued on a scale of one per fire team, ie, two per squad. The SAW may also replace some M60s in non-infantry units.

The M249 SAW is a development of the Belgian Fabrique Nationale (FN) "Minimi". Current orders are being met from the FN factory, but it is intended to set up a production line in the USA. Current requirements are for 26,000 M249s for the Army and 9,000 for the Marine Corps in a five-year program, but further orders will doubtless follow.

The M249 is very smooth in operation and displays a reliability that is considered exceptional in light machine guns. Fully combat ready, with a magazine of 200 rounds, bipod, sling, and cleaning kit, the M249 weighs 22lb (9·97kg), which is still 1lb (0·4kg) less than an empty M60 machine gun. The M855 ball round fired from the M249 will penetrate a US steel helmet at a range of 1,421 yards (1,300m).

Overall, the M249 is superior to the Soviet PKM 7·62mm (bigger, heavier smaller mag), and the RPK 5·45mm (bigger, lighter, smaller mag).

Above: Largely replaced now by the M203/M16A1 rifle combination, the M79 fires the full range of 40mm grenades.

Above: The M249, which is better than the M16, especially at extended ranges. It is left-hand fed from a 200-round container.

Vehicles

Far less glamorous and eye-catching than tanks or armored personnel carriers, there is a vast range of support and logistic vehicles vital to any modern army. Some of these vehicles are simply adapted for the particular environment of the battlefield, such as passenger-carrying vehicles which are "ruggedized" and fitted with four-wheel drive.

Hummer

Type: High mobility, multi-purpose wheeled vehicle (HMMWV).
Dimensions: Length 15ft (4·57m); width 7ft (2·15m); height 5ft 9in (1·75m).
Weights: Empty 4,969lb (2,254kg); maximum 8,532lb (3,870kg).
Engine: General Motors V-8, 6·2 liter diesel, 130hp at 3,600rpm.
Performance: Maximum road speed 65mph (105km/h); road range 351 miles (565km); gradient 60 per cent.

Modern armies are very dependent upon wheeled vehicles of all types, and perhaps the most important of these is the field car; exemplified in the US Army by the ubiquitous Jeep and in the British Army by the Land Rover. The quantity of vehicles needed is enormous, and the importance of the Hummer can be gauged from the fact that some 40,000 will be bought by the US Army, with a further 11,000 going to the USAF and 14,000 to the USMC.

A "drive-off" was held in 1982 for the three competitors for this lucrative contract, the winner being American Motors General. Following the

There are also, however, numerous types of highly specialized vehicles, ranging from recovery trucks ("wreckers") through ammunition delivery and ambulances to bridging launchers, and just a very few selected types are shown here. It is doubtful whether even the US Army knows how many vehicles it possesses, but the scale of numbers may be assessed from the fact that the new commercial utility ¼-ton truck is the subject of an order for 53,248 vehicles (most for the Army, but some for the other services) with an option for a 100 per cent increase. Planned procurement for the US Army and USMC on just four new types of vehicle amounts to $1,704 million in Fiscal Year 1985.

---

announcement of this success in March 1983, AM General was bought by the ever-growing LTV Corporation for $170 million. Production has begun and first deliveries are due in 1984.

The Hummer is intended by the US Army to replace several vehicles: the early model M151 quarter-ton Jeep; M274 half-ton Mule; M880 1¼-ton pick-up truck; M561 Gama Goat articulated utility vehicle; and M792 1¼-ton ambulance. The Hummer has four road wheels driven through geared hubs, enabling the vehicle to be no more than 5ft 9in (1·75m) high and thus bettering the design requirement of 6ft (1·82m). Considerable attention has been paid to a comfortable ride and to weight saving. Some 18 variations on the design are already planned, ranging from a simple pick-up to ambulances and a TOW missile launcher.

With its massive US order-book and its clear potential for large-scale overseas sales, there is no doubt that the Hummer is destined to become as familiar as its famous predecessor, the Jeep.

Below: The versatile Hummer will be used in the airborne, airmobile and light infantry division as TOW missile carrier, and will also be used for recce, fire support, communications, command and control.

M60 (AVLB)

Type: Armored vehicle-launched bridge.
Crew: 2 (commander; driver).
Armament: None.
Armor: Front 4in-4·72in (101-120mm); sides 2in (51mm).
Dimensions (vehicle): Length 28ft 4in (8·648m); width 12ft (3·657m), height 10ft 4in (3·162m).
Weight (vehicle): 91,900lb (41,685kg).
Engine: Continental AVDS-1790-2A, 12-cylinder diesel; 750bhp at 2,400rpm.
Performance: Road speed 30mph (48·28km/h); range 310 miles (500km); fording 4ft (1·22m); gradient 60 per cent; vertical obstacle 3ft (0·91m); trench 8ft 6in (2·59m).

The US Army's requirement for a tactical bridge is met by the M60 AVLB although numbers of M48 AVLBs remain in service. So far as is known there are no current plans to develop an AVLB version of the M1.

The M60 AVLB can use a variety of bridges. The first weighs 31,900lb (14,470kg) and is made of aluminum. It is 63ft (19·2m) long and can span a gap of 60ft (18·3m), taking 3 minutes to launch and from 10 to 60 minutes to recover (depending on the ground). The second bridge weighs 19,000lb (8,618kg), has an overall length of 92ft 10in (28·3m), and can span 88ft 7in (27m). Both have a Bridge Classification of Type 60; ie, they will take a load of 60 tons.

Other types of bridging used by the US Army include the Mobile Assault Bridge/Ferry (MAB) and the British-designed Medium Girder Bridge (MGB).

Below: The highly mobile M60 chassis without turret, fitted with a hydraulic cylinder assembly and a scissors bridge.

Above: An M113 mounted with Vulcan air defense system trundles across an AVLB emplaced by the M60 chassis parked on the bank.

M88A1

Type: Medium armored recovery vehicle.
Crew: 4 (commander, driver, co-driver, mechanic).
Armament: One 0·50 M2 HB machine gun.
Dimensions: Length (without dozer blade): 27·15ft (8·267m); width 11·24ft (3·428m); height with anti-aircraft machine gun 10·58ft (3·225m).
Weight: 111,993lb (50,800kg).
Ground pressure: 1·63lb/in^2 (0·74kg/cm^2).
Engine: Continental AVSI-1790-2DR diesel engine developing 750bhp at 2,400rpm.
Performance: Road speed 26mph (42km/hr); range 280 miles (450km); vertical obstacle 3·49ft (1·066m); trench 8·58ft (2·61m); gradient 60 per cent.

The standard medium armored recovery vehicle used by the US Army in the early 1950s was the M74. This was based on a Sherman tank chassis but could not handle the heavier tanks which were then entering service. In 1954, work on a new medium armored recovery vehicle commenced and three prototypes, designated the T88, were built by Bowen-McLaughlin-York. After trials, a batch of pre-production vehicles was built and then Bowen-Laughlin-York were awarded a production contract for the vehicle which was standardized as the M88. Just over 1,000 M88s were built between 1961 and 1964, and some were also exported abroad. The M88 uses many automotive components of the M48 tank, and can recover AFVs up to and including the M60 MBT. Its role on the battlefield is to recover damaged and disabled tanks and other AFVs, and it can, if required remove major components from tanks such as complete turrets. When the M88 first entered service it was armed with a 0·50 caliber machine gun mounted in a turret but this was subsequently replaced by a simple pintle mounted 0·50 machine gun.

The hull of the M88 is of cast armor construction and provides the crew with protection from small arms fire and shell splinters. The crew compartment is at the front of the hull and the engine and transmission are at the rear. A hydraulically operated dozer blade is mounted at the front of the hull and this is used to stabilize the vehicle when the winch or "A" frame is being used, and can also be used for normal dozing operations. The "A" type frame is pivoted at the front of the hull, and when not required this lies in the horizontal position on top of the hull. This frame can lift a maximum load of

six tons (5,443kg), or 25 tons (22,680kg) with the dozer blade in the lowered position.

The M88 is provided with two winches and both of these are mounted under the crew compartment. The main winch is provided with 200ft (61m) of 32mm cable and has a maximum pull of 40 tons, whilst the secondary winch, which is used for hoisting operations, has 200ft (61m) of 16mm cable. The vehicle is provided with a full range of tools and an auxiliary fuel pump. This enables the vehicle to transfer fuel to other armored vehicles.

All M88s of the US Army have now been brought up to M88A1 standard and are fitted with the Continental AVDS-1790-2DR diesel engine developing 750bhp at 2,400rpm. This gives the vehicle a longer operating range of 280 miles (450km) compared to the original M88. It is also fitted with an APU and can also be fitted with a NBC system. Current production model is M88A1 which has also been exported to many parts of the world.

M578

Type: Light armored recovery vehicle.
Crew: 3.
Armament: One 0·50 M2 HB machine gun.
Dimensions: Length overall 21ft (6·42m); width 10·331ft (3·149m); height with machine gun 11·20ft (3·416m).
Weight: 53,572lb (24,300kg).
Ground pressure: 1·56lb/in² (0·71kg/cm²).
Engine: General Motors Model 8V71T eight cylinder liquid diesel developing 425bhp at 2,300rpm.
Performance: Road speed 34mph (54·71km/h); range 450 miles (725km); vertical obstacle 3·3ft (1·016m); trench 7·76ft (2·362m); gradient 60 per cent.

In the mid-1950s, the Pacific Car and Foundry Company of Renton Washington, was awarded a contract by the US Army to build a new range of self-propelled artillery, all of which were to use the same common chassis. These three weapons were the T235 (which eventually entered service as the 175mm M107), the T236 (which entered service as the 8inch M110) and the T245 (this was a 155mm weapon but was not developed past the prototype stage). In 1957, it was decided to build a range of light armored recovery vehicles using the same chassis as the self-propelled guns. Three different prototypes were built. Further development resulted in the T120E1 which had a diesel engine, and this entered service as the M578.

The first production M578 was completed by the FMC Corporation in 1962, and since then the vehicle has been produced by the designers Pacific Car and Foundry, and more recently by Bowen-McLaughlin-York Between FY 1976 and FY 1978, the US Army requested some $64 million to purchase an additional 283 M578s.

The M578 is used by all arms, including self-propelled artillery battalions mechanized infantry battalions, and armored cavalry regiments. Apart from recovering such vehicles as the M110 and M109, the vehicle is also

used to change major components in the field, such as engines, transmissions, and tank barrels.

The hull of the M578 is identical to that of the M107 and M110 self-propelled guns, with the driver being seated at the front of the hull on the left side and the engine to his right. The crane is mounted at the rear of the hull and this can be traversed through a full 360 degrees. The commander and mechanic are seated in the turret and a standard 0·50 Browning M2 HB machine gun is mounted on the roof for anti-aircraft protection. The crane can lift a maximum of 13·38 tons (13,600kg) and the main winch is provided with 229ft (70m) of 25mm cable. This has a maximum capacity of 26·57 tons (27,000kg). A large spade is mounted at the rear of the hull to stabilize the vehicle when the winch or crane is being used; in addition, the suspension can be locked out if required. Unlike most MBTs, the M578 is not provided with a NBC system and it has no amphibious capability. Infra-red driving lights are normally fitted.

Above: The M578 is designed to recover vehicles up to 66,137lb (30,000kg), and therefore could recover the Army's SPGs and APCs (and engines, gun barrels and so on), but not main battle tanks (the M1 weighs 120,000lb/54,432kg). The tow-winch capacity is 60,000lb (27,216kg) bare drum, and hoisting capacity is 15,000lb (6,804kg). Besides the driver there are a commander and a mechanic, who normally enter the turret through side doors, although there are also double doors at the rear. They each have a single-piece hatch cover and six periscopes. A machine gun mounted in front of the left hatch cover is provided for use against attacking aircraft. The M578 uses the M110 chassis; there are no variants in service.

M992 FAASV

Type: Field artillery ammunition support vehicle (FAASV).
Crew: 9 (maximum).
Armament: One 0·5in Browning MG.
Dimensions: Length overall 22ft 3in (6·7m); width 10ft 10in (3·295m); height 10ft 7½in (3·24m).
Weights: Loaded 57,500lb (26,082kg); cargo capacity 18,920lb (8,582kg).
Engine: Detroit Diesel Model 8V71T, 8-cylinder turbocharged diesel; 405bhp at 2,350rpm.
Performance: Road speed 35mph (56km/h); road range 220 miles (354km); vertical obstacle 1ft 9in (0·53m); trench 6ft (1·83m).

Many armies are searching for an answer to the ammunition resupply problem created by the ever-increasing capability of modern artillery. This problem has a number of facets. First, most artillery is now on highly mobile self-propelled tracked chassis, and is thus able to move more often, faster and to more inaccessible sites. Secondly, rates of fire are increasing and

Inset: M992 will support M109 and M110 battalions in Europe from 1985. Note armored overhead protection provided by rear door.

Below: Capable of carrying 48 8in (203mm) rounds for the M110A2 SP howitzer, the highly-mobile FAASV will speed up rates of fire.

hus creating a greater quantitative requirement. Finally, increases in caliber have led to larger and heavier rounds which are more difficult for the "ammunition numbers" to handle.

The US Army's solution to this problem is the FAASV, which entered production in 1983, with introduction to service scheduled for 1985-86. The FAASV is based on the well-proven M109A2 chassis, but with a large armored housing in place of the turret. This housing contains removable vertical racks which are hoisted aboard by a 1,500lb (680kg) capacity, extendible-boom crane on the front of the vehicle. On arrival at the gun position, projectiles and charges are removed from these racks by an automatic stacker, assembled, fuzed, and then passed by an hydraulic conveyer directly into the supported gun.

The FAASV can carry 90 155mm projectiles and charges, or 48 8in rounds. The rate of passing rounds to the guns is 8 rounds per minute, which handsomely exceeds current rates of fire. An additional feature is that the armored rear door swings up to provide overhead protection during the transfer process.

This very promising vehicle is designed and built by Bowen-McLaughlin-York and 144 units are currently on order, although the US Army's requirement is for at least 250 units.

Mines

The mine is a weapon which seems always to be on the verge of a major comeback, but never quite making it. There is no doubt as to its value in at least delaying (if not actually stopping) either armored or infantry advances or deployments. The major problem, however, is the time taken to lay

---

GEMSS
Ground-Emplaced Mine-Scattering System

All NATO armies are seeking to enhance their ability to stop and defeat armored thrusts by the numerically superior Warsaw Pact forces. To this end, all forms of anti-tank weapons are being developed, and over the past decade there has been a marked revival of interest in anti-tank mines, interest both in the effect of the mines themselves and in rapid methods of laying them. The Ground-Emplaced Mine-Scattering System (GEMSS) is particularly effective, since it is mounted on a trailer that can be towed by any suitable tracked (M548 cargo carrier, M113 APC) or wheeled (5-ton truck) prime mover. GEMSS's primary purpose is quickly to lay minefields that will force attacking enemy armored vehicles into constricted areas where they will provide a rewarding target for killing weapons.

GEMSS is the M128 mine dispenser, holding up to 800 4lb (1·8kg) mines which are deployed at intervals of 32 or 64 yards (30 or 60m), the

mines, assuming that it is most unlikely that any will be laid in peacetime. Thus, great efforts have been devoted to rapid minelaying systems, using either mechanical layers or helicopters. Much attention is also being paid to delivering large quantities of very small mines ("minelets"), using artillery shells or missiles as the delivery agent. The full range of US Army mines covers the spectrum from small anti-personnel mines, through anti-tank mines, to the Atomic Demolition Mines (ADMs) which will soon be withdrawn from Western Europe where they have been deployed for many years. The mine is an ideal defensive weapon—provided that it can be laid in time.

interval being determined by the rate of launch and the speed of the vehicle. The M128 dispenser is mounted on the M794 trailer.

The mines are laid on the surface and a 2,734 yard (2,500m) field can be laid in less than six hours. The anti-tank mine has a magnetic influence field; this means that it can attack the whole width of the target and does not need to be run over by the tracks. There is also an anti-personnel mine, a fragmentation weapon activated by automatically deployed trip-wire sensors. Both types of mine have anti-disturbance devices to inhibit clearance, but both also have a built-in self-destruct device which neutralizes the minefield after a pre-determined interval.

Fiftynine GEMSS units were procured by the US Army in FY 1982 and a further 52 units in FY 1983.

Below: The Army's FASCAM (family of scatterable mines) program is designed to lay minefields rapidly to force enemy armor into "ambush" situations. It includes GEMSS (below) as well as mine systems seeded by artillery and aircraft.

Uniforms and Personal Equipment

The uniforms of the United States Army must cover every military requirement, from formal parades at the White House, through combat in any possible condition of terrain or climate, to fatigues and NBC warfare. The Army has usually managed to meet these requirements although, like all soldiers, the American always thinks that someone else has something just that little bit better. There has been a perceptible change in some areas. There has, for example, been a gradual increase in the wearing of berets, the merits of this ubiquitous item of military headgear have been realized. Also, a barrack uniform of olive-green trousers and the now virtually universal woolen pullover has been adopted, a relaxed form of day-to-day wear which originated with the British Army and its "wooly pully".

The olive-drab fatigues formerly intended to be worn in combat have been replaced by a properly camouflaged outfit, with basic colors and patterns varied for different climates, from European temperate to African desert. Materials are also more up-to-date, and in addition to being more weather-proof also incorporate a certain degree of resistance to chemical and infra-red detection. Special combat clothing is available for extremes of climate, such as Arctic or jungle environments.

Above: Paratrooper of 1st/502d Infantry, 101st Airborne Division, in desert combat uniform, in the Sinai Multinational Force, 1983.

Left: A soldier of 4th Infantry Division decontaminating his over-shoes in a special bath. Note the detection paper on his left sleeve.

A recent introduction is the new "military helmet". This was the result of years of research and much agonized appraisal. The helmet is made of laminated Kevlar and weighs only 51oz (1·45kg). It is much more resistant to projectiles than the previous model. Its most obvious characteristic, however, is its shape—the principal aim being to avoid the notorious and widely recognizable shape of the German World War II helmet. Despite this, the new helmet, especially with its camouflage cover, does bear a resemblance to the German helmet, and this led to some comment during the first use of the new headwear during the freeing of Grenada. ▶

► Web equipment has evolved gradually over the years, but even th
Americans have not yet found a really satisfactory answer to the problem o
providing a really comfortable method of carrying the impedimenta neede
by a modern soldier. As was discovered by British infantrymen during the
1982 war in the Falklands, an APC or truck will not always be available t
carry it all.

Much publicity is given to the overpressure systems now being fitted to a
AFVs to ensure a degree of NBC protection for the crew. The vast majorit
of soldiers on the modern battlefield will, however, not have such protectio
and will still have to rely on respirators and protective suits. In the earl
1980s, the US Army found itself so lacking in this area that it had to bu
some 200,000 British Mark 3 NBC suits and boots for US troops in
Western Europe, to cover the gap pending issue of new American equip
ment. What still has to be determined—and not just by the US Army—i
just how long soldiers will be able to continue fighting and working in suc
conditions, because nobody can pretend that wearing the full NBC equip
ment for protracted periods is anything other than a very trying experience

Most US Army uniforms and items of personal equipment are well-de
signed and popular with the troops. There has been a noticeable increase in
the smartness and bearing of American soldiers since the bad days of the
aftermath of Vietnam, and they now—especially since the success in
Grenada—appear proud and confident once again, which bodes well for
their many allies around the world.

**Below: US Army infantrymen on exercise in northern Norway mov
equipment on a Norwegian "pulk". This is just one of the very many
deployment options for which the Army is constantly training.**

Above: An infantry soldier in his combat suit and boots, holding an M16 rifle. The helmet is the new model, made of Kevlar, which is lighter, more comfortable, and offers better protection.

Radars and Communications

In any future conflict one of the major battlefields will be an invisible one—the electromagnetic spectrum—but the outcome will be crucial to overall success. Today's sophisticated, highly mobile, rapidly moving armies are totally dependent upon radars and telecommunications systems for their survival; inevitably, none more so than the US Army.

Currently, the US Army uses tactical radio systems based on the traditional radio nets using the High Frequency (HF) and Very High Frequency (VHF) bands, with some specialized needs (eg, ground-to-air) using even higher bands. A major program is now under way for the Single-Channel Ground and Airborne Radio Subsystem (SINCGARS-V) which will provide the next generation of sets. These will be light in weight, secure, and will use the most modern microprocessor techniques. They will be capable not only of voice transmissions, but also of passing data, an ever-increasing requirement on today's battlefield. The most interesting aspect, however, is that a technique known as "frequency hopping" will be used to provide a major degree of Electronic Counter-counter Measure (ECCM) protection. This means that the set transmits on any one frequency for only a micro-second at a time. For an enemy, therefore, the intercept problem becomes very acute, although the technique is not without its problems at the transmitting end as well.

As with other major armies, the US Army is putting a major effort into developing a Maneuver Control System (MCS) to provide a field commander and his staff with automated assistance in controlling the battle. The long term system will be known as Sigma, and is likely to be very sophisticated indeed. Currently in service are a microcomputer called the Tactical Computer Terminal (TCT) and a rather more powerful device, the Tactical Computer System (TCS). One particular device under development would put the entire battlefield map into the data base, which would not only give a picture similar to that of a current paper map, but would also give a 3-D picture from any point on the map in any requested direction. Thus, a commander would be able to "look" at his positions from the enemy's viewpoint, a unique capability.

The major strategic communications system for the US Department of

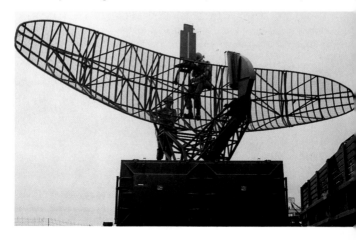

Defense is the Defense Satellite Communication System (DSCS), and the Army is responsible for developing, procuring, and operating the earth terminals. This involves equipment of many kinds, ranging from huge stations with antenna dishes several hundred feet in diameter to the latest vehicle-borne tactical terminals.

The command, control, and communications (C^3) areas are becoming ever more sophisticated, and ever more demanding in manpower and resources. There is no doubt that modern forces need a major control effort, and that the amount of intelligence and information flowing in the system is growing at a great rate as sensors become more effective; but some are beginning to feel that the limit is being approached.

The US Army also uses a great variety of radars and other electronic sensors. These range in size and role from the small, tripod-mounted infantry radars such as the AN-PPS-15 to large gun- and mortar-locating and air-defense radars. The gun- and mortar-locating radars are of especial importance to the Army in central Europe for their contribution to countering the massive fire support capability of the Warsaw Pact. Such radars can pinpoint an enemy round within seconds of its leaving the barrel, analyse its trajectory and backplot to the point of origin, and then pass the information to the counter-battery gun positions before the round has landed.

Far left: AN/MPQ-50 pulse-acquisition radar being set up by men of 38th Air Defense Artillery Brigade in Korea.

Left: An infantry company commander using a VHF radio command link. Such forward nets are simple to intercept.

Below: US Army operator using teleprinter GRC-12 radio link.

157

General Logistics and Resupply

According to legend, a US Army general was being briefed on the then newly discovered "science" of logistics in the early 1940s. After listening for some time with increasing bewilderment he got to his feet and said to his staff: "I still don't know what these goddam logistics are—but, whatever they are, make sure I get a lot of them!" Any logistician would say that the attitudes of commanders and their operations staffs have changed little over the years: they still do not want to be bothered with the details, but heaven help the logistics specialist who fails to deliver the goods. The US Army's logistics problem is severe, because virtually any operation will be mounted at a very considerable distance from the Continental USA. Some of these can be carefully planned and prepared for in peace; eg, West Germany or South Korea, where in-place units are supported by a well prepared logistic system. Other deployment options are recognized but are subject to peacetime limitations; for example, the Norwegians will not permit troops or stores to be positioned on their soil in peacetime. Finally there are the open options, such as those facing the Rapid Deployment Force.

One of the logistic problems which causes US military planners most concern is the air/sea bridge across the North Atlantic, over which, in the early days of any future conflict or crisis, vast amounts of men and materiel would have to flow. The great increase in strength of the Soviet Navy is a direct threat to these plans, and, as in World War II, some of the most crucial battles will be fought in the open expanses of the Atlantic.

A second major logistic problem facing the US forces in Europe is that in peacetime the French will not permit US military stores to be landed in or transported across, Metropolitan France. These stores must instead be

Above: A vehicle-mounted 25-ton crane on road test for the US Army. This is one of many thousands of support vehicles of differing types necessary to a modern army.

Left: M60 tanks are unloaded from a ship. US supply lines must use the vulnerable routes across the Pacific and Atlantic Oceans; this constitutes a major risk.

landed at North Sea ports and then moved by road and rail south to the US areas along a supply route which is parallel to—and dangerously near—the inner German Border. This is a bad situation to be in, although it must be hoped that in war the French would relent. Further in-theater problems would arise in war with the roads being crammed with refugees and vehicles trying to move in the opposite direction to the military units and supplies.

One of the major logistic problems in terms of commodities is likely to be fuel. There has recently been a major switch-over to diesel to reduce demand—but there are vast numbers of vehicles and the allied logistic services are going to be very hard pressed to meet the demands. Obviously, reserves exist, but these would not sustain a war effort for very long. Thus, the fuel resupply lines back across the oceans to the point of production will be crucially important and, again, the Soviet Fleet seems poised to threaten these.

A further problem for the logistic services in a future war will be that of dealing with casualties, especially those from chemical, biological, or nuclear attack. This is a task of awesome proportions.

Section Two

NAVAL WEAPONS AND EQUIPMENT

Contents of Section Two

Introduction

The geographical situation of the United States, separated from Europe by the Atlantic and from the mainland of Asia by the even broader expanses of the Pacific, makes the possession of a strong navy imperative. The United States Navy is the primary instrument for the projection of American military power and political influence into these distant regions, and it is at the same time the means by which the United States maintains control over the seas in order to ensure the

curity of its maritime com-
unications and of its territory in
e event of hostilities with
other power.

These twin missions of power
ojection and sea control can-
t be considered in total isola-
n from one another. In order

to project power against a distant
land mass a navy must be able to
exercise control over the seas
which its forces will have to

**Below: USS *Carl Vinson*
(CVN 70), the epitome of US
Navy power projection.**

transit in order to reach their objective and over the operating area from which the air strikes and amphibious assault will be made. Similarly, the job of exercising sea control over broad ocean areas is made much easier if forward-deployed power projection forces compel the enemy to adopt a defensive posture. The power projection and sea control missions should therefore be seen as two sides of the same coin. The problem is that of finding the right balance between those forces required for "offensive"—ie, power projection—missions and those required for "defensive"—ie, sea control— missions.

In time of war, when funds and resources are virtually unlimited, there is no conflict of interests; a country the size of the United States simply builds what it needs. In peacetime, however, the inevitable constraints on the defence budget mean that difficult choices have to be made; more of one type of ship means less of another. Factions supporting a particular aspect of naval operations—the aviators, the submariners, the surface ship lobby—begin to dig their heels in, and bitter conflicts break out

over the crucial issue of wh sort of forces the navy shou have, and in what numbers. It against this background that t development of the US Na over the past three decades mu be seen.

The 1950s
The advent of the atomic bor threw American naval strategy the immediate postwar peri into a state of total confusic Many questioned the survivabil of any sort of task force in t face of the new weaponry. 1950, however, came a ne conflict, which served emphasise once again the val of traditional power projecti forces. The Korean War established the aircraft carri and the amphibious assault for as the twin central elements American sea-power, and set a massive naval reconstructic programme. Between 1955 a 1962 no fewer than seven sup carriers—one of which w nuclear-powered—were co pleted.

In addition to the standa light attack squadrons, th would be able to opera strategic bombers (A—3 Sl warriors) which could laun

Above: The A-3 launched from carriers was one of the Navy's early answers to strategic power projection problems.

Below: Versatility of all forces has for several years been a keynote of the Navy's shipbuilding programme which is leading to a 600-ship goal, including 15 Carrier Battle Groups, 4 Battleship Surface Action Groups, 100 SSNs, 10 Underway Replenishment Groups, 14 Mine Countermeasures ships, and amphibious ships sufficient to lift the assault echelons of a Marine Amphibious Force plus a Marine Amphibious Brigade. Shown are (left to right) *Oliver Hazard Perry* (FFG-7), top; *Luce* (DDG-38), a Coontz class guided missile destroyer; *Stein* (FF-1065); and *Moinester* (FF-1097). They all represent vessels which are part of a massive modernization programme, besides the new-build ships.

US Fleet Organisation

The basic units of organisation for the purposes of deployment
are as follows:—

Carrier Battle Group

Centred around a single carrier (CV), this generally includes an
escort group of four to six ships. The typical composition
of such a group would be:

1 or 2 CGs armed with Terrier
1 DDG armed with Tartar
2 or 3 ASW destroyers (DD) or frigates (FF)

Nuclear-powered carriers (CVN) are usually deployed with a
homogeneous group of nuclear-powered escorts (CGN).

Amphibious Squadron (PhibRon)

Composed of between three and five amphibious vessels and two
escorts (FF/FFG). The typical composition of a PhibRon would be:

1 LPH
1 LPD, 1 LSD
2 LST

A PhibRon based on an LHA would omit the LPH and LSD.

Before the crisis in the Arabian Gulf US Navy deployments were
maintained on the following pattern:

Forward Deployed Forces

Pacific Fleet

Third Fleet

4 Carrier Battle Groups
2 PhibRons

Seventh Fleet
(NW Pacific, SE Asia)
2 Carrier Battle Groups
2 PhibRons

Atlantic Fleet

Second Fleet

4 Carrier Battle Groups
3 PhibRons

US Naval Forces Europe

Sixth Fleet
Mediterranean)
2 Carrier Battle Groups
1 PhibRon

Middle East Force

1 flagship (AGF)
2 FF

Since late 1979, however, one of the Seventh Fleet and one of the
Sixth Fleet Carrier Battle Groups have been deployed to the Indian
Ocean on a regular basis. They have been reinforced by one of the
Seventh Fleet PhibRons.

nuclear strikes deep into the heart of the Soviet Union. The primary mission of the large numbers of war-built surface units—destroyers and cruisers—would continue to be the protection of the carriers, with a subsidiary fire-support role in amphibious operations.

Although the development of both surface-to-surface and surface-to-air missiles proceeded simultaneously throughout the 1950s, submarine- and ship-launched SSMs did not find favour in the US Navy in the way that they did in the Soviet Navy because of the renewed confidence in carrier-borne aviation. Surface-to-air missiles, on the other hand, received massive development funds because of their potential value in defence of the carrier task force, and an entire "family" of missiles—Talos, Terrier and Tartar—was in service aboard a variety of US ships by the early 1960s.

The first missile ships were converted war-built cruisers

(CAGs and CLGs) but, with the tailing-off of the carrier programme, funds became available for three classes each of ten "frigates" (DLGs) armed with the Terrier long-range missile, and a large class of destroyers (DDGs) armed with the medium-range Tartar. A programme for the development of the even more capable—and costly—Typhoon missile was set in motion. (This particular project was to founder but was later revived as Aegis.).

In the 1950s the threat to US

Above Test launches of Tartar and Terrier surface-to-air missiles. These represent a whole family of SAMs which first saw service aboard US Navy warships in the 1960s. By virtue of constant updating to keep abreast of growing threats, they developed within a programme which persisted for thirty years and also produced some useful surface-to-surface and air-to-surface missiles.

Above: USS *Hornet,* one of the Essex class carriers built during World War II and modernised in the 1950s-60s to serve as ASW carriers to guard against the growing Soviet submarine threat. She is seen here with Tracker and Tracer fixed-wing ASW aircraft and Sea King helicopters.

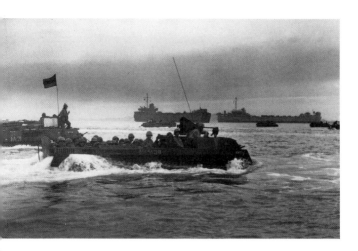

Above: During the Korean War, United States forces enjoyed unopposed amphibious landings. It would be different today.

Below: An A-7 ready for catapult launch during the Vietnam War, which reinforced the Navy's power projection mission bias.

sea control was minimal. The Soviet Navy, although growing rapidly in size, was still little more than a coast defence force. The air strikes and amphibious assaults of the Korean War had been unopposed. The only US ships specifically built for the sea control mission in this period were a handful of diesel-powered destroyer escorts (DEs), which were not much of an improvement on their war-built counterparts.

Only in the NATO Eastlant area, which was threatened by a growing Soviet submarine fleet based on the Kola Peninsula, was sea control thought to merit any serious attention, and a number of war-built Essex-class carriers were modified as ASW carriers (CVSs) carrying S-2 Tracker aircraft and HSS-1 helicopters. They would form the centre of submarine hunter-killer groups and convoy escort groups. As far as possible the sea control mission in the European Theatre would be devolved onto the NATO navies, which were boosted by American construction and American finance under the Mutual Defense Aid Program (MDAP).

US Navy Classification System

Note:
In June 1975 a new system of classification was adopted. Vessels formerly classified as "Frigates" (DLG/DLGN) became "Cruisers" (CG/CGN), and "Destroyer Escorts" (DE/DEG) became "Frigates" (FF/FFG).

CVN (ex-CVAN)	nuclear-powered aircraft carrier
CV (ex-CVA)	aircraft carrier
CGN (ex-CLGN/DLGN)	nuclear-powered misisle cruiser
CG (ex-DLGN)	missile cruiser
DDG	missile destroyer (AAW)
DD	destroyer (ASW)
FFG (ex-DEG)	missile frigate (AAW)
FF (ex-DE)	frigate (ASW)
PHM	missile patrol hydrofoil
LCC	amphibious command ship
LHA	amphibious assault ship (multi-purpose)
LPH	amphibious assault ship
LPD	amphibious transport dock
LSD	dock landing ship
LST	tank landing ship
AD	destroyer tender
AS	submarine tender
AE	ammunition ship
AFS	combat support ship
AO	oiler
AOE	fast combat support ship
AOR	replenishment oiler

The classification system used by the US Navy is frequently extended—often incorrectly—to ships of other navies. Note the distinction between the suffix "G" (=surface-to-air) and the suffix "M" (=antiship) used for missile ships.

1960s—More of the same

From 1960 onwards the mission of nuclear strike on the Soviet Union was transferred from the big carriers to the Polaris submarine. No sooner was the latter programme under way, however, than the value of conventional power projection forces in a limited conflict was reaffirmed by American involvement in the Vietnam War.

For nearly a decade the big carriers conducted sustained strike operations against targets in North Vietnam and in support of friendly forces in the South. Studies were undertaken for new classes of nuclear-powered carriers (CVANs) and nuclear-powered missile escorts (DLGNs), and a massive programme of amphibious construction—some 60 vessels in all—was institute to replace the aging force c war-built vessels.

The escort problem

While attention was focused ye again on the construction of eve more capable—and costly power projection units, th forces of sea control continue to be neglected. Many of th war-built destroyers underwer extensive FRAM (Fleet Rehabil tation And Modernisation) refit in the early 1960s to equip ther with ASROC, new sonars, an DASH (Drone Anti-Submarin Helicopters), and these no became the workhorses of th sea control mission. But the onl new vessels completed durin the 1960s were a handful c "convoy escorts" (DEs), begin

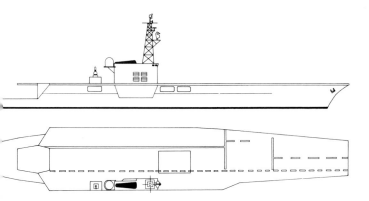

Above: Profile and plan views of the Sea Control Ship (SCS) proposed in the early 1970s by Admiral Zumwalt.

ning with the two prototypes of the Bronstein class.

The new ships, which aimed to avoid the high costs increasingly associated with fleet escorts while providing a first-class ASW capability which would enable them to deal effectively with the new generation of fast, nuclear-powered Soviet submarines, were designed on traditional American "all-or-nothing" principles. They were fitted with the most advanced anti-submarine weapons and sensors: the massive SQS-26 bow sonar, ASROC and DASH. The "platform" characteristics, on the other hand, were distinctly second-rate, with only a single screw and a maximum speed of only 25 to 27kts. AAW capabilities were minimal except in the Brooke class, which proved too expensive for construction beyond six units.

In the mid-1960s, with block obsolescence looming for the large number of war-built destroyers, orders began to be placed for the 46-strong Knox class. But the new escorts were not popular with some factions in the naval community; concern was expressed about the limited military capabilities of the ships and about their one-shaft propulsion plant. The next escort design, the DDX, which began as an attempt to provide a simple ASW destroyer for fleet work, resulted in the controversial Spruance class, which came out at 8,000 tons—three times the displacement of the war-built destroyers they were to replace—and were the ultimate in sophistication.

By 1970 the only designs on the drawing board were sophisticated power projection types: the Nimitz-class CVANs, the Tarawa-class LHAs, the Virginia-class DLGNs, the Spruance-class DDs and the Los Angeles-class SSNs (all three of the last-named types designed primarily for fleet work in support of the carrier battle groups).

Zumwalt and Project 60

Such was the situation that confronted Admiral Elmo Zumwalt when he became Chief of Naval Operations in 1970. Unlike his three predecessors, who were all aviators, Zumwalt was a surface navy man, and he immediately set about changing what he regarded as an alarming imbalance in the Navy's construction programme. Zumwalt felt that American naval commitment in South Asia over the previous two decades had distorted the strategic picture in favour of projection forces and that the growing threat posed by the Soviet Navy to American control of the seas in the event of war between NATO and the forces of the Warsaw Pact had been seriously neglected. The war-built destroyers and the

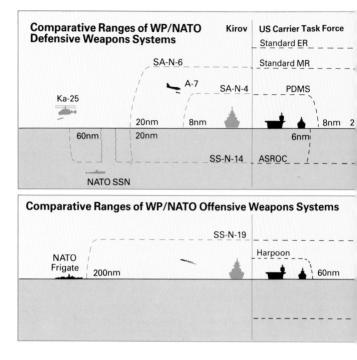

Comparative Ranges of WP/NATO Defensive Weapons Systems — Kirov — US Carrier Task Force

Standard ER
Standard MR
SA-N-6
A-7   SA-N-4   PDMS
Ka-25
20nm   8nm   8nm   2
60nm   20nm   6nm
SS-N-14   ASROC
NATO SSN

Comparative Ranges of WP/NATO Offensive Weapons Systems

SS-N-19
NATO
Frigate   Harpoon
200nm   60nm

Above: A comparison of the offensive and defensive capabilities of a US carrier battle group (CBG) with those of a Soviet surface action group centred on the cruiser *Kirov* reveals why the US Navy is so reluctant to abandon the large-deck carrier.

Below: A carrier battle group (CBG) centred on the carrier *Midway* (CV-41) operating in the Indian Ocean.

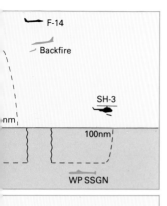

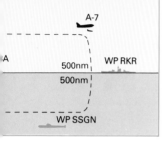

Essex-class CVs on which the Navy still largely depended to perform the sea control mission were by now 25 years old, yet even with the 30-strong Spruance class the US Navy would possess only 180 out of the 250 escorts which it regarded as the minimum figure required to perform its missions. The US Navy needed large numbers of new hulls, and quickly.

Zumwalt elevated his own "High-Low" concept to the level of a philosophy. The "high" end of the Navy would be the high-performance ships and weapon systems needed to perform the projection mission in high-threat areas. The "low" end would consist of moderate-performance ships which, because of their low cost, could be produced in large numbers for the sea control mission.

Within 60 days of his accession Zumwalt produced Project 60, which was to form the basis for major changes in the Navy's construction policy during the 1970s. The "high" programme was already in full swing, and the only modification made to it was the cancellation of the last four of nine projected LHAs.

But it was now to be balanced by a "low" programme financed in part by the premature retirement of large numbers of war-built ships and based on four new classes. Of these the most important were the Patrol Frigate (PF) and the Sea Control Ship (SCS). The PF, which became the FFG 7 class, was a development of the convoy escort types built during the 1960s, but with enhanced AAW and anti-surface capabilities in order to counter the new Soviet long-range maritime bombers and forward deployment of surface units.

The SCS was an austere ASW carrier designed to operate 14 SH-3 ASW helicopters and three AV-8A Harrier V/STOL aircraft. The SCS was affordable in large numbers—eight could be purchased for the price of one CVAN—and was the obvious replacement for the CVSs of the Essex class. Zumwalt went further and suggested that in peacetime the SCSs would take the place of the big carriers on forward deployments in order to blunt the threat posed by Soviet surface action groups (SAGs), and that the big carriers would be held back in low-threat areas until hostilities began, when they would exchange places with the SCSs.

Other important related projects were the acceleration of the LAMPS manned helicopter programme in order to increase the number of air-capable platforms, and of the development of the Harpoon SSM, which would spread offensive capabilities throughout the fleet instead of leaving them concentrated on the decks of a handful of strike carriers.

In order to provide the necessary coordination for these various weapons platforms Zumwalt initiated the development of a network of satellite-based communication and surveillance systems.

Above: The battleship *New Jersey* (BB-62) has been reactivated and armed with Harpoon and Tomahawk missiles.

Below: US design philosophy favours sophisticated multi-function weapons systems and radars whereas the Soviet Navy favours larger numbers of single-purpose systems. The Soviet Kara (above) and USS *Virginia* (below) illustrate this contrast.

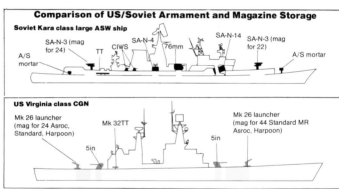

Comparison of US/Soviet Armament and Magazine Storage

Soviet Kara class large ASW ship

SA-N-3 (mag for 24)   CIWS   SA-N-4   76mm   SA-N-14   SA-N-3 (mag for 22)

A/S mortar   TT   A/S mortar

US Virginia class CGN

Mk 26 launcher (mag for 24 Asroc, Standard, Harpoon)   Mk 32TT   Mk 26 launcher (mag for 44 Standard MR Asroc, Harpoon)

5in   5in

A continuing struggle

When Zumwalt retired as CNO in 1974, the battle between the power projection and sea control factions resumed in earnest. The first victim of the new battle was the Sea Control Ship, which, following evaluation trials employing the LPH *Guam*, was declared to be unable to defend itself against the growing threat from Soviet long-range bombers.

The real reason for its demise, however, was undoubtedly the fear of the aviators that the project would reduce the funds available for attack carrier con-struction and for the purchase of carrier aircraft, and that by taking the place of the big carriers in the "front line" in peacetime the SCS would seriously reduce their credibility—and consequently the willingness of Congress to continue to provide virtually unlimited funds to maintain force levels.

The aviators were, however, compelled to make one significant concession. From 1975 the big carriers ceased to be designated Attack Carriers (CVA) instead they become "Multi-Mission" Carriers (CV) and accep-

ed squadrons of S-3A Viking ASW aircraft and SH-3H Sea King ASW helicopters in place of some of their strike aircraft. This modification equipped them to provide more effective distant cover for convoys and to perform more general sub-hunting operations, using data from the SOSUS seabed surveillance system. it also provided an increasingly necessary long-range ASW defence capability to a battle group faced by growing numbers of submarines armed with cruise missiles.

Harpoon and Tomahawk

By the late 1970s large numbers of the Navy's ships had been fitted with the Harpoon SSM and there was the prospect of a follow-on, Tomahawk, with a range comparable to that of the largest cruise missiles in service with the Soviet Navy. The development of long-range cruise missiles, however, has inevitably led to increased polarisation of the aviation and surface ship camps. Long-range cruise missiles in a maritime environment need an extensive—and costly—satellite-based Extended Horizon Command and Control (EHC) system on the Soviet pattern. They would also be most effective if used in conjunction with VTOL aircraft scattered among a number of surface warships.

Proposals such as these have attracted considerable criticism from the aviation lobby, who have pointed out that distributing aircraft among a variety of small hulls is uneconomic in terms of ship space and maintenance facilities. Supporters of the big carriers claim, with some justification, that the carrier battle group is still the most capable, versatile and cost-effective strike weapon available, and that to adopt an essentially "defensive" sea control posture is to play into the hands of the Soviet Navy.

Present and future

The dramatic increase in defence spending established by the Reagan Administration in its first term of office has served to ease—temporarily, at least—some of these conflicts. Under an increased budget there is no reason why the construction of high-value super-carriers and their large, sophisticated escorts should not go hand in hand with a large programme of cheap frigates and the widespread fitting of Tomahawk missiles.

With the application of additional resources, however, thinking has grown more conservative. There have been proposals to drag some of the older carriers, and even the four Iowa-class battleships, out of retirement in order to re-establish mastery over the seas, while new technology programmes such as the Surface Effect Ship (SES) have foundered without trace.

A 600-ship Navy is planned instead of the present total of 450. There are strong indications, however, that the US budget is in trouble and will not be able to sustain this level of expansion. In the Navy's case the problem will be exacerbated by manning difficulties and the additional strain on its resources imposed by new commitments in the Indian Ocean. It therefore appears inevitable that before long the battle between the advocates of power projection and sea control forces will be renewed with even greater intensity.

Aircraft Carrier

CVN
Nimitz

Completed: 1975 onwards.
Names: CVN 68 *Nimitz;* CVN 69 *Dwight D. Eisenhower;*
CVN 70 *Carl Vinson;* CVN 71 *Theodore Roosevelt,*
CVN 72 *Abraham Lincoln,* CVN 73 *George Washington* (
Displacement: 81,600t standard; 91,400t full load.
Dimensions: 1,092 oa x 134 wl, 251 flight deck x 37ft
(332.8 x 40.8, 76.4 x 11.3m).
Propulsion: 4-shaft nuclear; 2 A4W reactors; 260,000shp = 30kts.
Armament: *AAW:* 3 BPDMS launchers Mk 25 (3x8).
Aircraft: 24 F-14A Tomcat; 24 A-7E Corsair; 10-A6E Intruder
+ 4 KA-6D; 4 E-2C Hawkeye; 4 EA-6B Prowler;
10 S-3A Viking; 6 SH-3H Sea King.
Sensors: *Surveillance:* SPS-48, SPS-43A, SPS-10.
Fire Control: 3 Mk 115.

The large aircraft carrier remains the "capital ship" of the US Navy. At present thirteen carriers, each serving at the centre of a Carrier Battle Group (CBG), are maintained in the active fleet, while a fourteenth ship—at present *Independence* (CV-623)—undergoes a major modernisation as part of the Service Life Extension Programme. All except the older Midway class carriers (to be replaced by two new CVNs) now operate squadrons of ASW aircraft in addition to their attack and fighter squadrons.

The Nimitz class was originally envisaged as a replacement for the three Midway-class carriers. The completion of the first nuclear-powered carrier, *Enterprise*, had been followed by the construction of two conventionally powered ships, *America* and *John F. Kennedy*. The latter had, however, only ever been thought of as "interim" designs to plug the gap between *Enterprise* and a second generation of nuclear carriers which would employ smaller numbers of more advanced reactors to provide the necessary power, and which would, it was hoped, cost less to build. The two A4W reactors which power the Nimitz class each produce approximately 130,000shp compared with only 35,000shp for each of the eight A2W reactors aboard *Enterprise*. Moreover, the uranium cores need replacing far less frequently than those originally used in *Enterprise*, giving a full 13-year period between refuellings.

The reduction in the number of reactors from eight to two allowed for major improvements in the internal arrangements below hangar-deck level. ▶

Below: A carrier of the Nimitz class underway. Note the massive "hurricane" bow and the overhang of the angled deck.

►Whereas in *Enterprise* the entire centre section of the ship is occupied by the machinery rooms, with the aviation fuel compartments and munitions machinery is divided into two separate units, with the magazines between machinery is dvided into two separate units, with the magazines between them and forward of them. The improved arrangement has resulted in an increase of 20 per cent in aviation fuel capacity and a similar increase in the volume available for munitions and stores.

Flight-deck layout is almost identical to that of *John F. Kennedy*. At hangar-deck level, however, there has been a significant increase in the provision of maintenance workshops and spare parts stowage. Maintenance shops have all but taken over the large sponson which supports the flight deck, and at the after end of the hangar there is a large bay for aero-engine maintenance and testing. The increased competition for internal volume even in a ship of this size is illustrated by the need to accommodate a total complement of almost 6,300 men, compared with only 4,900 for *Enterprise*—the original *Forrestal* design on which both ships are based provided for 3,800!

Sensor provision and defensive weapons are on a par with *John F. Kennedy*. The SPS-33/34 "billboard" radars fitted to *Enterprise* and the cruiser *Long Beach* proved to be a maintenance nightmare, and *Nimitz* has been provided with conventional rotating 3-D and air search models. The position of the SPS-48 and SPS-43 antennae is reversed in comparison with *John F. Kennedy*. *Nimitz* and *Eisenhower* are scheduled to be fitted with an

Right: *Eisenhower* (CVN-69), showing her vast expanse of flight deck. Two SH-3 Sea King helicopters can be seen on the port side, with a single A-7 Corsair to starboard.

Below: *Nimitz* (CVN-68) during underway replenishment operations. The lifts are in the lowered position to receive stores. Aircraft on deck include the F-4, A-6 and E-2C.

▶ ASW Control Centre and specialised maintenance facilities for the S-3 Viking anti-submarine aircraft; these features were incorporated into *Carl Vinson* while building. The fourth ship of the class may receive the fixed SPY-1 planar antennae associated with Aegis.

Three Mk 25 BPDMS launchers are fitted at present, but these will shortly be replaced by the Mk 29 launcher for NATO Sea Sparrow (IPDMS). The class is also scheduled to receive three Phalanx CIWS guns.

Problems were experienced from the outset in the construction of the ships. *Nimitz* was four years late in commissioning and took seven years to build (*Enterprise* took only four). Her construction was plagued by a shortage of skilled labour and frequent strikes at the Newport News Shipyard. When she was finally completed in 1973, vital components for the A4W reactors had still not been delivered, and a further two years were to elapse before commissioning. This delayed the start of *Eisenhower* by a further four years, and produced a knock-on effect which resulted

cketing costs. President Carter attempted, unsuccessfully, to block the
uthorisation of funds for the construction of a fourth carrier in favour of the
maller, less capable, but less costly CVV design. The CVV, however, was
ever popular with the Navy, and the Reagan administration has now
ommitted itself to the continuation of the CVN programme.

Both *Nimitz* and *Eisenhower* serve in the Atlantic, and besides the
ustomary deployment to the Mediterranean they have recently seen service
the Indian Ocean. *Vinson* and *Roosevelt* serve in the Pacific.

elow left: The Air Traffic Control Centre of *Eisenhower*.

**ottom: *Eisenhower* (CVN-69) in company with the replenishment
iler *Kalamazoo* (ACR-6) and the destroyer *Coontz* (DDG-40).**

elow: *Nimitz* (CVN-68) operating in the Mediterranean.

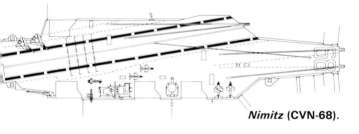

***Nimitz* (CVN-68).**

CVN
Enterprise

Completed: 1961
Name: CVN 65 *Enterprise*
Displacement: 75,700t standard; 89,600t full load.
Dimensions: 1,123 oa x 133 wl, 248 flight deck x 36ft (342.3 x 40.
75.7 x 10.9m).
Propulsion: 4-shaft nuclear; 8 A2W reactors; 280,000shp = 30kts
Armament: 3 NATO Sea Sparrow launchers Mk 29 (3x8); 3 Phalan
CIWS (3x6).
Aircraft: 24 F-14A Tomcat; 24A-7E Corsair; 10 A-6E Intruder + 4
KA-6D; 4 E-2C Hawkeye; 4 EA-6B Prowler; 10 S-3A
Viking; 6 SH-3H Sea King.
Sensors: *Surveillance:* SPS-48C, SPS-49, SPS-65.
Fire Control: 3 Mk 91.

Laid down shortly after the US Navy's first nuclear-powered surface ship
the cruiser *Long Beach, Enterprise* was completed in the remarkably sho
space of 3 years 9 months. The initial development work on her propulsio
plant had begun as early as 1950, and the design of the reactors ha
benefited from the evaluation of early models installed in submarines. Eve
so, the problem of producing the required 280,000shp on four shaf
employing first-generation reactors resulted in a solution that was costly i
terms of internal volume; two A2W reactors are coupled to each shaft an
the entire centre section of the ship is taken up by machinery.

Enterprise was also costly in terms of the initial purchase price—nearly double that of her conventionally-powered contemporaries of the Kitty Hawk class—but a number of strong arguments were advanced in favour of nuclear power. Reduced life-cycle costs due to infrequent refuellings made the nuclear-powered carrier a more economic proposition in the longer term, and the CVAN would be capable of undertaking lengthy transits and operations in high-threat areas at a high sustained speed. Moreover, the elimination of ship's fuel bunkers in *Enterprise* allowed a 50 per cent increase in aviation fuel capacity, and consequently in the number of consecutive days of strike operations she could sustain. ▶

Below left: Stern view of *Enterprise* (CVN-65). Note the overhang of the flight deck to port and to starboard.

Below: *Enterprise* in the late 1970s. She was the first US Navy carrier to operate the F-14 Tomcat, of which six can be seen on the after part of the flight deck.

▶ In size and general layout *Enterprise* is similar to *Kitty Hawk*. The most significant difference as completed was in the shape of the island, which comprised a "box" structure on which were mounted SPS-32/33 "billboard" radars, surmounted by a large cone for ECM and ESM antennae. The SPS-32/33 radars proved difficult to maintain, however, and when *Enterprise* was refitted in 1979-81, the entire island was removed and replaced by a more conventional structure similar to that of the *Nimitz*. As refitted, she now carries conventional rotating radars of the latest types.

Like the carriers of the Kitty Hawk class *Enterprise* was to have received two Mk 10 launchers for Terrier missiles. She was completed with the large sponsons aft, but Terrier was not installed initially in a bid to keep down costs. When Terrier lost favour as a carrier weapon in the mid-1960s, it was decided instead to fit two BPDMS Sea Sparrow launchers on the after sponsons. After her recent refit *Enterprise* now carries three Mk 29 launchers for NATO Sea Sparrow, and three Phalanx CIVVS guns.

Enterprise began her operational life in the Atlantic, but was transferred together with her nuclear-powered escort group to the Pacific during the Vietnam War and has remained there ever since. A second ship of the class was to have been authorised in the early 1960s but the project was deferred on grounds of cost (see *John F. Kennedy*).

Right: *Enterprise* (CVN-65) underway in the Pacific. In this view she is still operating the F-4 Phantom.

Below: *Enterprise* in company with *Ranger* (CV-61). In her recent refit the superstructure was completely rebuilt.

CV
Kitty Hawk

Completed:	1961-8.
Names:	CV63 *Kitty Hawk;* CV64 *Constellation;* CV 66 *America;* CV 67 *John F. Kennedy.*
Displacement:	60,100-61,000t standard; 80,800-82,000t full load.
Dimensions:	1,048-1,073 oa x 130 wl, 250-268 flight deck x 36ft. (319.3-326.9 x 39.6, 76.2-81.5 x 11m).
Propulsion:	4-shaft geared steam turbines; 280,000shp = 30kts.
Armament:	2 NATO Sea Sparrow launchers Mk29 (2x8); CV 64: 2 twin Mk 10 launchers (40 + 40) for Terrier missiles; CV 66-7: 3 BPDMS launchers Mk 25 (3x8), 3 Phalanx CIWS.
Aircraft:	24 F-14A Tomcat; 24 A-7E Corsair; 10 A-6E Intruder + 4 KA-6D; 4 E-2C Hawkeye; 4 EA-6B Prowler; 10 S-3A Viking; 6 SH-3H Sea King.
Sensors:	*Surveillance:* SPS-48C, SPS-49 (SPS-37A in CV 63), SPS-10, SPS-65 (CV 67 only). *Fire Control:* 4 SPG-55A (CV 64), 2 Mk 91 (CV 63), 3 Mk 115 (CV 66-7). *Sonars:* SQS-23 (CV 66 only).

Although there are significant differences between the first pair completed and the last two vessels—*John F. Kennedy* is officially considered as a separate single-ship class—these four carriers are generally grouped together because of their common propulsion system and flight-deck layout.

Kitty Hawk and *Constellation* were ordered as improved Forrestals, incorporating a number of important modifications. The flight deck showed a slight increase in area, and the arrangement of the lifts was revised to improve aircraft-handling arrangements. The single port-side lift, which on the Forrestals was located at the forward end of the flight deck—and was therefore unusable during landing operations—was repositioned at the after end of the overhang, outside the line of the angled deck. The respective positions of the centre lift on the starboard side and the island structure were reversed, so that two lifts were available to serve the forward catapults. A further improved feature of the lifts was that they were no longer strictly rectangular, but had an additional angled section at their forward end which enabled longer aircraft to be accommodated. The new arrangement proved so successful that it was adopted by all subsequent US carriers. ▶

Below left: USS *Kitty Hawk* (CV-63), with over 30 aircraft on deck. The SPS-48 3-D radar is visible aft of the island.

Below: *Kitty Hawk* (CV-63) underway in the Pacific. Four E-2C Hawkeye AEW aircraft are parked on the flight deck.

► *Kitty Hawk* and *Constellation* were designed at a time when long-range surface-to-air missiles were just entering service with the US Navy. In place of the eight 5-inch (127mm) guns of the Forrestal class these ships therefore received two Mk 10 launchers for Terrier missiles positioned on sponsons aft just below the level of the flight deck, with their 40-missile magazines behind them. The SPG-55 guidance radars were fitted close to the launchers and on the island, which became far more cluttered than that of the *Forrestal* because of the need to accommodate a much larger outfit of air search and height-finding radars. To help solve this problem a separate tall lattice mast was placed immediately aft of the island. This has carried a

succession of large 3-D radars, beginning with the SPS-8B, subsequently replaced by the SPS-30, and eventually by the planar SPS-48.

America, the third ship of the class, was completed after a gap of four years and therefore incorporated a number of further modifications. She has a narrower smokestack and is fitted with an SQS-23 sonar—the only US carrier so equipped.   ▶

Below: *Constellation* (CV-64) during underway replenishment operations with an oiler of the Mispillion class and a missile destroyer of the Charles F. Adams class.

▶ In 1963 it was decided that the new carrier due to be laid down in FY 1964 would be nuclear-powered, but Congress baulked at the cost, and the ship was finally laid down as a conventionally powered carrier of a modified Kitty Hawk design. *John F. Kennedy* can be distinguished externally from her near-sisters by her canted stack—designed to keep the corrosive exhaust gases clear of the flight deck—and by the shape of the forward end of the angled deck.

Of even greater significance was the abandonment of the expensive long-range Terrier system, which took up valuable space and merely duplicated similar area defence systems on the carrier escorts, in favour of the Basic Point Defence Missile System (BPDMS), for which three octuple launchers were fitted. The SPS-48 radar, carried on a rather slimmer mast aft of the island, was fitted from the outset. Provision was made, as in *America*, for an SQS-23 sonar, but this was never installed.

John F. Kennedy marks the high point of US carrier construction, and it is significant that the later CVNs of the Nimitz class are almost identical in flight-deck layout, armament, and sensor outfit. The earlier three ships of the Kitty Hawk class are now being refitted to the same standard. In particular the Terrier launchers, together with the fire control radars, are being removed and replaced by Mk 29 launchers for NATO Sea Sparrow. It is envisaged that all four ships will eventually carry three Mk 29 launchers and three Phalanx CIWS guns. All vessels in the class are now fitted with the SPS-48 3-D radar, and the SPS-37A air search radar is being replaced by the much more compact SPS-49.

Kitty Hawk and *Constellation* have served since completion in the Pacific. *America* and *John F. Kennedy* serve in the Atlantic, with frequent deployments to the Mediterranean.

Above: An aerial view of *America* (CV-66) testing the washdown system which would protect her from nuclear fall-out.

Below: *John F. Kennedy* (CVN-67). Note the distinctive canted smoke-stack. Aircraft include F-14, A-7 and A-6.

Forrestal

Completed: 1952-5.

Names: CV 59 *Forrestal;* CV 60 *Saratoga;* CV 61 *Ranger;*
CV 62 *Independence.*

Displacement: 60,000t standard; 78,000t full load.

Dimensions: 1,039-1,047 oa x 130wl, 238 flight deck x 37ft
(316.7-319 x 38.5, 72.5 x 11.3m).

Propulsion: 4-shaft geared steam turbines; 260-280,000shp = 33kts

Armament: CV 59-60: 2 BPDMS launchers Mk 25 (2x8);
CV 61-62: 2 NATO Sea Sparrow launchers Mk 29 (2x8

Aircraft: 24 F-4J Phantom; 24 A-7E Corsair; 10 A-6E Intruder
+ 4 KA-6D; 4 E-2C Hawkeye; 4 EA-6B Prowler;
10 S-3A Viking; 6 SH-3H Sea King.

Sensors: *Surveillance:* SPS-48, SPS-43A, SPS-10, SPS-58
(not in CV 61).
Fire Control: 2 Mk 115 (CV 59-60), 2 Mk 91 (CV 61-62

Authorisation of the Forrestal class was a direct consequence of the Korea
War, which re-established the value of the carrier for projecting air powe
against land targets. The new class was to operate the A-3 Skywarric
strategic bomber, which weighed fully 78,000lb (35,455kg) and dimension
and hangar height were increased accordingly. The original design was for
carrier similar in configuration to the ill-fated *United States,* which had
flush deck, together with a retractable bridge, and two waist catapult
angled out on sponsons in addition to the standard pair of catapults forward

Above: *Saratoga* (CV-60) underway. In 1980-83 she underwent
a major refit as part of the Service Life Extension Programme.

Below: *Forrestal* (CV-59) underway in the Mediterranean. Unlike
more recent carriers she continues to operate the F-4 Phantom.

▶   The advent of the angled deck, which was tested by the US Navy in 1952 on the Essex-class carrier *Antietam,* led to the modification of *Forrestal* while building to incorporate this new development. The result was the distinctive configuration which has been adopted by all subsequent US carrier construction: a massive flight deck with considerable overhang supported by sponsons to the sides, with a small island incorporating the smokestack to starboard. The Forrestals were the first US carriers to have the flight deck as the strength deck – in previous ships it was the hangar deck – and in consequence side lifts were adopted in preference to centreline lifts and

ncorporated in the overhang. This resulted in a large uninterrupted hangar n which more than half the ship's aircraft could be struck down. The layout of the four side lifts proved less than satisfactory, however; in particular the port-side lift, which is at the forward end of the angled deck, cannot be used during landing operations, and the Kitty Hawk class which followed had a modified arrangement.

All four ships of the class were completed with eight 5-inch (127mm) single mountings on sponsons fore and aft. The forward sponsons created problems in heavy seas, however, and the three ships based in the Atlantic had both guns and sponsons removed in the early 1960s (*Ranger* lost her forward guns but retained the sponsons). During the 1970s all guns were replaced by BPDMS Mk 25 or IPDMS Mk 29 launchers. Eventually all four ships will have three Mk 29 launchers and three Phalanx CIWS guns.

The electronics suite has undergone considerable change and expansion since the 1950s. Large SPS-43A long-range air search aerials have been fitted on outriggers to the starboard side of the island, and the distinctive SPS-30 3-D radar was carried above the bridge from the early 1960s until replaced in the late 1970s by the SPS-48. *Saratoga* was taken in hand in October 1980 for a 3-year major modernisation (SLEP) which included replacement of the SPS-43 by the new SPS-49.

Unlike later carriers, the Forrestal class do not operate the F-14 Tomcat, but retain the F-4 Phantom. It is envisaged that the latter will eventually be replaced by the F-18 Hornet.

Left: ***Independence*** **(CV-62) operating in the Mediterranean. A BPDMS launcher can be seen below the level of the flight deck.**

Below: A recent view of ***Forrestal*** **(CV-59). She now has the SPS-48 planar radar above the bridge in place of the SPS-30.**

CV

Midway

Completed:	1945-7.
Names:	CV 41 *Midway*; CV 43 *Coral Sea*.
Displacement:	51-52,000t standard; 64,000t full load.
Dimensions:	979 oa x 121 wl, 259/236 flight deck x 36ft (298.4 x 36.9, 78.8/71.9 x 11m).
Propulsion:	4-shaft geared steam turbines; 212,000shp = 32kts.
Armament:	2 BPDMS launchers Mk 25 (2x8–CV 41 only); 3 Phalanx CIWS.
Aircraft:	24 F-4J Phantom; 24 A-7E Corsair; 10 A-6E Intruder + 4 KA-6D; 4 E-2C Hawkeye; 4 EA-6B Prowler.
Sensors:	*Surveillance:* (CV 41) SPS-48A, SPS-37A, SPS-10; (CV 43) SPS-30, SPS-43A, SPS-10. *Fire Control:* 2 Mk 115.

These ships were the last war-built US carriers. Three units were completed but *Franklin D. Roosevelt* was stricken in 1977. As built, the Midway class had an axial flight deck with two centre-line lifts and a side lift amidships on the port side. They were armed with a heavy battery of 14-18 5-inch (127mm) guns and numerous smaller AA weapons. The original design was quickly overtaken by developments in jet aircraft, and the class underwent a major modernisation during the 1950s in which an 8-degree angled deck was built, incorporating the side lift at its forward end; the after lift, which would have obstructed landing operations, was removed and replaced by a second side lift to starboard aft of the island. The armament was significantly reduced and the latest 3-D and air search radars fitted. C-11 steam catapults were installed to enable the ships to operate the new generation of various types of jet aircraft.

Right: *Midway* (CV-41) operating in the Western Pacific. She is the only US carrier home-ported outside the United States.

Below: Aerial view of *Coral Sea* (CV-43). Aircraft on deck include F-4s, A-7s, A-6s and the E-2C Hawkeye AEW aircraft.

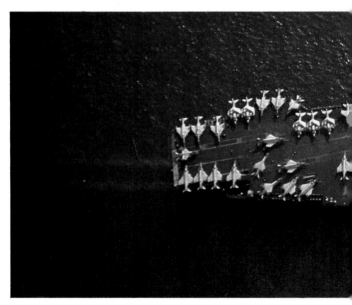

197

▶ *Coral Sea*, which was the last of the three to the modernised, incorporated a number of further modifications as a result of experience with her two sisters and with the Forrestal class. The position of the port-side lift was found to be unsatisfactory, and it was moved aft to clear the angled deck altogether. This enabled the angled deck itself to be extended forward with consequent increase in deck space, and a third C-11 catapult was installed. The position of the forward centre-line lift was found to be equally unsatisfactory, as it was situated between the forward catapults and was therefore unusable during take-off operations. It was therefore removed and replaced by a third side lift forward of the island. New sponsons were built for the six remaining guns, which were now just below flight-deck level.

The conversion of *Coral Sea* was particularly successful, and she remained largely unaltered – except for the removal of the remaining guns – throughout the following two decades. Since 1978 she has been the thirteenth carrier in a 12-carrier force and has only recently been reactivated to replace *Saratoga* while the latter undergoes her SLEP.

In 1966 *Midway* was taken in hand for a major modernisation which would enable her to operate the same aircraft as the more modern US carriers. The flight deck was completely rebuilt – its total area was increased by approximately one-third – and the lifts rearranged on the pattern established by *Coral Sea*. (The new lifts are much larger, however, and have a capacity of 130,000lb (59,100kg) compared with 74,000lb (33,636kg) for those of her sister-ship). Two C-13 catapults were installed forward, enabling *Midway* to handle the latest aircraft. The armament was reduced to three 5-inch (127mm) guns (these were replaced in 1979 by two BPDMS launchers). NTDS was installed during the modernisation and the island has recently been extended to incorporate the latest sensors. Three Phalanx CIWS guns are to be fitted in the near future.

Midway, which is based in Japan, is due to remain in service until 1988, when she will replace *Coral Sea* as a training ship. Her principal limitations compared with later carriers are those inherent in the initial design; a hangar height of only 5.3m (17ft 6in) – the E-2 Hawkeye AEW aircraft needs 5.6m (18ft 4in) clearance – and a limited aviation fuel capacity – 365,000 gallons compared with 750,000 gallons in the Forrestal design. In spite of their CV designation neither *Midway* nor *Coral Sea* operate fixed- or rotary-wing ASW aircraft, and both continue to operate the F-4 Phantom in place of the F-14 Tomcat.

Below: A Soviet AGI shadows *Coral Sea* (CV-43) in the Gulf of Tonkin during the Vietnam War. An A-3 Skywarrior is refuelling.

Bottom: *Midway* (CV-41) now has a new lattice mast aft of the funnel. It is intended to fit the planar SPS-48 3-D radar.

Cruisers

CG

Ticonderoga

Completed: 1983 onwards.
Names: CG 47 *Ticonderoga;* CG 48 *Yorktown;* CG 49. . . .;
   CG 50. . . .; CG 51. . . .; CG 52. . . .
Displacement: 9,100t full load.
Dimensions: 563 oa x 55 x 31ft (171.7 x 17 x 17.6 x 9.4m).
Propulsion: 2-shaft COGAG; 4 LM2500 gas turbines;
   80,000bhp = 30kts.
Armament: *AAW:* 2 twin Mk 26 launchers (44 + 44) for Standard MR
   SM-2 missiles; 2 5-inch (127mm) Mk 45 (2x1);
   2 Phalanx CIWS.
   ASW: ASROC missiles from Mk 26 launcher;
   2 LAMPS helicopters; 6 12.75-inch (324mm) torpedo
   tubes Mk 32 (2x3).
   SSM: 8 Harpoon missiles (2x4).
Sensors: *Surveillance:* 4 SPY-1A, SPS-49, SPS-55.
   Fire Control: 4 Mk 99, SPQ-9A.
   Sonars: SQS-53A, SQR-19 TACTAS.

Most of the cruisers in the US Fleet were completed during the 1960s. Their missiles and electronics have received constant updates to enable them to keep abreast of the threat to the carrier battle groups posed by long-range Soviet bombers. Conventional air defence systems are now considered inadequate to meet this threat and a large programme of new cruisers armed with the revolutionary AEGIS system is now underway. Five are in service and 11 more on order.

The new missile cruiser *Ticonderoga* will be the first operational vessel to be fitted with the AEGIS Combat System. It was originally envisaged that this system would be installed in nuclear-powered escorts such as the Strike Cruiser (CSGN) and the CGN 42 variant of the Virginia class, but the enormous cost of AEGIS combined with that of nuclear propulsion proved to be prohibitive under the restrictive budgets of the late 1970s. Moreover, two AEGIS escorts were required for each of the twelve carrier battle groups, and as not all of the carriers concerned were nuclear-powered, it was decided to utilise the growth potential of the fossil-fuelled Spruance design to incorporate the necessary electronics.

The AEGIS Combat System was developed to counter the saturation missile attacks which could be expected to form the basis of Soviet anti-carrier tactics during the 1980s. Conventional rotating radars are limited both in data rate and in number of target tracks they can handle, whereas saturation missile attacks require sensors which can react immediately and have a virtually unlimited tracking capacity. The solution adopted in the AEGIS system is to mount four fixed planar antennae each covering a sector of 45 degrees on the superstructures of the ship. Each SPY-1 array has ▶

Below: *Ticonderoga* (CG-47), the first of the new AEGIS cruisers, is docked after her launch at the Ingalls Yard.

▶ more than 4000 radiating elements that shape and direct multiple beams. Targets satisfying predetermined criteria are evaluated, arranged in sequence of threat and engaged, either automatically or with manual override, by a variety of defensive systems.

At longer ranges air targets will be engaged by the SM-2 missile, fired from one of two Mk 26 launchers. The SM-2 differs from previous missiles in requiring target illumination only in the terminal phase of flight. In the initial and mid-flight phase the missile flies under auto-pilot towards a predicted interception point with initial guidance data and limited mid-course guidance supplied by the AEGIS system. This means that no less than 18 missiles can be kept in the air in addition to the four in the terminal phase, and the Mk 99 illuminators switch rapidly from one target to the next under computer control. At closer ranges back-up is provided by the two 5-inch guns, while "last-ditch" self-defence is provided by two Phalanx CIWS guns, assisted by ECM jammers and chaff dispensers.

Ticonderoga and her sisters are designed to serve as flagships, and will be equipped with an elaborate Combat Information Centre (CIC) possessing an integral flag function able to accept and coordinate data from other ships and aircraft. Eighteen units are currently projected, and it is envisaged that they will operate in conjunction with specialised ASW destroyers of the Spruance class and a new type of AAW destroyer (Arleigh Burke class).

Above right: Port bow view of *Ticonderoga* (CG-47) prior to launching. The basic design is that of the Spruance-class DD.

Below: Starboard quarter view of *Ticonderoga* (CG-47) prior to launch. One of the large CP propellers is visible.

Ticonderoga (CG-47).

Virginia

Completed: 1976-80.
Names: CGN 38 *Virginia;* CGN 39 *Texas;* CGN 40 *Mississippi;*
CGN 41 *Arkansas.*
Displacement: 11,000t full load.
Dimensions: 585 oa x 63 x 30ft (178 x 19 x 9m).
Propulsion: 2-shaft nuclear; 2 D2G reactors; 60,000shp = 30kts.
Armament: *AAW:* 2 twin Mk 26 launchers (44 + 24) for Standard MR
missiles; 2 5-inch (127mm) Mk 45 (2x1).
ASW: 1 LAMPS helicopter (see notes); ASROC missiles
from fwd Mk 26 launcher; 6 12.75-inch (324mm)
torpedo tubes Mk 32 (2x3).
SSM: 8 Harpoon missiles (2x4) being fitted.
Sensors: *Surveillance:* SPS-48C, SPS-40B, SPS-55.
Fire Control: 2 SPG-51D, SPG-60, SPQ-9A.
Sonars: SQS-53A.

Following closely upon the two CGNs of the California class, the *Virginia*
incorporated a number of significant modifications. While the basic layout of
the class is identical to that of their predecessors, the single-arm Mk 13
launchers of the *California* were superseded by the new Mk 26 twin

ASROC launcher forward, and a helicopter hangar was built into the stern.

The magazine layout and missile-handling arrangements of the Mk 26 constitute a break with previous US Navy practice. In earlier missile cruisers and destroyers booster-assisted missiles such as Terrier were stowed in horizontal magazine rings, and the shorter Tartar missiles in cylindrical magazines comprising two concentric rings of vertically stowed missiles. The magazine associated with the Mk 26 launcher, however, has a continuous belt feed system with vertical stowage capable of accommodating a variety of missiles. This means that ship's length is the only limiting factor on the size of the magazine, which is capable of being "stretched" or "contracted" to suit the dimensions of the vessel in which it is to be installed. It has also eliminated the requirement for a separate launcher for ASROC. In the Virginia class ASROC rounds are carried in the forward magazine alongside Standard MR surface-to-air missiles. The elimination of the ASROC launcher and its associated reloading deckhouse has saved 5m (16.4ft) in length compared with *California*.

The installation of an internal helicopter hangar in a ship other than an aircraft carrier is unique in the postwar US Navy. The hangar itself is 42ft by 14ft (12.8 x 4.3m) and is served by a stern elevator covered by a folding hatch. Although it is envisaged that SH-2F helicopters will eventually be ▶

Below: *Virginia* (CGN-38) underway. The class was designed to escort the nuclear-powered carriers of the Nimitz class.

Above: Stern view of *Mississippi* (CGN-40). The twin-arm Mk 26 launchers distinguish her from the earlier California class.

assigned, the ships do not at present have helicopters embarked.

The electronics outfit is on a par with *California*, with two important differences. The first is the replacement of the SQS-26 sonar by the more advanced solid-state SQS-53, and the older Mk 114 ASW FC system by the digital Mk 116. The second is the retention of only the after pair of SPG 51 tracker/illuminators, reducing the number of available channels (including the SPG-60) from five to three. This modification looks forward to the conversion of the ships to fire the SM-2 missile, which requires target illumination only in the terminal phase. The ships are also scheduled to receive Harpoon, Tomahawk, and two Phalanx CIWS guns at future refits.

The original requirement was for eleven ships of this class, which would then combine with earlier CGNs to provide each of the CVANs projected at that time with four nuclear-powered escorts. After only four units of the class had been laid down, however, further orders were suspended while consideration was given first to the Strike Cruiser (CSGN) and then to a modified CGN 38 design with AEGIS. Both these projects were abandoned in favour of the conventionally powered CG-47 now under construction, but the CGN42 AEGIS proposal was recently revived and dropped again.

All ships of the class serve as CGN escorts; two in the Atlantic Fleet and two in the Pacific Fleet.

Texas (CGN-39).

Below: *Virginia* (CGN-38) underway in the Indian Ocean. Nuclear power makes these ships well-suited to long-range operations.

California

Completed:	1974-5.
Names:	CGN 36 *California*; CGN 37 *South Carolina*.
Displacement:	10,150t full load.
Dimensions:	596 oa x 61 x 32ft (182 x 18.6 x 9.6m).
Propulsion:	2-shaft nuclear; 2 D2G reactors; 60,000shp = 30kts.
Armament:	*AAW:* 2 single Mk 13 launchers (40 + 40) Standard MR missiles, 2 5-inch (127mm) Mk 45 (2x1). 2 Phalanx 20mm CIWS.
	ASW: ASROC launcher Mk 16 (1x8, reloads); 4 12.75-inch (324mm) torpedo tubes (4x1, fixed).
	SSM: 8 Harpoon missiles (2x4).
Sensors:	*Surveillance:* SPS-48C, SPS-40B, SPS-10.
	Fire Control: 4 SPG-51D, SPG-60, SPQ-9A.
	Sonars: SQS-26CX.

California and her sister *South Carolina* were built in response to the need for a new class of nuclear escorts to accompany the CVNs of the *Nimitz* class. A third ship was approved in FY 1968, but this was later cancelled.

Compared with previous CGNs, *California* is a much larger, more sophisticated vessel. The design reverted to the "double-ended" layout of *Bainbridge*, but single Mk 13 Tartar launchers were adopted in preference to the Mk 10. This was in some ways a retrograde step in that it limited the ship to the medium-range (MR) version of the Standard missile, whereas earlier

CGs and CGNs could be retro-fitted with the extended-range (ER) version. It also necessitated the provision of a separate ASROC launcher, forward of which there is a magazine surmounted by a prominent deckhouse into which the missiles are hoisted before reloading.

California was the first ship to be fitted with the new lightweight 5-inch (127mm) gun, and the first to have the digital Mk 86 FC system installed. The anti-surface element of the latter—the SPQ-9 antenna—is housed within a radome on the after side of the mainmast, while the SPG-60 antenna, which besides tracking air targets can serve as a fifth illuminating channel for the missiles, is located directly above the bridge.

One ship serves in the Atlantic, the other in the Pacific. Both have recently been fitted with Harpoon and Phalanx CIWS, and will be fitted with Tomahawk.

California (CGN-36).

Below: *California* (CGN-36) underway off Puerto Rico. Note the single Mk 13 launchers which distinguish her from later CGNs. *California* was the first US ship to receive the 5-inch Mk 45 together with the digital Mk 86 fire control system.

Truxtun

Completed: 1967.
Name: CGN 35 *Truxtun*.
Displacement: 8,200t standard; 9,200t full load.
Dimensions: 564 oa x 58 x 31ft (172 x 17.7 x 9.4m).
Propulsion: 2-shaft nuclear; 2 D2G reactors; 60,000shp = 30kts.
Armament: *AAW:* twin Mk 10 launcher (60) for Standard ER missiles;
1 5-inch (127mm) Mk 42.
ASW: ASROC missiles from Mk 10 launcher;
1 SH-2F helicopter; 4 12.75-inch (324mm) torpedo tubes
Mk 32 (4x1, fixed).
SSM: 8 Harpoon missiles (2x4).
Sensors: *Surveillance:* SPS-48, SPS-40, SPS-10.
Fire Control: 2 SPG-55B, 1 SPG-53F.
Sonars: SQS-26.

Originally requested as one of seven Belknap-class frigates in the FY 1962 programme, *Truxtun* was given nuclear propulsion at the insistence of Congress. She emerged from the drawing board with tall, distinctive lattice masts in place of the twin macks of the oil-burning ships.

While she carried an identical weapons outfit to her near-sisters, major modifications were made to the layout. The positions of the Mk 10 launcher and the 5-inch (127mm) Mk 42 and their respective fire-control radars were reversed, and the ASROC/Terrier magazine rings were therefore located beneath the flight deck and not forward of the bridge. In place of the triple Mk 32 torpedo tubes of the Belknaps *Truxtun* has two fixed tubes located in the superstructure on either side amidships. The helicopter hangar, which is

40ft by 17ft (12.3 x 5m), is shorter and wider than that of the Belknaps.

Truxtun originally had twin 3-inch (76mm) mountings amidships, but these were replaced in the late 1970s by quadruple launchers for Harpoon. The two Mk 25 stern tubes have also been removed. Two Phalanx CIWS guns will be fitted in the near future.

Truxtun has served since completion in the Pacific Fleet, where she has combined with *Long Beach* and *Bainbridge* to form the nuclear-powered escort squadron which accompanies the carrier *Enterprise*.

Below: ***Truxtun* (CGN-35) underway in the Pacific. Note the distinctive lattice masts which carry the surveillance radars.**

Bottom: Port-side view of *Truxtun*. Her armament is similar to that of the Belknap class but the layout is reversed.

CG
Belknap

Completed: 1964-7.
Names: CG 26 *Belknap;* CG 27 *Josephus Daniels;*
CG 28 *Wainwright;* CG 29 *Jouett;* CG 30 *Horne;*
CG 31 *Sterett;* CG 32 *William H. Standley;* CG 33 *Fox;*
CG 34 *Biddle.*
Displacement: 6,570t standard; 7,930t full load.
Dimensions: 547 oa x 55 x 29ft (166.7 x 16.7 x 8.7m).
Propulsion: 2-shaft geared steam turbines; 85,000shp = 33kts.
Armament: *AAW:* twin Mk 10 launcher (60) for Standard ER missiles;
1 5-inch (127mm) Mk 42; 2 Phalanx CIWS being fitted.
ASW: ASROC missiles from Mk 10 launcher;
1 SH-2F helicopter; 6 12.75-inch (324mm) torpedo
tubes Mk 32 (2x3).
SSM: 8 Harpoon missiles (2x4).
Sensors: *Surveillance:* SPS-48, SPS-40 (CG 29, 31-34) *or*
SPS-43 (CG 27-28, 30) *or* SPS-49 (CG 26), SPS-10F.
Fire Control: 2 SPG-55B, 1 SPG-53.
Sonars: SQS-26BX (except CG 26, SQS-53C)

he nine ships of the Belknap class, together with their nuclear-powered alf-sister *Truxtun*, constitute the final group of AAW "frigates" completed or the US Navy during the 1960s. Outwardly they resemble their redecessors of the Leahy class, with which they share a common hull-form nd superstructure layout. A closer look, however, reveals a shift in mphasis in favour of significantly increased anti-submarine capabilities.

In the Belknaps the "double-ended" missile launcher arrangement was bandoned and the 5-inch gun reinstated—a reflection, in part, of concern bout the diminishing number of vessels capable of fire support operations. he Mk 10 Terrier launcher was given a third 20-round magazine ring ocated below and between the other two. The extra capacity was used, owever, not to compensate for the reduction in Terrier rounds compared vith the *Leahy*, but in order to dispense with a separate ASROC launcher. he upper two rings carry alternate Terrier/Standard and ASROC rounds, vhile the third, which carries only SAM rounds, serves as a feed for the two pper rings.

The additional deck space gained as a result of these modifications was tilised to provide a helicopter platform and hangar immediately aft of the ▶

Below: *William H. Standley* (CG-32) in the Mediterranean. The Mk 10 launcher fires both Standard ER and ASROC missiles.

▶ second mack. It was envisaged that the Belknaps would operate the ill-fated drone anti-submarine helicopter (DASH) but the programme was abandoned before any drones were embarked. Instead, the Belknaps became the trial class for the LAMPS helicopter programme in the early 1970s, and introduced manned ASW helicopters to the US Navy with conspicuous success.

***Wainwright* (CG-28).**

Below: Aerial view of *Jouett* (CG-29) off Hawaii. The Belknap class is the standard conventional AAW escort in the US Navy

Below right: Stern view of a Belknap. Note the 5-inch gun.

The Belknaps carried an altogether more advanced electronics outfit to the Leahy class. In particular the SQS-23 sonar was replaced by the much more powerful SQS-26, while the new planar SPS-48 3-D radar replaced the older SPS-39. Target and fire control data were coordinated by the US Navy's first computer-based Naval Tactical Data System (NTDS). Moreover, these systems have been constantly updated in order to keep abreast of the aerial threat. In 1977 *Wainwright* was modified to conduct evaluation of the SM-2 missile, following which it is now carried by all ships of the class. *Belknap*, which had her entire upper works destroyed by fire following a collision with the carrier *John F. Kennedy* in 1975, has been rebuilt with a completely updated sensor outfit, including an SPS-49 air search radar, an SQS-53A sonar, and SLQ-32(V)3 ECM antennae. All ships have now been fitted with quadruple Harpoon launchers in place of the former 3-inch (76mm) AA guns amidships, and each will receive two Phalanx CIWS guns in the near future.

Four units of the Belknap class currently serve in the Atlantic, and five in the Pacific. They are employed as AAW escorts for the conventionally powered carriers.

CGN
Bainbridge

Completed: 1962.
Names: CGN 25 *Bainbridge.*
Displacement: 7,700t standard; 8,580t full load.
Dimensions: 565 oa x 58 x 29ft (172.5 x 17.7 x 7.9m).
Propulsion: 2-shaft nuclear; 2 D2G reactors; 60,000shp = 30kts.
Armament: *AAW:* 2 twin Mk 10 launchers (40 + 40) for Standard ER missiles; 2 20mm (2x1).
ASW: ASROC launcher Mk 16 (1x8);
6 12.75-inch (324mm) torpedo tubes Mk 32 (2x3).
SSM: 8 Harpoon missiles (2x4).
Sensors: *Surveillance:* SPS-48, SPS-37, SPS-10D.
Fire Control: 4 SPG-55B.
Sonars: SQS-23.

Like the later *Truxtun, Bainbridge* is an offshoot of a larger class of conventionally powered AAW "frigates". She is a near-sister of the Leahy class, with which she initially shared an identical outfit of weapons and electronics. As completed, she presented a more streamlined profile than the *Leahy* because her nuclear propulsion enabled her to dispense with the tall macks of the latter.

The layout of *Bainbridge's* weapons is identical to that of the *Leahy,* with twin Mk 10 Terrier launchers fore and aft and an ASROC box launcher forward of the bridge. From 1974 onwards the ship underwent an extensive refit aimed at upgrading her electronics. The refit included not only the installation of new surveillance radars and NTDS but also the complete remodelling of her superstructure, which now comprises two distinct blocks with much greater internal volume. The forward block is surmounted by a broad lattice mast and the after block by a heavy pole mainmast. The former 3-inch (76mm) AA guns have been replaced by quadruple Harpoon launchers, and two Phalanx CIWS guns will be fitted abreast the after SPG-55 tracker/illuminators in the near future.

Bainbridge has served since completion in the Pacific, where she has combined with *Truxtun* and *Long Beach* to form the nuclear-powered escort squadron which accompanies the carrier *Enterprise.*

Above: *Bainbridge* (CGN-25) was the US Navy's first nuclear-powered AAW escort. She has recently undergone modernisation.

Below: *Bainbridge* underway in the Pacific. Note the "double-ended" missile launcher layout and the absence of major guns.

CG
Leahy

Completed: 1962-4.
Names: CG 16 *Leahy;* CG 17 *Harry E, Yarnell;* CG 18 *Worden;*
CG 19 *Dale;* CG 20 *Richmond K. Turner;* CG 21 *Gridley;*
CG 22 *England;* CG 23 *Halsey;* CG 24 *Reeves.*
Displacement: 5,670t standard; 7,800t full load.
Dimensions: 553 oa x 55 x 25ft (162.5 x 16.8 x 7.6m).
Propulsion: 2-shaft geared steam turbines; 85,000shp = 32kts.
Armament: *AAW:* 2 twin Mk 10 launchers (40 + 40) for Standard
ER missiles.
2 Phalanx CIWS.
ASW: ASROC launcher Mk 16 (1x8); 6 12.75-inch
(324mm) torpedo tubes Mk 32 (2x3).
SSM: 8 Harpoon missiles (2x4) fitted in place
3-inch (76mm) guns.
Sensors: *Surveillance:* SPS-48, SPS-43 (SPS-49 in CG 19), SPS-10.
Fire Control: 4 SPG-55B.
Sonars: SQS-23.

The nine ships of the Leahy class, together with their nuclear-powered half
sister *Bainbridge,* constitute the second group of AAW "frigates" completed
for the US Navy during the 1960s. They were designed at a time when it was
thought that guns would disappear altogether from the inventory of naval
weapons. They were therefore the first US Navy ships to have an all-missile
main armament. They also introduced the "mack" (combined mast and
stack) to US Navy construction as a means of conserving valuable centre
line deck space.

**Right: Stern view of *Leahy* (CG-16) in the Pacific. The class
underwent a major AAW modernisation in the early 1970s.**

**Below: The cruiser *Halsey* (CG-23). The "double-ended" missile
launcher layout distinguishes her from the later Belknap class.**

▶ A "double-ended" layout was adopted with twin Mk 10 Terrier launchers fore and aft. There are 20-round magazine rings in line with each launcher arm, and the missiles are lifted from the top of the ring and run up at an angle of 15 degrees through a wedge-shaped deckhouse onto the launcher. Target tracking and illumination are provided by paired SPG-55B FC radars mounted atop the fore and after superstructures.

As in the earlier Coontz class, there is an 8-round ASROC launcher forward of the bridge, but no reloads are carried.

From 1967 until 1972 the Leahy class underwent an extensive modernisation programme aimed at bringing their electronics up to the same standard as the Belknaps. A large planar SPS-48 3-D radar replaced the original SPS-39, and NTDS was installed. *Dale* has now received the new SPS-49 air search radar in place of her SPS-43, and this modification will eventually be extended to all ships of this class and the Belknap class.

All ships have had their 3-inch (76mm) AA guns removed and have received eight Harpoon in their place. They have also received two Phalanx CIWS guns.

Only three units of this class are based in the Atlantic, the remaining six being allocated to the Pacific Fleet. These dispositions are almost certainly related to their much greater cruising range as compared with the preceding Coontz class, and also to their limited ASW capabilities. Two of these AAW ships would normally be allocated to each non-nuclear carrier battle group.

Dale **(CG-19).**

Above: *Leahy* (CG-16) underway in the Pacific. The large planar antenna atop the foremast is an SPS-48 3-D radar.

Below: *Halsey* (CG-23) in the Pacific. Only three ships of the class serve with the Atlantic Fleet.

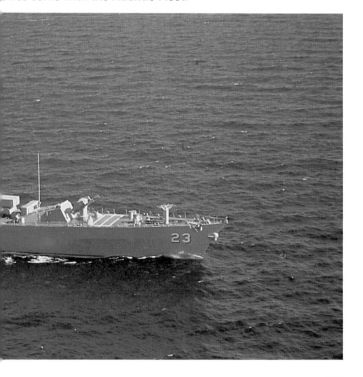

CGN
Long Beach

Completed: 1961.
Name: CGN 9 *Long Beach.*
Displacement: 14,200t standard; 17,350t full load.
Dimensions: 721 oa x 73 x 29ft (219.8 x 22.3 x 8.8m).
Propulsion: 2-shaft nuclear; 2 C1W reactors; 80,000shp = 30kts.
Armament: *AAW:* 2 twin Mk 10 launchers (40 + 80) for Standard
ER missiles; 2 5-inch (127mm) Mk 30 (2x1).
ASW: ASROC launcher Mk 16 (1x8); 6 12.75-inch
(324mm) torpedo tubes Mk 32 (2x3).
SSM: 8 Harpoon missiles (2x4).
Sensors: *Surveillance:* SPS-48C, SPS-49, SPS-65.
Fire Control: 4 SPG-55A.
Sonars: SQQ-23.

Long Beach was the US Navy's first all-missile warship, and the first surface
ship with nuclear power. She was designed as an escort for the carrier
Enterprise, and has performed this role throughout the past two decades.

As completed she had two Mk 10 Terrier launchers forward and a Mk 12
launcher aft for the long-range Talos. The depth of the hull enabled an extra
pair of magazine rings to be worked in beneath the second Mk 10 launcher,
giving *Long Beach* a total capacity of no less than 166 surface-to-air missiles.
There was an ASROC box launcher amidships, and shortly after the ship
entered service two 5-inch (127mm) guns of an older pattern were fitted to
provide defence against small surface craft.

Electronics were on a par with *Enterprise* herself, with large fixed SPS-
32/33 "billboard" radars mounted on a similar "turret" superstructure
block. The latter proved to be a major maintenance problem, and the FY
1978 budget provided funds to fit *Long Beach* with the AEGIS system. The
proposed conversion was quickly cancelled, however, as it was feared that
this expenditure might result in reductions in the new CG 47 programme.

Talos was removed in 1979 and the after launcher replaced by quadruple Harpoon launchers. The following year *Long Beach* began a major refit at which the SPS-32/33 radars were removed and their functions taken over by an SPS-48 3-D radar and an SPS-49 air search radar—the latter atop lattice mainmast. Two Phalanx CIWS guns were installed on the after superstructure, and there will eventually be launchers for Tomahawk aft.

Below: Aerial view of *Long Beach* (CGN-9) underway in the Pacific. The Talos launcher has already been removed.

Bottom: *Long Beach* come alongside at San Diego; in her recent refit the SPS-32 and SPS-33 planar radars were removed.

Destroyers

Kidd

Completed:	1981-2.
Names:	DDG 993 *Kidd;* DDG 994 *Callaghan;* DDG 995 *Scott;* DDG 996 *Chandler.*
Displacement:	8,140t full load.
Dimensions:	563 oa x 55 x 30ft (171.1 x 16.8 x 8.1m).
Propulsion:	2-shaft COGAG; 4 LM2500 gas turbines; 80,000bhp = 30kts.
Armament:	*AAW:* 2 twin Mk 26 launchers (24 + 44) for Standard MR missiles; 2 5-inch (127mm) Mk 45 (2x1) 2 Phalanx CIWS. *ASW:* ASROC missiles from Mk 26 launcher; 2 LAMPS helicopters; 6 12.75-inch (324mm) torpedo tubes Mk 32 (2x3). *SSM:* 8 Harpoon missiles (2x4).
Sensors:	*Surveillance:* SPS-48, SPS-55. *Fire Control:* 2 SPG-51, SPG-60, SPQ-9A. *Sonars:* SQS-53.

The four ships of the Kidd class are AAW modifications of the Spruance-class destroyer originally ordered by Iran but acquired by the US Navy in 1979 following the fall of the Shah.

The allowances made in the Spruance design for the modular installation of a number of weapon systems then in production or under development made redesign a simple matter, as the AAW modification had been one of the variations originally envisaged. In the Kidd class twin-arm Mk 26 launchers have been fitted fore and aft in place of the ASROC and Sea Sparrow launchers of the ASW version. The forward magazine is the smaller of the two, the original intention being to fit the now-defunct 8-inch (205mm) Mk 71 gun in place of the forward 5-inch (127mm) mounting. Contrary to US Navy practice, an SPS-48 3-D radar is fitted, but there is no independent air

***Callaghan* (DDG-994).**

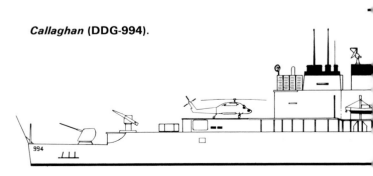

224

In the US Fleet structure the destroyer is a fleet unit, with adequate speed to keep pace with a carrier battle group. Destroyers are divided into those with an air defence function (DDG) and those with an antisubmarine mission (DD). Most of the DDGs were completed in the early 1960's and therefore need replacing in the not-so-distant future. The ASW destroyers of the Spruance class, however, are large modern units. The older DDGs—and CGs— will eventually be replaced by a new design, the DDGX.

---

search radar. There are also only two SPG-51 tracker/illuminators—one above the bridge and the other on a raised superstructure immediately abaft the mainmast. The electronics outfit is therefore austere by US Navy standards, but this will be remedied over the next few years by the addition of systems currently being fitted to other ships of similar capabilities. Two Phalanx CIWS guns have recently been installed.

The Kidd-class destroyers can fire ASROC missiles from their forward Mk 26 launcher, resulting in an ASW capability not far short of that of the standard Spruance.

The provision of extra air-conditioning capacity and dust separators for the gas-turbine air intakes makes these ships well suited to operations in tropical conditions.

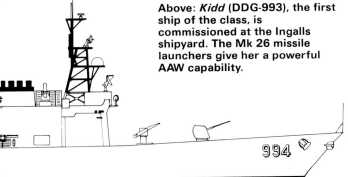

Above: *Kidd* (DDG-993), the first ship of the class, is commissioned at the Ingalls shipyard. The Mk 26 missile launchers give her a powerful AAW capability.

DD
Spruance

Completed: 1975-82.
Names: DD 963 *Spruance;* DD 964 *Paul F. Foster;* DD 965 *Kinkaid,*
DD 966 *Hewitt;* DD 967 *Elliott;*
DD 968 *Arthur W. Radford;* DD 969 *Peterson;*
DD 970 *Caron;* DD 971 *David W. Ray;* DD 972 *Oldendorf*
DD 973 *John Young;* DD 974 *Comte De Grasse;*
DD 975 *O'Brien;* DD 976 *Merrill;* DD 977 *Briscoe;*
DD 978 *Stump;* DD 979 *Conolly;* DD 980 *Moosbrugger;*
DD 981 *John Hancock;* DD 982 *Nicholson;*
DD 983 *John Rodgers;* DD 984 *Leftwich;* DD 985 *Cushing*
DD 986 *Harry W. Hill;* DD 987 *O'Bannon;* DD 988 *Thorn;*
DD 989 *Deyo;* DD 990 *Ingersoll;* DD 991 *Fife;*
DD 992 *Fletcher;* DD 997 *Hayler.*
Displacement: 7,800t full load.
Dimensions: 563 oa x 55 x 29ft (171.1 x 16.8 x 8.8m).
Propulsion: 2-shaft COGAG; 4 LM2500 gas turbines;
80,000bhp = 30 + kts.

Armament: ASW: ASROC launcher Mk 16 (1x8, 24 reloads);
2 SH-2F helicopters (only one embarked); 6 12.75-inch
(324mm) torpedo tubes Mk 32 (2x3).
AAW: NATO Sea Sparrow launcher Mk 29 (1x8, 16
reloads). 2 5-inch (127mm) Mk 45 (2x1); 2 Phalanx
CIWS being fitted.
SSM: 8 Harpoon missiles (2x4).

Sensors: *Surveillance:* SPS-40, SPS-55.
Fire Control: SPG-60, SPQ-9A, Mk 91.
Sonars: SQS-53.

The most controversial ships to be built for the US Navy since World War II,
the Spruance class was designed to replace the war-built destroyers of the
Gearing and Allen M. Sumner classes, which had undergone FRAM ASW
modification programmes during the 1960s but by the early 1970s were
nearing the end of their useful lives.

At 7,800t full load – more than twice the displacement of the destroyers it
was to replace – the *Spruance* epitomised the US Navy's design philosophy ▶

**Below: *Oldendorf* (DD-972) underway. The Spruance class have
recently been fitted with canister launchers for Harpoon SSMs.**

of the 1970s. This philosophy envisaged the construction of large hulls with block superstructures which maximised internal volume, fitted out with machinery that could be easily maintained and, if necessary, replaced, and equipped with high-technology weapon systems that could be added to and updated by modular replacement at a later stage. The object was to minimise "platform" costs, which have no military pay-off, in favour of greater expenditure on weapon systems ("payload") in order to ensure that the ships would remain first-line units throughout the 30-year life-expectancy of their hulls.

In a further attempt to minimise "platform" costs the entire class was ordered from a single shipbuilder, the Litton/Ingalls Corporation, which invested heavily in a major production facility at Pascagoula, using advanced modular construction techniques.

The only "visible" weapons aboard *Spruance* when she was completed were 5-inch (127mm) Mk 45 lightweight gun mountings fore and aft and an ASROC box launcher forward of the bridge. In view of the size and cost of the ships this caused an immediate public outcry.

The advanced ASW qualities of the Spruance class are, however, largely hidden within the hull and the bulky superstructures. The ASROC launcher

or example, has a magazine beneath it containing no less than 24 reloads. The large hangar to port of the after-funnel uptakes measures 49·54ft by 21·3ft (15-16.5m x 6.47m) and can accommodate two LAMPS helicopters. And to either side of the flight deck there are sliding doors in the hull which conceal triple Mk 32 torpedo tubes and torpedo-handling rooms.

Of even greater significance are the advanced submarine detection features of the class. The bow sonar is the new SQS-53, a solid-state improved version of the SQS-26, which can operate in a variety of active and passive modes, including direct path, bottom bounce and convergence zone. The SQS-53 has proved so successful that the SQS-35 VDS initially scheduled to be installed in these ships will not now be fitted. The adoption of an all-gas-turbine propulsion system, which employs paired LM2500 turbines *en echelon* in a unit arrangement, and which was selected partly because of the ease with which it can be maintained and because of its low ▶

Below: *Elliott* (DD-967) underway. Gas-turbines give her rapid response and a low noise signature—a crucial factor in ASW operations. In the interests of fuel economy the ships generally trail one of their two shafts at cruise speed.

▶manning requirements, has resulted in a significant reduction in underwater noise emission. The Spruance is therefore capable of near-silent ASW operations.

The class is also fitted with the latest computerised data systems in a well designed Combat Information Centre (CIC), and has the latest digital fire control systems—the Mk 86 GFCS and the Mk 116 underwater FC system.

Moreover, besides the weapon systems fitted on completion, the Spruance class was designed to accept a variety of other systems then at the development stage. All ships have now received the Sea Sparrow Improved Point Defence Missile System (IPDMS), Harpoon anti-ship missiles (aft of the first funnel), and Whiskey-3 (WSC-3) satellite communications antennae. SLQ-32(V)2 ECM antennae are now being fitted, and provision has been made for the future replacement of the ASROC and Sea Sparrow launchers by Mk 26 launchers. Eventually these will be replaced by Mark 41 Vertical Launch Systems (VLS), each of which comprises a 29- or 61-missile box able to accommodate AAW, anti-ship, and ASW missiles. The Spruance class is scheduled to receive the SQR-19 TACTAS towed array when it becomes available.

The flexibility of the Spruance design is such that it has formed the basis both for the AAW destroyers originally ordered for Iran (see Kidd class) and of the new AEGIS cruiser (see Ticonderoga class).

One additional ship of the Spruance class was ordered in 1979. DD 997 was originally to have had increased hangar and flight-deck space for helicopter and VTOL operations, but it was a modification which found greater favour with Congress than with the US Navy, which has since decided to complete the ship to the standard Spruance configuration.

Above right: An early view of *Spruance* (DD-963) on sea trials in 1975. Note the layout of the funnels, which are en echelon.

Below: *Elliott* (DD-967) underway. Early criticism of the Spruance design has generally given way to praise.

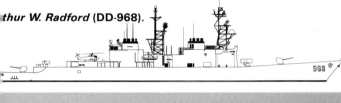

thur W. Radford (DD-968).

Decatur

Completed: 1956-9.
Names: DDG 31 *Decatur;* DDG 32 *John Paul Jones;*
DDG 33 *Parsons;* DDG 34 *Somers.*
Displacement: 4,150t full load.
Dimensions: 418 oa x 45 x 20ft (127.5 x 13.8 x 6.1m).
Propulsion: 2-shaft geared steam turbines; 70,000shp = 32.5kts.
Armament: *AAW:* single Mk 13 launcher (40) for Standard MR missiles;
1 5-inch (127mm) Mk 42.
ASW: ASROC launcher Mk 16 (1x8); 6 12.75-inch
(324mm) torpedo tubes Mk 32 (2x3).
SSM: Harpoon missiles will be fired from Mk 13 launcher.
Sensors: *Surveillance:* SPS-48, SPS-29E (SPS-40 in DDG 34),
SPS-10B.
Fire Control: 1 SPG-51C, 1 SPG-53B.
Sonars: SQS-23.

These four ships were originally conventionally armed destroyers of the
Forrest Sherman class. From 1965 until 1968 they underwent a major
conversion to bring them up to a similar standard to the DDGs of the Charles
F. Adams class.

The three-year refit included the removal of the after 5-inch (127mm)
guns and their replacement by the Tartar missile system. A Mk 13 single-arm
launcher together with its cylindrical magazine replaced the after gun
mounting, and immediately forward of it a large deckhouse carrying a

single SPG-51 tracker/illuminator was constructed. Two massive lattice masts replaced the original tripods, giving the ships a distinctive profile. The purpose of the new mainmast was to carry the large SPS-48 3-D radar, which was just entering service. *Somers*, the last ship converted, also had her original SPS-29 air search radar replaced by an SPS-40. The initial conversion plan envisaged the operation of DASH anti-submarine drones, but when the DASH programme ran into problems, it was decided to fit an ASROC launcher instead.

It was originally intended that the entire Forrest Sherman class should undergo a similar conversion, but the cost of the programme proved to be prohibitive. Nor has the conversion proved to be particularly successful; the Decatur class suffers from excessive topweight, and although costly long-range detection and tracking facilities have been provided, the ships are limited to a single tracker/illuminator. All are now in reserve.

Top: *Parsons* (DDG-33). The single Mk 13 Tartar launcher is aft, with its SPG-51 FC radar mounted on a new deckhouse.

Above: A port bow view of *Somers* (DDG-34) underway off Hawaii. All four ships of the class are now in reserve.

Left: *John Paul Jones* (DDG-32) underway. These are the only US ships of their size to be fitted with the SPS-48 radar.

DDG
Charles F. Adams

Completed:	1960-4.
Names:	DDG 2 *Charles F. Adams;* DDG 3 *John King;* DDG 4 *Lawrence;* DDG 5 *Claude V. Ricketts;* DDG 6 *Barney;* DDG 7 *Henry B. Wilson;* DDG 8 *Lynde McCormick;* DDG 9 *Towers;* DDG 10 *Sampson;* DDG 11 *Sellers;* DDG 12 *Robison;* DDG 13 *Hoel;* DDG 14 *Buchanan;* DDG 15 *Berkeley;* DDG 16 *Joseph Strauss;* DDG 17 *Conyngham;* DDG 18 *Semmes;* DDG 19 *Tattnall;* DDG 20 *Goldsborough;* DDG 21 *Cochrane;* DDG 22 *Benjamin Stoddert;* DDG 23 *Richard E. Bird;* DDG 24 *Waddell.*
Displacement:	3,370t standard; 4,500t full load.
Dimensions:	437 oa x 47 x 22ft (133.2 x 14.3 x 6.7m).
Propulsion:	2-shaft geared steam turbines; 70,000shp = 31.5kts.
Armament:	*AAW:* twin Mk 11 launcher (42) *or* single Mk 13 launcher (40) for Standard MR missiles; 2 5-inch (127mm) Mk 42 (2x1). *ASW:* ASROC launcher Mk 16 (1x8); 6 12.75-inch (324mm) torpedo tubes MK 32 (2x3). *SSM:* Harpoon misiles from Mk 13 launcher.
Sensors:	*Surveillance:* SPS-39, SPS-29/37 (DDG 2-14) *or* SPS 40 (DDG-15-24), SPS-10C/D. *Fire Control:* 2 SPG-51C, 1 SPG-53A/E/F. *Sonar:* SQS-23.

The Charles F. Adams class is derived from the Forrest Sherman, with a Tartar launcher in place of the third 5-inch (127mm) gun mounting. It is still the standard AAW destroyer in service with the US Navy, and is employed together with the larger CGs to provide anti-air defence for the carrier battle groups.

The first 13 ships of the class were fitted with the twin-arm Mk 11 launcher but later ships have the single-arm Mk 13. The Mk 13 is a lightweight launcher with a high rate of fire—8 rounds per minute—which compensates in part for the single arm. Both launchers employ a cylindrical magazine containing two concentric rings of missiles. Overall length was increased by about 9m (29.5ft) to accommodate a Mk 16 ASROC launcher between the funnels. The installation of Tartar and ASROC made the *Charles F. Adams* one of the most formidably armed destroyers of its period, and the design was adopted by the Federal German and the Australian Navies.

In spite of their age these ships are still highly regarded in the US Navy. They have proved to be extremely useful, well balanced ships, whose only major defect has been their temperamental high-pressure boilers. In the late 1970s it was therefore proposed that they should undergo a major modernisation programme which would extend their service life beyond the nominal 30-year mark. Funding was to have been authorised in FY 1980-3 ▶

Below left: An aerial view of *Waddell* (DDG-24) underway in the Pacific. She has the single Mk 13 Tartar launcher aft.

Below: A DDG of the Charles F. Adams class in heavy weather. This unit has the older Mk 11 twin-arm Tartar launcher aft.

▶but it was feared that expenditure of this magnitude would adversely affec the programme of new construction, and it was then proposed that the las ten ships would receive a less fundamental modernisation, but this was rejected by Congress.

In a revised plan just three ships (DDG-14, -20, -22) will be modernised using 'fleet maintenance funds'. The SPS-39 3-D radar will be replaced by the SPS-52B, the SPS-29/37 by an SPS-40C, and the SPS-10 by an SPS-65. The original Gun Fire Control System (GFCS) will be replaced by the digital Mk 86, with SPG-60 and SPQ-9A antennae, and the NTDS wil be updated, with provision of the SYS-1 integrated automatic detection and tracking system. An SQQ-23 PAIR active/passive sonar will replace the SQS-23, and ECM capabilities will be greatly enhanced by the installation of two SLQ-32(V)2 antennae. The modernisation will require at least 18 months per ship. It is envisaged that these vessels will eventually be replaced by the DDGX now under development.

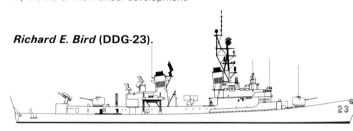

Richard E. Bird **(DDG-23).**

Right: Bow view of a DDG of the Charles F. Adams class. This unit has the SPS-40 air search radar on the foremast.

Below: *Henry B. Wilson* **(DDG-7) underway in the Pacific. She has the twin-arm Mk 11 Tartar launcher aft.**

DDG
Coontz

Completed: 1959-61.

Names: DDG 37 *Farragut;* DDG 38 *Luce;* DDG 39 *Macdonough;* DDG 40 *Coontz;* DDG 41 *King;* DDG 42 *Mahan;* DDG 43 *Dahlgren;* DDG 44 *Wm. V. Pratt;* DDG 45 *Dewey;* DDG 46 *Preble.*

Displacement: 4,700t standard; 5,800t full load.

Dimensions: 513 oa x 53 x 25ft (156.2 x 15.9 x 7.6m).

Propulsion: 2-shaft geared steam turbines; 85,000shp = 33kts.

Armament: *AAW:* twin Mk 10 launcher (40) for Standard ER missiles; 1 5-inch (127mm) Mk 42.
ASW: ASROC launcher Mk 16 (1x8); 6 12.75-inch (324mm) torpedo tubes Mk 32 (2x3).
SSM: 8 Harpoon missiles (2x4).

Sensors: *Surveillance:* SPS-48 (SPS-49 in DDG 43, 46), SPS-29/37, SPS-10.
Fire Control: 2 SPG-55B, 1 SPG-53A.
Sonars: SQS-23.

The ten ships of the Coontz class constitute the first group of AAW "frigates" completed for the US Navy during the 1960s. Unlike the later ships of the Leahy and Belknap classes they have a flush-decked hull, and this feature, together with their twin lattice mast/funnel arrangement, reveals their derivation from the all-gun DLs of the early 1950s. They also have much lower endurance than later ships, and this factor appears to have been largely responsible for their redesignation as DDGs in 1975 (the Leahy and Belknap classes became CGs). They nevertheless carry a similar armament to the later ships, have been brought up to the same standard as regards electronics, and perform an identical mission in defence of the carrier battle groups which are described and shown on pages 10-13.

Above: The destroyer *Luce* (DDG-38) seen here in the Mediterranean. These ships were formerly classified as DLG.

Below: *Macdonough* (DDG-39). She and her sister ships underwent a major AAW modernisation programme in the early 1970s.

► The *Coontz* has a twin Mk 10 launcher aft, a single 5-inch (127mm) gu
forward, an ASROC box launcher above it in "B" position, and triple ant
submarine tubes amidships. From 1968 until 1976 the class underwent
major modernisation similar to that of the *Leahy*. The SPS-39 3-D radar wa
replaced by an SPS-48, the Terrier guidance system was changed from
command (employing SPG-49 radars) to semi-active guidance (employing
the SPG-55), and a computer-based NTDS was installed – *Mahan* and *King*
which had been trials ships for the system 1961-2, had theirs updated
Farragut had her ASW capability enhanced by the provision of a reloading
magazine for ASROC at the forward end of the superstructure, but she

emained the only ship thus fitted. All ships had the original 3-inch (76mm) AA guns removed, and these were later replaced by Harpoon. In 1979 *Mahan* received the SM-2 missile, and this was subsequently fitted to the rest of the class. They have also received the SQQ-23 PAIR sonar, but will not be fitted with Phalanx.

All except *Preble* currently serve in the Atlantic, where their limited endurance is of less consequence than in the broader reaches of the Pacific.

Below: The destroyer *Coontz* (DDG-40) underway. She established the armament pattern for the US Navy's carrier escorts.

DD
Forrest Sherman

Completed:	1955-9.
Names:	DD 931 *Forrest Sherman;* DD 942 *Bigelow;*
	DD 944 *Mullinix;* DD 945 *Hull;* DD 946 *Edson* (NRF).
	DD 951 *Turner Joy.* (ASW conversions).
	DD 937 *Davis;* DD 938 *Jonas Ingram;* DD 940 Manley;
	DD 941 *Du Pont;* DD 943 *Blandy;* DD 948 *Morton;*
	DD 950 *Richard S. Edwards.*
Displacement:	2,800t standard, 4,050t full load.
Dimensions:	418 oa x 45 x 22ft (127.5 x 13.7 x 6.7m).
Propulsion:	2-shaft geared steam turbines; 70,00shp = 32.5kts.
Armament:	(Unmodified units).*ASW:* 6 12.75-inch (324mm) torpedo
	tubes Mk 32 (2x3).
	AAW: 3 5-inch (127mm) Mk 42 (3x1).
	(ASW Conversions).*ASW:* ASROC launcher Mk 16 (1x8);
	6 12.75-inch (324mm) torpedo tubes Mk 32 (2x3).
	AAW: 2 5-inch (127mm) Mk 42.
Sensors:	*Surveillance:* SPS-37 or SPS-40, SPS-10.
	Fire Control: SPG-53.
	Sonars: SQS-23, SQS-35 IVDS in ASW-modified ships.

The Forest Sherman class were the first postwar US destroyers. Although conventionally armed, they followed current tactical thinking in abandoning anti-ship torpedoes, which were replaced by four fixed 21-inch (533mm) "long" ASW torpedoes, and in mounting a lesser number of guns with higher performance than those of their war-built predecessors.

The conventional armament was quickly overtaken by new technological developments--in particular the advent of the nuclear submarine and the surface-to-air missile—and an extensive conversion programme was drawn up. Four ships were given the Tartar missile system (see Decatur class) but the cost of the conversion precluded its extension to the rest of the class. Eight ships were therefore given a limited ASW conversion between 1967 and 1971. The second gun mounting was replaced by an ASROC launcher and the fixed A/S tubes by triple Mk 32 trainable tubes; surveillance radars were updated and an independent variable depth sonar fitted above the stern.

Even this limited conversion programme ran into cost problems, and the remaining six ships of the class received only those modifications which entailed a minimum of structural alterations. They retained all three 5-inch (127mm) guns and were not fitted with ASROC or VDS.

From 1975 onwards *Hull* served as trial ship for the 8-inch (205mm) Mk 71 Major Calibre Light Weight Gun (MCLWG). The mounting replaced the forward gun until 1979, when it was removed. All are in reserve, except for DD-933, which is now a floating museum.

Below left: The destroyer *Forrest Sherman* (DD-931) underway. She retains her original configuration with three 5-inch guns.

Below: An aerial view of an ASW conversion of the Forest Sherman class, showing clearly the ASROC launcher aft.

Frigates

Oliver Hazard Perry

Completed: 1977 onwards.
Names: FFG 7 *Oliver H. Perry;* FFG 8 *McInerney;*
FFG 9 *Wadsworth;* FFG 10 *Duncan;* FFG 11 *Clark;*
FFG 12 *George Philip;* FFG 13 *Samuel E. Morison;*
FFG 14 *Sides;* FFG 15 *Estocin;* FFG 16 *Clifton Sprague;*
FFG 19 *John A. Moore;* FFG 20 *Antrim;* FFG 21 *Flatley;*
FFG 22 *Fahrion;* FFG 23 *Lewis B. Puller;*
FFG 24 *Jack Williams;* FFG 25 *Copeland;* FFG 26 *Gallery;*
FFG 27 *Mahlon S. Tisdale;* FFG 28 *Boone;*
FFG 29 *Stephen W. Groves;* FFG 30 *Reid;* FFG 31 *Stark;*
FFG 32 *John L. Hall;* FFG 33 *Jarret;* FFG 34 *Aubrey Fitch;*
FFG 36 *Underwood;* FFG 37 *Crommelin;* FFG 38 *Curts;*
FFG 39 *Doyle;* FFG 40 *Halyburton;* FFG 41 *McClusky;*
FFG 42 *Klakring;* FFG 43 *Thach;* FFG 45 *De Wert;*
FFG 46 *Rentz;* FFG 47 *Nicholas;* FFG 48 *Vandegrift;*
FFG 49 *Robert G Bradley;* FFG 50 *Taylor;* FFG 51 *Gary;*
FFG 52 *Carr;* FFG 53 *Hawes;* FFG 54 *Ford;* FFG 55 *Elrod;*
FFG 56 *Simpson;* FFG 57 *Reuben James;*
FFG 58 *Samuel B Roberts;* FFHG 59 *Kauffman;*
+ 2 building.
Displacement: 3,710t full load.
Dimensions: 445 oa x 45 x 25ft (135.6 x 13.7 x 7.5m).
Propulsion: 1-shaft COGAG; 2 LM2500 gas turbines;
40,000bhp = 28kts.
Armament: *AAW:* single Mk 13 launcher (40) for Standard MR missiles;
1 76mm (3-inch) Mk 75; 1 Phalanx CIWS being fitted.
ASW: 2 LAMPS helicopters; 6 12.75-inch (324mm)
torpedo tubes Mk 32 (2x3).
SSM: Harpoon missiles from Mk 13 launcher.
Sensors: *Surveillance:* SPS-49, SPS-55.
Fire Control: STIR (modified SPG-60).
Sonars: SQS-26.

The FFG 7 design has its origins in the Patrol Frigate first proposed in
September 1970. The latter was to constitute the "low" end of the so-called
"high/low" mix, providing large numbers of cheap second-rate escorts with
reduced capabilities to counterbalance the sophisticated but costly specialist
ASW and AAW vessels whose primary mission was to protect the carriers.
Strict limitations were therefore imposed on cost, displacement and
manpower requirements.

Unlike its near-contemporary, the high-value *Spruance,* which had its own
specialised production facility, the FFG 7 was designed to be built anywhere

Right: *Oliver Hazard Perry* **(FFG-7) underway. The single Mk 13
Tartar launcher is visible on the forecastle.**

The US frigate is essentially a cheap, simpler type designed to escort convoys and groups of amphibious ships. One-shaft operation and a modest speed are therefore acceptable, although good endurance is essential. As with destroyers, some frigates are configured for air defence (FFG) while others are primarily for ASW (FF). The latest ships of the Oliver Hazard Perry class can perform both missions. Plans for a new design (FFGX) have been shelved.

▶Simple construction techniques were encouraged, making maximum use of flat panels and bulkheads, and passageways are generally straight. The hull structure can be prefabricated in modules of 35, 100, 200 or 400 tons, allowing the various shipyards to use the most convenient size. As a result the programme is running well to schedule with some units being delivered early, and costs have been kept remarkably close to the original estimates.

The application of the USAF-derived "fly-before-buy" concept to the FFG 7 programme has meant a two-year gap between the completion of the first ship and the rest of the class, making it possible to iron out any problems experienced during trials with the first ship, and to incorporate any necessary modifications into the following units while buildilng. Moreover, before even the lead ship had been completed, the individual systems with which she was to be equipped had already been tested on ships of other classes.

Like the frigates which preceded her, the *Oliver Hazard Perry* has a

"second-class" propulsion plant on one screw. The layout is, however, much more compact than that of the *Knox* as a result of the adoption of gas turbines. Two LM2500s – the same model as that installed in the *Spruance* – are located side-by-side in a single engine room. Two small retractable propulsion pods fitted just aft of the sonar dome provide back-up during docking procedures, and these can drive the ship at 6 knots in an emergency.

The balance of the armament is more closely oriented to AAW than that of the *Knox*, which was a specialist ASW design. The FFG 7 has a Mk 13 launcher forward for Standard MR surface-to-air missiles and Harpoon anti-ship missiles, and an OTO-Melara 76mm (3-inch) quick-firing gun atop the ▶

Below: *Oliver Hazard Perry* **(FFG-7) is the first of the new Patrol Frigates. The single Mk 13 Tartar launcher and the SPS-49 radar are prominent features. Large numbers have been constructed.**

▶bulky superstructure block. ASROC has been abandoned altogether, but there is a broad hangar aft for two LAMPS helicopters. The sonar, which is hull-mounted inside a rubber dome, is a new austere type which has neither the long range nor the multi-mode capability of the SQS-26 fitted to previous frigates. It is, however, envisaged that the FFG 7 would operate in conjunction with other frigates equipped with the SQS-26 and would receive target information from their sonars via data links.

Whereas the *Spruance* was designed to incorporate a large amount of space for future growth, the FFG 7 has been strictly tailored to accommodate only those systems envisaged in the near future. These include the SH-60 Seahawk LAMPS III (together with its RAST recovery system), the SQR-19 tactical towed array, fin stabilisers, a Link 11 data transfer system, and a single Phalanx CIWS gun. These items alone represent a lot of growth. Once these modifications have been made, however, there remains only a 50-ton margin for further growth, and if any additional items of equipment are to be fitted, others will have to be removed.

Right: *Oliver Hazard Perry* (FFG-7). The surveillance radar is the new SPS-49, which replaces the SPS 37/43 series.

Below: *Oliver Hazard Perry* (FFG-7) on sea trials. Note the large double hangar and the short, stubby funnel.

Knox

Completed: 1969-74.

Names: FF 1052 *Knox;* FF 1053 *Roark;* FF 1054 *Gray;*
FF 1055 *Hepburn;* FF 1056 *Connole;* FF 1057 *Rathburne;*
FF 1058 *Meyerkord;* FF 1059 *W.S. Sims;* FF 1060 *Lang;*
FF 1061 *Patterson;* FF 1062 *Whipple;* FF 1063 *Reasoner;*
FF 1064 *Lockwood;* FF 1065 *Stein;*
FF 1066 *Marvin Shields;* FF 1067 *Francis Hammond;*
FF 1068 *Vreeland;* FF 1069 *Bagley;* FF 1070 *Downes;*
FF 1071 *Badger;* FF 1072 *Blakely;*
FF 1073 *Robert E. Peary;* FF 1074 *Harold E. Holt;*
FF 1075 *Trippe;* FF 1076 *Fanning;* FF 1077 *Ouellet;*
FF 1078 *Joseph Hewes;* FF 1079 *Bowen;* FF 1080 *Paul,*
FF 1081 *Aylwin;* FF 1082 *Elmer Montgomery;*
FF 1083 *Cook;* FF 1084 *McCandless;*
FF 1085 *Donald B. Beary;* FF 1086 *Brewton;*
FF 1087 *Kirk;* FF 1088 *Barbey;* FF 1089 *Jesse L. Brown;*
FF 1090 *Ainsworth;* FF 1091 *Miller;*
FF 1091 *Miller;* FF 1092 *Thomas C. Hart;*
FF 1093 *Capodanno;* FF 1094 *Pharris;* FF 1095 *Truett;*
FF 1096 *Valdez;* FF 1097 *Moinester.*

Displacement: 3,011t standard; 4,100t full load.

Dimensions: 438 oa x 47 x 25ft (133.5 x 14.3 x 7.6m).

Propulsion: 1-shaft geared steam turbines; 35,000shp = 27kts.

Armament: *ASW:* ASROC launcher Mk 16 (1x8, reloadable);
1 SH-2F helicopter; 4 12.75-inch (324mm) torpedo
tubes Mk 32 (4x1).
AAW: BPDMS launcher Mk 25 (1x8) in 31 ships;
1 5-inch (127mm) Mk 42.
SSM: Harpoon missiles from ASROC Launcher.

Sensors: *Surveillance:* SPS-40, SPS-10.
Fire Control: SPG-53A/D/F, Mk 115.
Sonars: SQS-26CX, SQS-35 IVDS in some ships.

The Knox class began as a Design Work Study of the Brooke-class missile
escort. Congressional opposition to the mounting costs of fitting escorts
with the Tartar system resulted, however, in the abandonment of the latter
class after only six units had been laid down, The *Knox* was therefore
redesigned as an ASW Escort.

Above: A bow view of *Moinester* (FF-1097), the last ship of the Knox class. The ASROC launcher is visible behind the 5-inch gun.

Below left: *Joseph L. Hewes* (FF-1078) soon after completion. The helicopter platform and hangar have yet to be modified.

Below: An aerial view of *Stein* (FF-1065) in the Pacific. Note the enlarged helicopter platform and the telescopic hangar.

▶ Although the *Knox* retained the one-shaft propulsion system of the Garcia/Brooke design, the complex pressure-fired boilers of the latter were abandoned in favour of a "safer", more conventional steam plant. This necessitated an increase in size without creating any extra space for weapons.

Originally the two 5-inch (127mm) Mk 38 guns of the *Garcia* were to have been replaced by a combination of a single 5-inch Mk 42 and the ill-fated Sea Mauler point-defence missile. The Sea Mauler was eventually replaced by the Sea Sparrow BPDMS—a system not contemplated when the *Knox* was designed.

Other "hiccups" in the development of the *Knox* include the abandonment of a fixed "billboard" ECM antenna which influenced the design of the tall mack, of the pair of fixed torpedo tubes (for Mk 37/Mk 48 torpedoes) which were to have been fitted in the stern, and of the DASH programme.

Ultimately the abandonment of DASH worked to the ships' advantage, as it was replaced by the LAMPS I manned helicopter. As with the previous two classes of escort, the hangar received a telescopic extension, giving overall dimensions of 42-47ft by 15-18ft (12.6-14.3m x 4.4-5.6m). Taken together

with the reloadable ASROC launcher and the SQS-26 sonar, this gave the *Knox* a first-class anti-submarine outfit, which rescued the design from an unpromising beginning.

Besides the Sea Sparrow BPDMS, many ships have received the SQS-35 independent variable depth sonar since completion. All will receive the SQR-18 towed array in the near future. Most ships have now had their ASROC launchers modified to fire Harpoon, and it is planned to replace Sea Sparrow with a single Phalanx CIWS mounting.

In spite of the early problems experienced the *Knox* has become one of the most useful and versatile classes of US warship. It is also the largest class of major combatants completed in the West in the postwar era, and would have been larger still but for the cancellation of ten ships authorised in FY 1968 to finance other programmes.

Below: The frigate *Connole* (FF-1056) underway in the Atlantic. The Knox class is now being fitted with bow bulwarks in order to improve sea-keeping. The class has proved successful in service, despite initial criticism of the design.

FFG
Brooke

Completed: 1966-8.
Names: FFG 1 *Brooke;* FFG 2 *Ramsey;* FFG 3 *Schofield;*
FFG 4 *Talbot;* FFG 5 *Richard L. Page;* FFG 6 *Julius A. Furer.*
Displacement: 2,640t standard; 3,245t full load.
Dimensions: 415 oa x 44 x 24ft (126.3 x 13.5 x 7.3m).
Propulsion: 1-shaft geared steam turbine; 35,000shp = 27kts.
Armament: *AAW:* single Mk 22 launcher (16) for Standard MR missiles;
1 5-inch (127mm) Mk 30.
ASW: ASROC launcher Mk 16 (reloadable in FFG 4-6);
1 SH-2F helicopter; 6 12.75-inch (324mm) torpedo
tubes Mk 32 (2x3).
Sensors: *Surveillance:* SPS-52D, SPS-10F.
Fire Control: 1 SPG-51C, Mk35.
Sonars: SQS-26AX.

The Brooke class is a Tartar modification of the Garcia class of ASW escorts.
The two classes share the same basic hull, single-shaft propulsion plant, and
general layout, but the *Brooke* has a single Mk 22 Tartar launcher in place of
the second 5-inch (127mm) Mk 30 of the *Garcia.*

The Mk 22 launcher has a single-ring magazine with a much-reduced capacity of 16 rounds compared with the 40-round installation which is standard to larger vessels. The above-water sensor outfit is also comparatively austere; there is an SPS-52 3-D radar but no independent air search antenna, and only a single SPG-51 tracker/illuminator. In spite of this Congress baulked at the $11m increase in cost compared with the gun-armed *Garcia*, and rejected the proposal for a further 10 units in FY 1964.

Since completion, the Brooke class has undergone similar modifications to the Garcia. The two Mk 25 torpedo tubes initially incorporated in the stern have been removed and, following the abandonment of the DASH programme, the hangar has been enlarged and fitted with a telescopic extension to accommodate a LAMPS helicopter. Overall hangar dimensions are now 40-52ft by 15-17ft (12-15.8m x 4.4-5.1m).

In 1974 *Talbot* was refitted to evaluate various systems which were to be installed in the FFG 7, including the OTO Melara 76mm gun, the Mk 92 and STIR fire control systems, and the SQS-56 sonar. She has since reverted to her original configuration.

Below: *Julius A. Furer* (FFG-6). The sloping bridge-face conceals an ASROC reload magazine, fitted only in the last three ships of the class. The single Mk 16 Tartar launcher and its SPG-51 FC radar are amidships, just forward of the helicopter hangar.

FF
Garcia

Completed: 1964-68.
Names: FF 1040 *Garcia;* FF 1041 *Bradley;*
FF 1043 *Edward McDonnell;* FF 1044 *Brumby;*
FF 1045 *Davidson;* FF 1047 *Voge;* FF 1048 *Sample;*
FF 1049 *Koelsch;* FF 1050 *Albert David;* FF 1051 *O'Callahan*
Displacement: 2,620t standard; 3,400t full load.
Dimensions: 415 oa x 44 x 24ft (126.3 x 13.5 x 7.3m).
Propulsion: 1-shaft geared steam turbine; 35,000shp = 27kts.
Armament: *ASW:* ASROC launcher Mk 16 (1x8) reloadable in FFG
(1047-51). 1 SH-2F helicopter (except FF 1048, 1050)
6 12.75-inch (324mm) torpedo tubes Mk 32 (2x3).
AAW: 2 5-inch (127mm) Mk 30 (2x1).
Sensors: *Surveillance:* SPS-40, SPS-10.
Fire Control: Mk 35.
Sonars: SQS-26AXR (FF 1040-45) *or*
SQS-26BX (FF 1047-51), SQR-15 TASS
(FF 1048, 1050 only).

The Garcia-class ocean escort was evolved from the Bronstein design which
although similar in size to contemporary European escorts, proved too small
for the US Navy. Improvements included a larger, flush-decked hull, a
heavier gun armament, and the provision of a hangar aft for DASH anti-
submarine drones. The last five units were also given a reload magazine for
ASROC at the forward end of the bridge, which has a distinctive sloping face
in these ships. The earlier units were initially fitted with two stern tubes for
Mk 25 torpedoes, but these have now been removed.

Only *Bradley* is thought to have operated DASH before the programme
was abandoned. All except *Sample* and *Albert David* (which are fitted instead
with a towed array) subsequently had their hangars enlarged and a

256

telescopic extension fitted to enable them to operate manned LAMPS helicopters. This modification has brought with it a significant increase in ASW capabilities.

A compact one-shaft steam propulsion plant employing pressure-fired boilers was adopted to maximise the internal volume available for weapons and electronics. The pressure-fired boilers proved complex to operate and maintain, however, and concern about the reliability of such a high-technology system—especially in a ship with only a single shaft—led to a reversion to conventional boilers in the succeeding Knox class.

Below: Stern view of a frigate of the Garcia class. Note the helicopter hangar, which now has a telescopic extension.

Bottom: The frigate *Voge* (FF-1047) comes alongside the carrier *America* (CV-66). The second 5-inch gun is visible amidships.

Bronstein

Completed:	1963.
Names:	FF 1037 *Bronstein*; FF 1038 *McCloy*.
Displacement:	2,360t standard; 2,650t full load.
Dimensions:	372 oa x 41 x 23ft (113.2 x 12.3 x 7m).
Propulsion:	1-shaft geared steam turbine; 20,000shp = 24kts.
Armament:	*ASW:* ASROC launcher Mk 16 (1x8);
	6 12.75-inch (324mm) torpedo tubes Mk 32 (2x3).
	AAW: 2 3-inch (76mm) Mk 33 (1x2).
Sensors:	*Surveillance:* SPS-40, SPS-10.
	Fire Control: Mk 35.
	Sonars: SQS-26, SQR-15 TASS.

The development of high-speed nuclear-powered submarines by the Soviet Union in the late 1950s effectively outdated even those US Navy DEs which were under construction at that time. The US Navy responded by designing a new type of ocean escort radically different from its predecessors in every respect. The result was the two ships of the Bronstein class.

Steam propulsion was adopted in place of the traditional diesels, although, contrary to European practice, the single shaft of the DE was retained. The most revolutionary feature of the design, however, was that the entire ship was built around a first-class ASW outfit comprising the latest weapons and sensors. The slim, tapered bow conceals a massive SQS-26 sonar dome, which was originally to be matched with the ASROC anti-submarine missile and a DASH drone, for which a flight deck was provided immediately abaft the superstructure. When DASH was cancelled, however, the superstructure arrangement proved too cramped to fit a hangar large enough to take a LAMPS helicopter, and only ASROC and the triple Mk 32 tubes remain.

The gun armament was on a par with previous DEs. A third 3-inch (76mm) gun on the low quarterdeck was removed in the mid-1970s to make room for a large towed array. The superstructure comprises a single compact block surmounted by a tall mack carrying the air search radar and ECM aerials.

Although unsatisfactory in some respects, these two ships set the pattern for all ocean escorts built for the US Navy over the next two decades.

Above: Bow view of a Bronstein-class frigate. Later frigates have a single 5-inch gun in place of the twin 3-inch mounting.

Below left: The frigate *Bronstein* (FF-1037) underway. This ship was the first of a series of large ocean-going escorts.

Below: *McCloy* (FF-1038), showing the large helicopter deck from which DASH antisubmarine drones were to have been operated.

Patrol Combatants

Pegasus

Completed: 1977-82.
Names: PHM 1 *Pegasus;* PHM 2 *Hercules;* PHM 3 *Taurus;* PHM 4 *Aquila;* PHM 5 *Aries;* PHM 6 *Gemini.*
Displacement: 231t full load.
Dimensions: 132 x 28 x 6ft (40 x 8.6 x 1.9m).
Propulsion: (hullborne) 2 Mercedes-Benz diesels; 1600bhp = 12kts. (foilborne) 1 General Electric gas-turbine; 18,000bhp = 40kts.
Armament: 8 Harpoon (2x4); 1 3-inch (76mm) Mk 75.
Sensors: *Fire Control:* 1 Mk 92 (Mk 94 in PHM 1).

The PHM was one of the four new designs in the "low" programme advocated in Zumalt's Project 60 (see Introduction). It was envisaged that squadrons of these fast patrol craft would be deployed at the various choke points—in particular those in the Mediterranean and the NW Pacific—through which the surface units of the Soviet Navy needed to pass in order to reach open waters. High speed and a heavy armament of anti-ship missiles would enable the PHM to make rapid interceptions, and the relatively low unit cost meant that large numbers could be bought.

The US Navy has traditionally shown little interest in small patrol craft, and has concentrated on ocean-going construction to meet its maritime commitments. Seventeen gas-turbine-powered gunboats (PG) were built in the mid-1960s to counter Cuban-inspired insurgency in the Caribbean, and these saw extensive employment in Vietnam. Only two remain in service, and they are used only for training. The six missile hydrofoils of the Pegasus class are all that remain of 30 planned in the 1970s.

The Italian and Federal German Navies, with similar requirements in the Mediterranean and the Baltic respectively, participated in the development of the design. The Germans planned to build 12 units of their own in addition to the 30 originally projected for the US Navy.

Technical problems with the hydrofoil system resulted in cost increases, and opponents of the PHM programme, pointing to the limited capabilities of the design, tried to obtain cancellation of all except the lead vessel. Congress insisted, however, on the construction of the six units for which funds had already been authorised.

The propulsion system of the PHM comprises separate diesels driving two waterjets for hullborne operation and a single gas turbine for high-speed foilborne operation.

In order to fit in with the requirements of the NATO navies the OTO-Melara 76mm gun and a Dutch fire control system were adopted. The Mk 94 GFCS on Pegasus was bought direct from HSA but the Mk 92 systems on the other five are being manufactured under licence. The original anti-ship missile armament has been doubled, with two quadruple mounts replacing the four singles first envisaged.

Below: *Pegasus* (PHM-1) at speed. She can make 40 knots on her foils. She is exceptionally well-armed for a vessel of her size, with quadruple canisters of Harpoon antiship missiles aft and an OTO-Melara 76mm (3-inch) automatic gun forward.

Amphibious Warfare Vessels

LCC
Blue Ridge

Completed:	1970-71
Names:	LCC 19 *Blue Ridge;* LCC 20 *Mount Whitney.*
Displacement:	19,290t full load.
Dimensions:	620 oa x 82 wl, 108 upper deck x 27ft. (188.5 x 25.3, 33 x 8.2m).
Propulsion:	1-shaft steam turbine; 22,000shp = 20kts.
Armament:	2 BPDMS launchers Mk 25 4 3-inch (76mm) Mk 33 (2x2).
Sensors:	*Surveillance:* SPS-48, SPS-40, SPS-10. *Fire Control:* 2 Mk 115, 2 Mk 35.

These two vessels were built to provide specialised command facilities for the amphibious fleets in the Pacific and Atlantic respectively. They replaced the more numerous war-built AGFs, which had inadequate speed for the new 20-knot amphibious squadrons. The basic design is that of the Iwo Jima-class LPH, with the former hangar occupied by command spaces, offices and accommodation. Prominent sponsons for LCPLs and ships boats project from the sides, and the broad flat upper deck is lined with a variety of surveillance, ECM/ESM and communications aerials. The LCCs

The bulk of the US Navy's Amphibious fleet was built in the late 1950s and the 1960s. It comprises ships for vertical assault employing helicopters (LHPs), and others for the landing of troops, vehicles and stores via landing craft (LPDs/LSDs) or by direct beaching (LSTs). In the 1970s a new class incorporating all but the last of these functions (the LHA) was completed. The oldest LSDs will be replaced by a new design (LSD-41), while the LPHs will be replaced by amphibious transport docks (LHDs)

are fitted with the Naval Tactical Data System (NTDS), the Amphibious Command Information System (ACIS) and the Naval Intelligence Processing System (NIPS). As completed, they had only two twin 3-inch (76mm) mountings for defence against aircraft, but two BPDMS launchers were added in 1974. Two utility helicopters are generally operated from the flight pad aft but there are no hangar or maintenance facilities.

The command facilities originally provided for a naval Commander Amphibious Task Group (CATG), a Marine Landing Force Commander (LFC), Air Control Group Commander, and their respective staffs, with accommodation for up to 200 officers and 500 enlisted men in addition to the 780-man crew.

There were plans for a third ship (AGC 21), which would have provided both fleet command and amphibious command facilities, but inadequate speed for fleet work was an important factor in her cancellation. With the demise of the Cleveland-class CGs fleet flagships in the late 1970s, however, *Blue Ridge* and *Mount Whitney* became flagships of the Seventh (W. Pacific) and the Second (Atlantic) Fleets respectively.

Below left: The Amphibious Command Ship *Blue Ridge* (LCC-19) off Hawaii. She now serves as flagship of the US 7th Fleet.

Below: An aerial view of *Blue Ridge*. The flat upper deck carries a variety of communications aerials.

LHA

Tarawa

Completed: 1976-80.
Names: LHA 1 *Tarawa;* LHA 2 *Saipan;* LHA 3 *Belleau Wood;*
LHA 4 *Nassau;* LHA 5 *Peleliu.*
Displacement: 39,300t full load.
Dimensions: 820 oa x 107 wl. 126 flight deck x 26ft
(249.9 x 32.5, 38.4 x 7.9m)
Propulsion: 2-shaft geared steam turbines; 70,000shp = 24kts.
Armament: 2 BPDMS launchers Mk 25 (2x8); 3 5-inch (127mm)
Mk 45 (3x1); 6 20mm (6x1).
Aircraft: 30 helicopters (CH-46D, CH-53D/E, AH-1T, UH-1N).
Troops: 2,000.
Landing-craft: 4 LCU, 2 LCM.
Sensors: *Surveillance:* SPS-52B, SPS-40B, SPS-10F.
Fire Control: SPG-60, SPQ-9A, 2 Mk 115.

The last in a series of ocean-going amphibious vessels ordered during the
1960s, the Tarawa-class LHAs were to combine in a single hull capabilities
which had previously required a number of separate specialist types—the

LPH, the LSD, the LPD, the LCC and the LKA (see following entries). The result is a truly massive ship with more than twice the displacement of any previous amphibious unit and with dimensions approaching those of a conventional aircraft carrier. Nine ships were originally projected, to be constructed by means of advanced modular techniques at the same Litton/Ingalls yard that built the Spruance-class destroyers. In 1971, however, with the Vietnam War drawing to a close, the order was reduced to five, resulting in some financial penalties.

The increase in size of these ships is a direct consequence of the need to provide a helicopter hangar *and* a docking-well. The hangar is located directly above the docking-well; both are 268ft in length and 78ft wide (81.6 x 23.7m), and the hangar has a 20ft (6.5m) overhead to enable the latest heavy-lift helicopters to be accommodated. In order to maximise internal capacity the ship's sides are vertical for two-thirds of its length. Hangar capacity is greater than that of the Iwo Jima class, and all the helicopters can be struck down if necessary. The customary loading would include about 12 CH-46D Sea Knights, six of the larger CH-53D Sea Stallions, four AH1▶

Below: *Tarawa* **(LHA-1), displaying her massive flight deck. Note the vertical sides of the hull, which testify to the presence of a capacious docking well in the after part of the ship.**

►SeaCobra gunships, and a couple of UH-1N utility helicopters. The Pacific based ships have operated AV-8 Harriers and have their flight decks marked out accordingly. The flight deck is served by a side lift to port and a large centre-line lift set into the stern. The latter can handle the new CH-53E Super Stallion heavy-lift helicopter.

The docking-well can accommodate four of the big LCUs, which can each lift three M-48 or M-60 tanks, or 150 tons of cargo. Two LCM-6 landing craft, which can each carry 80 troops or 34 tons of cargo, are stowed immediately aft of the island and are handled by a large crane. The docking-well is divided into two by a central support structure incorporating a conveyor belt, which runs forward onto the vehicle decks. The conveyor belt is served by a group of three cargo elevators at its forward end, and by a further two elevators in the docking-well area. The elevators bring supplies for the landing force, stored in pallets each weighing approximately one ton, up from the cargo holds deep in the ship. The pallets are transferred to the

landing-craft by one of 11 monorail cars which work overhead in the welldeck area. The after pair of elevators can also lift pallets directly to the hangar deck, where they are loaded onto transporters. An angled ramp leads from the hangar deck to the forward end of the island, enabling the transfer of pallets to the flight deck for loading onto the helicopters.

Forward of the docking-well are the vehicle decks, interconnected by a series of ramps and able to accommodate some 200 vehicles. Tanks, artillery and trucks are generally stowed at the forward end, and up to 40 LVTP-7 amphibious personnel carriers, each with a capacity of 25 troops, can be accommodated. Eight LVTPs can be launched from the welldeck simultaneously with the four big LCUs. ▶

Below: ***Tarawa*** **underway in the Gulf of Mexico. Two CH-46 Sea Knight helicopters are positioned on the flight deck, with another landing on. Note the side lift to port.**

▶ Above the vehicle decks is the accommodation deck, with berths for some 2,000 troops in addition to the 900 crew. At the forward end there is a combined acclimatisation room/gymnasium, in which humidity and temperature can be controlled to simulate the climate in which the troops will be operating. At the after end there is a large, well equipped hospital, which can if necessary expand into accommodation spaces. Separate personnel elevators serve the hospital and the accommodation area, enabling rapid transfers to and from the flight deck.

The large block superstructure houses extensive command facilities, with accommodation for both the Commander Amphibious Task Group (CATG) and the Landing Force Commander (LFC) and their respective staffs. To enable these officers to exercise full tactical control over amphibious operations the LHAs are provided with a computer-based Integrated Tactical Amphibious Warfare. Data System (ITAWDS), which keeps track of the position of troops, helicopters, vehicles, landing-craft and cargo after they leave the ship. The system also tracks the position of designated targets ashore, and aims and fires the ship's armament, which is orientated towards fire support and short-range anti-aircraft defence.

The versatility of the LHAs enables them to combine with any of the other amphibious types in the US Navy inventory. A typical PhibRon deployment would combine an LHA with an LPD and one/two LSTs. The only major limitation of the design appears to be the inability to accommodate more than one of the new air-cushion landing-craft (AALC) because of the layout of the docking-well.

Right: *Nassau* (LHA-4) running sea trials in 1979. Vehicles can transfer from the hangar area to the flight deck via ramps.

Below: The stern of an LHA of the Tarawa class. The heavy stern doors give access to the large docking well.

Tarawa (LHA-1).

LPH
Iwo Jima

Completed:	1961-70.
Names:	LPH 2 *Iwo Jima;* LPH 3 *Okinawa;* LPH 7 *Guadalcanal;* LPH 9 *Guam;* LPH 10 *Tripoli;* LPH 11 *New Orleans;* LPH 12 *Inchon.*
Displacement:	17,000t light; 18,300t full load.
Dimensions:	592 oa x 84 wl, 112 flight deck x 26ft (180 x 25.6, 34.1 x 7.9m).
Propulsion:	1-shaft geared steam turbine; 22,000shp = 20kts.
Armament:	2 BPDMS launchers Mk 25 (2x8); 4 3-inch (76mm) Mk 33 (2x2).
Aircraft:	25 helicopters (CH-46D, CH-53D, AH-1T, UH-1N).
Sensors:	*Surveillance:* SPS-40, SPS-10. *Fire Control:* 2 Mk 115.

The US Marine Corps had initiated experiments in helicopter assault techniques as early as 1948, and in 1955 the former escort carrier *Thetis Bay* underwent a major conversion to test the "vertical envelopment" concept. Two years later the escort carrier *Block Island* was taken in hand for a similar conversion, but this was halted as an economy measure. The concept proved such a success, however, that the Navy embarked on a programme of new purpose-built helicopter carriers, which became the Iwo Jima class. As an interim measure three Essex-class carriers were modified for helicopter operations and reclassified as amphibious assault ships. These and the converted escort carriers took the "missing" LPH numbers in the series until their demise in the late 1960s.

As the ships of the Iwo Jima class were amphibious—not fleet—units, many of the refinements associated with first-line vessels were dispensed with in the interests of economy. The design was based on a mercantile hull with a one-shaft propulsion system capable of a sustained 20 knots. A large central box hangar was adopted with 20ft (6.5m) clearance, a capacity of about 20 helicopters, and with side lifts disposed *en echelon* at either end. The lifts, 50ft x 34ft (15.2 x 10.4m) and with a capacity of 44-50,000lb (20-22,725kg), can be folded upwards to close the hangar openings. Fore and aft of the hangar there is accommodation for a Marine battalion, and the ships have a well equipped hospital with 300 beds. ▶

Right: *Tripoli* (LPH-10) entering Subic Bay after mine-clearance operations off North Vietnam employing RH-53 helicopters.

Below: *Guadalcanal* (LPH-7) in the Atlantic. The helicopters are CH-46 Sea Knights and CH-53 Sea Stallions.

► The flight deck is marked out with five helo spots along the port side and two to starboard. No catapults or arresting wires are fitted. Helicopter assault operations are directed from a specialised Command Centre housed in the island. The radar outfit is austere: air search and aircraft control antennae are fitted but these ships do not have the large 3-D antennae of the first-line carriers.

As completed, the *Iwo Jima* class had two twin 3-inch (76mm) mountings at the forward end of the island and two further mountings just below the after end of the flight deck. Between 1970 and 1974 the after port mounting and the first of the two forward mountings were replaced by BPDMS launchers.

From 1972 until 1974 *Guam* was test ship for the Sea Control Ship concept. In this role she operated ASW helicopters and a squadron of marine AV-8 Harrier aircraft. A new tactical command centre was installed and carrier-controlled approach (CCA) radar fitted. Although operations with the Harrier were particularly successful and have been continued on a routine basis in the larger Tarawa-class LHAs, the Sea Control Ship did not find favour with the US Navy, and *Guam* has since reverted to her assault ship role.

The Iwo Jima class generally operates in conjunction with ships of the LPD, LSD and LST types. Although *Inchon,* the last ship built, carries two LCVPs, the LPHs have no significant ability to land troops, equipment and supplies by any means other than by helicopter. The troops are therefore lightly equipped and would be employed as an advance echelon, landing behind the enemy's shore defences and relying on a follow-up frontal assault staged by more heavily equipped units brought ashore by landing-craft from the other vessels in the squadron.

Above: A Marine AV-8A Harrier STOVL aircraft on the after aircraft elevator of an assault ship of the Iwo Jima class.

Below: Bow view of *Guam* (LPH-9). A BPDMS launcher is visible immediately forward of the island.

LPD
Austin

Completed: 1965-71.
Names: LPD 4 *Austin;* LPD 5 *Ogden;* LPD 6 *Duluth;*
LPD 7 *Cleveland;* LPD 8 *Dubuque;* LPD 9 *Denver;*
LPD 10 *Juneau;* LPD 12 *Shreveport.*
LPD 13 *Nashville;* LPD 14 *Trenton;* LPD 15 *Ponce.*
Displacement: 10,000t light; 16,900t full load.
Dimensions: 570 oa x 84 x 23ft (173.3 x 25.6 x 7m).
Propulsion: 2-shaft geared steam turbines; 24,000shp = 20kts.
Armament: 4 3-inch (76mm) Mk 33 (2x2).
Aircraft: up to 6 CH-46D (see notes).
Troops: 840-930.
Landing-craft: 1 LCU, 3 LCM-6.
Sensors: *Surveillance:* SPS-40, SPS-10.

The Austin class is a development of the Raleigh class, which instituted th
LPD concept. The major modification was the insertion of a 50ft (15.2m) hu
section forward of the docking-well. This resulted in a significant increase i
vehicle space and cargo capacity (3,900 tons compared to only 2,000 ton
for the Raleigh class). The additional length available for flying operation
enabled a large telescopic hangar to be worked in immediately aft of th
superstructure, giving these ships the maintenance facilities which wer
lacking in the Raleigh class. The main body of the hangar is 58-64ft (17.7
19.5m) in length and 19-24ft (5.8-7.3m) in width; the telescopic extensio
increases overall length to 80ft (24.4m).

Troop accommodation and docking-well capacity are identical to those c
Raleigh, except that LPD 7-13 are configured as amphibious squadro
(PhibRon) flagships and can accommodate only 840 troops. The latter ship
can be outwardly distinguished by their extra bridge level.

Two of the original four twin 3-inch (76mm) mountings, together with a
fire-control radars, were removed in the late 1970s. The class is schedule
to receive two Phalanx CIWS guns as soon as these become available.

In October 1980 *Coronado* was temporarily redesignated AGF as
replacement for the Command ship *La Salle* (see Raleigh class), which wa
undergoing refit, but has since remained in that role.

Below: *Coronado* (LPD-11) in company with an Iwo Jima class assault ship (*Coronado* is now an AGF).

Bottom: *Juneau* (LPD-10) with CH-46 Sea Knight and CH-53 Sea Stallion assault helicopters on her flight deck.

LPD
Raleigh

Completed: 1962-63.
Names: LPD 1 *Raleigh;* LPD 2 *Vancouver.*
Displacement: 8,040t light; 13,900t full load.
Dimensions: 522 oa x 84 x 21ft (158.4 x 25.6 x 6.4m).
Propulsion: 2-shaft geared steam turbines; 24,000shp = 20kts.
Armament: 6 3-inch (76mm) Mk 33 (3x2).
Troops: 930.
Landing-craft: 1 LCU, 3 LCM-6.
Sensors: *Surveillance:* SPS-40, SPS-10.

Raleigh was the prototype of a new amphibious class employing the
"balanced load" concept. Previous amphibious task forces carried troops in
Attack Transports (APA), cargo in Attack Cargo Ships (AKA), and landing-
craft and tanks in Dock Landing Ships (LSD). The basic principle of the
"balanced force" concept is that these three capabilities are combined in a
single hull. The docking-well in the Raleigh class therefore occupies only the
after part of the ship, while forward of the well there are vehicle decks, cargo

276

holds and substantial troop accommodation decks. The well itself measures 168ft x 50ft (51.2 x 15.2m) – less than half the length of the docking-well in the most modern LSDs – and is served overhead by six monorail cars, which load cargo into the awaiting landing-craft. The docking-well can accommodate one LCU and three LCM-6s, or four LCM-8s. Two further LCM-6s and four LCPLs are carried at the after end of the superstructure, and are handled by a large crane.

The docking-well is covered by a helicopter landing platform, which can receive any of the major types of helicopter in service with the Marines. The Raleigh class, unlike the later Austins, has no hangar or maintenance facilities and therefore relies on an accompanying LPH or LHA to provide helicopters for vertical assault operations. The flight deck can also be used as additional vehicle space, and there are ramps connecting the flight deck, the vehicle decks and the docking-well.

A third ship of the class, *La Salle*, serves as a Command Ship for the US Middle East Force. She was specially converted for this role and is now numbered AGF 3.

Below: *Vancouver* (LPD-2), with marines on her flight deck. No hangar or maintenance facilities for helicopters are provided.

LSD 41

Completed:	1984 onwards.
Name:	LSD 41 *Whidbey Island,* LSD 42 *Germantown,* plus one building, 3 ordered.
Displacement:	11,140t light; 15,745t full load.
Dimensions:	609 oa x 84 x 20ft (185.6 x 25.6 x 5.9m).
Propulsion:	2-shaft diesels; 4 SEMT-Pielstick 16-cyl.; 34,000shp = 20k
Armament:	2 Phalanx CIWS
Troops:	340.
Landing-craft:	4 LCAC.
Sensors:	*Surveillance:* SPS-55.

The LSD 41 design was prepared in the mid-1970s as a replacement for the eight Thomaston-class ships. The project was subjected to delaying tactics by the Carter Administration pending a reassessment of the Navy's requirement for amphibious lift. In 1981, however, pressure from Congress compelled the Administration to order the prototype for the class, and nine follow-on ships are included in the first 5-year programme of the Reagan Administration.

Although not a particularly innovative design, the LSD 41 shows a number

f improvements over its immediate predecessor, the Anchorage class. The large flight deck aft extends right to the stern, and is strong enough to accept he powerful CH-53E Super Stallion cargo-carrying helicopter now entering service with the Marines. The docking-well is identical in width to that of earlier LSDs but is 10ft (3m) longer than that of *Anchorage*. It is designed to accommodate four of the new air-cushion landing-craft (LCAC), with which it is intended to replace all conventional LCU-type landing-craft in the late 1980s. The two experimental craft at present being evaluated, the Jeff-A and Jeff-B AALCs, are 90ft (30.2m) and 87ft (26.4m) long respectively, and 47-8ft (14.3-14.6m) wide. Both have bow and stern ramps and can carry a single M-60 tank, with an alternative loading of six towed howitzers and trucks or 120,000lb (54,545kg) of cargo. This is a lower lift capacity than the conventional LCU, but the LCAC will compensate for this by carrying its load to the beach at a speed of 50 knots.

The LSD 41 is being built by modular construction techniques, and differs from previous amphibious vessels in adopting diesel propulsion in place of steam turbines. Four SEMT-Pielstick diesels manufactured under licence, are being installed in two independent paired units.

Below: Artist's impression showing how the new dock landing ships will be able to operate four air cushion landing craft, each capable of lifting an M60 tank or 120,000lb of cargo.

LSD

Anchorage

Completed: 1969-72.
Names: LSD 36 *Anchorage;* LSD 37 Portland; LSD 38 *Pensacola;* LSD 39 *Mount Vernon;* LSD 40 *Fort Fisher.*
Displacement: 8,600t light; 13,700t full load.
Dimensions: 553 oa x 84 x 19ft (168.6 x 25.6 x 5.6m).
Propulsion: 2-shaft geared steam turbines; 24,000shp = 20kts.
Armament: 6 3-inch (76mm) Mk 33 (3x2).
Troops: 375
Landing-craft: 3 LCU, 1 LCM-6.
Sensors: *Surveillance:* SPS-40, SPS-10.

The five dock landing ships of the Anchorage class were among the last units to be completed in the large amphibious ship programme of the 1960s. In spite of the advent of the LPD with its "balanced load" concept, there was still a requirement for LSDs to carry additional landing-craft to the assault area. The Anchorage class was therefore built to replace the ageing war-built vessels, which had inadequate speed for the new PhibRons. It is a

development of the Thomaston class, from which its ships can be distinguished by their tripod mast and their longer hull.

The docking-well measures 430ft by 50ft (131 x 15.2m)—an increase of 30ft (9m) in length over the Thomastons—and can accommodate three of the big LCUs or nine LCM-8s, with an alternative loading of 50 LVTP-7s. There is space on deck for a single LCM-6, and an LCPL and an LCVP are carried on davits. As in the Thomaston class, there are vehicle decks above the docking-well amidships, served by two 50-ton cranes. The Anchorage class was designed to transport up to 30 helicopters, and there is a removable flight deck aft for heavy-lift cargo helicopters.

The sensor outfit and armament are on a par with the contemporary LPDs of the Austin class (which are described on pages 114-115). Four twin 3-inch (76mm) mountings were originally fitted, but one was removed, together with all fire control radars, in the late 1970s. The mountings forward of the bridge are enclosed in GRP shields. Two Phalanx CIWS guns will be fitted when the mounting becomes available.

Below: *Pensacola* (LSD-38) with an LCU entering the large docking well. The flight deck is a temporary structure, and can be easily removed if required.

Thomaston

Completed:	1954-7.
Names:	LSD 28 *Thomaston;* LSD 29 *Plymouth Rock;* LSD 30 *Fort Snelling;* LSD 31 *Point Defiance;* LSD 32 *Spiegel Grove;* LSD 33 *Alamo;* LSD 34 *Hermitage;* LSD 35 *Monticello.*
Displacement:	6,880t light; 11,270-12,150t full load.
Dimensions:	510 oa x 84 x 19ft (155.5 x 25.6 x 5.8m).
Propulsion:	2-shaft geared steam turbines; 24,000shp = 22.5kts.
Armament:	6 3-inch (76mm) Mk 33 (3x2).
Troops:	340.
Landing-craft	3 LCU.
Sensors:	*Surveillance:* SPS-6, SPS-10.

The Thomaston class was the first postwar LSD design and was a result of the renewed interest in amphibious operations during the Korean War. The basic conception of the wartime LSD was retained but the Thomaston class incorporated a number of improvements. The ships have a large, more seaworthy hull, with greater sheer and flare in the bows, and can steam at a sustained speed of over 20 knots compared to only 15 knots for their war-built counterparts. The docking-well, which measures 391ft by 48ft (119.1 x 14.6m), is wider and more than half as long again, and can accommodate three LCUs or nine LCM-8s. There is a vehicle deck amidships but no access to the docking-well. Cargo and vehicles are therefore preloaded in the landing-craft or handled by the two 50-ton cranes. The after part of the docking-well is covered by a short removable platform for cargo-carrying helicopters, but there are no hangar or maintenance facilities.

As completed, the Thomaston class were armed with eight twin 3-inch (76mm) mountings but five of these, together with all fire-control radars, have since been removed.

In 1980 *Spiegel Grove* conducted evaluation trials for the Jeff-B aircushion landing-craft (AALC). Three such craft could be accommodated in the docking-well of the Thomaston class, but the class is now being placed in reserve.

**bove: An LCU is about to enter the docking well of an LSD
f the Thomaston class. Three LCUs can operate from the well.**

**eft: The dock landing ship *Hermitage* (LSD-34). These ships
ill shortly be replaced by the new LSD-41 class.**

LST
Newport

Completed: 1969-72.
Names: LST 1179 *Newport;* LST 1180 *Maniwotoc;*
LST 1181 *Sumter;* LST 1182 *Fresno;* LST 1183 *Peoria;*
LST 1184 *Frederick;* LST 1185 *Schenectady;*
LST 1186 *Cayuga;* LST 1187 *Tuscaloosa;*
LST 1188 *Saginaw;* LST 1189 *San Bernadino;*
LST 1190 *Boulder;* LST *1191 Racine;*
LST 1192 *Spartanburg County;* LST 1193 *Fairfax County;*
LST 1194 *La Moure County;* LST 1195 *Barbour County;*
LST 1196 *Harlan County;* LST 1197 *Barnstable County;*
LST 1198 *Bristol County.*
Displacement: 8,342t full load.
Dimensions: 562 oa x 70 x 18ft (171.3 x 21.2 x 5.3m).
Propulsion: 2-shaft diesels; 6 GM (1179-81)/Alco (others);
16,500bhp = 20kts.
Armament: 4 3-inch (76mm) Mk 33 (2x2).
Sensors: *Surveillance:* SPS-10.

The twenty LSTs of the Newport class are larger and faster than the war-buil
vessels they replaced. In order to match the 20-knot speed of the othe
amphibious units built during the 1960s the traditional bow doors were
suppressed in favour of a 112ft (34m) ramp which is lowered over the bow
of the ship between twin fixed derrick arms. This arrangement also allowed
for an increase in draught in line with the increase in displacement.

**Right: Amphibious personnel carriers (LVTP-7) return to the tan
landing ship *Newport* (LST-1179) during an Atlantic exercise.**

**Below: A tank landing ship of the Newport class unloads
vehicles via a bow ramp slung between its massive "jaws".**

There is a large integral flight deck aft for utility helicopters. Pontoons can be slung on either side of the flight deck for use in landing operations. Each can carry an MBT and they can be mated with the stern gate. They are handled by twin derricks located immediately aft of the staggered funnel uptakes.

Below decks there is a total parking area of 19,000sq ft (5,300m²) for a cargo capacity of 500 tons of vehicles. The forecastle is connected to the vehicle deck by a ramp and to the flight deck by a passageway through the superstructure. A through-hull bow thruster is provided to maintain the ship's position while unloading offshore.

The twin 3-inch (76mm) gun mounts, located at the after end of the superstructure will be replaced by Phalanx CIWS guns when these become available.

In 1980 *Boulder* and *Racine* were assigned to the Naval Reserve Force.

Replenishment Ships

Kilauea

Completed:	1968-72.
Names:	T-AE 26 *Kilauea;* AE 27 *Butte;* AE 28 *Santa Barbara;* AE 29 *Mount Hood;* AE 33 *Shasta;* AE 34 *Mount Baker;* AE 35 *Kiska.*
Displacement:	20,500t full load.
Dimensions:	564 oa x 81 x 26ft (171.9 x 24.7 x 7.8m).
Propulsion:	1-shaft geared steam turbine; 22,000shp = 20kts.
Armament:	4 3-inch (76mm) Mk 33 (2x2)—not in T-AE 26.
Helicopters:	2 UH-46 Sea Knight.
Sensors:	*Surveillance:* SPS-10.

The eight ammunition ships of the Kilauea class belong to the generation of
underway replenishment vessels constructed during the 1960s. They are
similar in size to the combat stores ships of the Mars class, but specialise in the

No other navy in the world can approach the underway replenishment capability of the US Fleet. The requirement for regular distant deployments far from the United States has brought with it the need for vast numbers of specialist auxiliary vessels to supply the fleet with oil, munitions and combat stores. Until recently these ships were manned by naval personnel, but a shortage of enlisted men has led to the transfer of a number of vessels to the civilian-manned Military Sealift Command (MSC).

---

transfer of missiles and other munitions. Improvements in layout include the merging of the bridge and hangar structures into a single block, leaving the entire forward and midships areas clear for transfer operations. The central section of the hull is a deck higher than that of the Mars class, providing the additional internal volume necessary for the stowage of missiles. Cargo capacity is approximately 6,500 tons. Four transfer stations are provided on either side forward of the bridge, and there is a further pair abreast the funnel and another at the after end of the hangar. The second and sixth pairs of transfer stations are fitted with booms in addition to the customary constant-tension gear. Fin stabilisers ensure a steady platform for the safe transfer of the ships' delicate cargo.

The twin hangars are 50ft long and 16-18ft (15.2 x 4.7-5.3m) wide and can accommodate two UH-46 VERTREP helicopters. All ships initially had two twin 3-inch (76mm) mounts and Mk 56 GFCS on the hangar roof but these were removed in the last 1970s. Two Phalanx CIWS guns have been fitted in AE-32 and will also be fitted in AE-27 to -29.

Below: The ammunition ship *Kilauea* (AE-26) underway.

AE
Suribachi

Completed: 1956-9.
Names: AE 21 *Suribachi;* AE 22 *Mauna Kea;* AE 23 *Nitro;*
AE 24 *Pyro;* AE 25 *Haleakala.*
Displacement: 10,000t standard; 17,500t full load.
Dimensions: 512 oa x 72 x 29ft (156.1 x 21.9 x 8.8m).
Propulsion: 1-shaft geared steam turbine; 16,000shp = 20.6kts.
Armament: 4 3-inch (76mm) Mk 33 (2x2).
Sensors: SPS-10.

Built from the keel up as Navy ships, the Suribachi class were among the first
specialised underway replenishment vessels built postwar. As completed,
they were equipped with conventional mercantile kingposts and booms for
the transfer of bombs and other munitions. Elevators were provided for the
internal handling of ammunition and explosives, and the design incorporated
air conditioning and the latest methods of stowage. A sixth ship was to have
been built under the FY 1959 Programme but was cancelled.

Soon after completion, all five ships underwent an extensive modernisation
to enable them to handle the new surface-to-air missiles. Three holds were
rigged for the stowage of missiles up to the size of Talos, and fully
mechanised handling facilities were provided to move the missiles to the
transfer stations. The Fast Automatic Shuttle Transfer (FAST) system
pioneered by the combat stores ships of the Mars class was installed,
resulting in safer missile handling and reduced transfer times. The Suribachi
class now has three kingposts, the first and third of which have constant-
tension transfer stations on either side.

As completed, these ships had two superfiring twin 3-inch mountings on the forecastle and a similar arrangement aft. Mk 56 and Mk 63 GFCS were provided. When the ships underwent modernisation in the mid-1960s, the after mountings and the fire-control systems were removed and a large flight deck for VERTREP helicopters was fitted above the stern. In some units the forward guns have been relocated side by side and given glass reinforced plastics (GRP) gunshields.

Below: The ammunition ship *Suribachi* (AE-21) one of the first underway replenishment vessels built postwar for the US Navy.

Bottom: *Suribachi* and her sisters were extensively modernised during the 1960s. Note the large helicopter platform aft.

AFS
Mars

Completed: 1963-70.
Names: AFS 1 *Mars;* AFS 2 *Sylvania;* AFS 3 *Niagara Falls;*
AFS 4 *White Plains;* AFS 5 *Concord;* AFS 6 *San Diego;*
AFS 7 *San Jose.*
Displacement: 16,500t full load.
Dimensions: 581 oa x 79 x 24ft (177.1 x 24.1 x 7.3m).
Propulsion: 1-shaft geared steam turbine; 22,000shp = 20kts.
Armament: 4 3-inch (76mm) Mk 33 (2x2).
Helicopters: 2 UH-46 Sea Knight.
Sensors: *Surveillance:* SPS-10.

The seven combat stores ships of the Mars class were the first of a new
generation of under-way replenishment vessels completed during the 1960
to support carrier task force deployments. They combine the functions o
store ships (AF), stores-issue ships (AKS), and aviation store ships (AVS
Unlike the contemporary AOEs of the Sacramento class, however, the
carry no fuel oil or other liquid cargo.

They were the first ships to incorporate the Fast Automatic Shuttle Transfer system (FAST), which revolutionised the handling of stores and munitions. Five "M" frames replace the conventional kingposts and booms of previous vessels and these have automatic tensioning devices to keep the transfer lines taut while replenishing. Cargo capacity is 7,000 tons in five cargo holds. Computers provide up-to-the-minute data on stock status, with the data displayed on closed-circuit television (CCTV). The propulsion system is also fully automated and can be controlled from the bridge to ensure quick response during transfer operations. The ships normally steam on only two boilers, with the third shut down for maintenance.

Twin helicopter hangars, 47-51ft long and 16-23ft wide (143-15.5 x 4.9-7m) are provided for VERTREP helicopters, enabling the ships to undertake vertical replenishment operations within a task force spread over a wide area.

As completed, the Mars class had four twin 3-inch mounts and the Mk 56 GFCS. Two of the twin mounts and the fire-control system were removed in the late 1970s.

Below: The combat stores ship *Mars* (AFS-1) underway off Hawaii. They were the first US ships to have the FAST transfer system.

AO
Cimarron

Completed: 1980 onwards.
Names: AO 177 *Cimarron;* AO 178 *Monongahela;*
AO 179 *Merrimack;* AO 180 *Willamette;* T-AO 186 *Platte.*
Displacement: 27,500t full load.
Dimensions: 592 oa x 88 x 34ft (178 x 26.8 x 10.2m).
Propulsion: 1-shaft geared steam turbine; 24,000shp = 20kts.
Armament: 2 Phalanx CIWS (not in T-AO 186).

The new fleet oilers of the Cimarron class are the first ships in that category
to be completed since the mid-1950s. Large numbers are planned as
replacements for the war-built oilers of the Mispillion and Ashtaboula
classes, which, although extensively modernised in the 1960s, are now

292

more than 35 years old. The US Navy has a requirement for 21 fleet oilers, and this figure can only be achieved by new construction on a massive scale.

The Cimarron-class oilers are significantly smaller than previous vessels. They have been deliberately "sized" to provide two complete refuellings of a fossil-fuelled carrier and six to eight escorts, and have a total capacity of 120,000 barrels of fuel oil. There are four replenishment stations to port and three to starboard, and there is a large platform aft for VERTREP helicopters, but no hangar or support facilities are provided.

These ships have a distinctive elliptical underwater bow for improved seakeeping. Unlike previous AOs, they have a single superstructure block aft incorporating the bridge. Originally it was envisaged that they would have a crew of only 135, but this was increased to 181 in order to provide sufficient personnel to carry out maintenance on prolonged deployments.

Plans for a further 17 were cancelled in 1979, although the US Navy requirement remains.

Left: The oiler *Cimarron* (AO-177) on sea trials in the Gulf of Mexico following her completion in 1980.

Below: *Cimarron* is smaller than previous US Navy oilers. Note the block bridge structure and the helicopter landing pad aft.

Bottom: The rig is biased towards replenishment operations on the port side to facilitate the refuelling of carriers.

AO
Neosho

Completed: 1954-56.
Names: T-AO 143 *Neosho;* T-AO 144 *Mississinewa;*
T-AO 145 *Hassayampa;* T-AO 146 *Kawishiwi;*
T-AO 147 *Truckee;* T-AO 148 *Ponchatoula.*
Displacement: 11,600t light; 38-40,000t full load.
Dimensions: 655 oa x 86 x 35ft (199.6 x 26.2 x 10.7m).
Propulsion: 2-shaft geared steam turbines; 28,000shp = 20kts.
Armament: removed.
Sensors: *Surveillance:* SPS-10.

These were the first major under-way replenishment vessels to be built
postwar, and they are the largest fleet oilers in the US Navy. They have a
capacity of approximately 180,000 barrels of fuel oil, and have been fitted
since the 1960s with a modern rig for abeam replenishment. There is a
separate bridge structure with a single pole mast and twin booms forward.

nd there are three kingposts and a second pole mast between the bridge nd the after structure. The ships of the Neosho class were designed to serve s flagships of the service forces, and were given accommodation for the ervice Force Commander and his staff.

As completed, they carried a powerful defensive battery of anti-aircraft uns, comprising single 5-inch (127mm) fore and aft, two twin 3-inch 76mm) mounts on the forecastle and four twin mounts at the corners of the fter superstructure. The 5-inch guns were removed in 1960 and three hips—Neosho, Mississinewa and Truckee—had helicopter platforms fitted bove the stern. The number of 3-inch weapons was steadily reduced and hey were removed altogether when the ships were transferred to the Military Sealift Comand (MSC) from 1976 onwards. The change in status as not affected their operational deployment in support of the carrier battle roups and amphibious squadrons, but they are now manned by civilians, ot regular Navy personnel.

Below: The oiler *Neosho* (AO-143) underway. These ships were he first major underway replenishment vessels built postwar.

AO
Mispillion/Ashtaboula

Completed:	1943-6.
Names:	T-AO 105 *Mispillion;* T-AO 106 *Navasota;*
	T-AO 107 *Passumpsic;* T-AO 108 *Pawcatuck;*
	T-AO 109 *Waccamaw;* AO 51 *Ashtaboula;*
	AO 98 *Caloosahatchee;* AO 99 *Canisteo.*
Displacement:	34,750t full load.
Dimensions:	646/644 oa x 75 x 36/32ft (196.9/196.3 x 22.9 x
	10.8/9.6m).
Propulsion:	2-shaft geared steam turbines; 13,500shp = 16-18kts.
Armament:	2 3-inch (76mm) Mk 26 (2x1) in AO only.
Sensors:	*Surveillance:* SPS-10.

These ships were originally of the war-built Maritime Administration
T3–S2–A1 type but were extensively modernised during the mid-1960s.
Modernisation included a concept known as ''jumboisation'' in which a 91-
3ft (28m) midships section was inserted, increasing cargo capacity by 50
per cent. A completely new transfer rig was installed. The five ships of the
Mispillion class have four fuelling stations to port and two to starboard.

There is a kingpost aft with constant-tension stations for the transfer of dry stores, and a large flight deck is marked out forward for the operation of VERTREP helicopters. Cargo capacity is 150,000 barrels of fuel oil.

The three ships of the Ashtaboula class underwent a different modification. The rig amidships is similar to that of the Mispillion class except that there is a third fuelling station to starboard. Forward, however, the helicopter landing area has been replaced by a second kingpost with constant-tension transfer stations, and there is a limited capacity for "dry" cargo. Besides fuel oil – 143,000 barrels – they can carry 175 tons of munitions, 250 tons of dry stores and 100 tons of refrigerated stores.

The original armament comprised 5-inch (127mm), 3-inch (76mm) and 40mm guns but these have since been progressively removed. The five ships of the Mispillion class, which were transferred to MSC in 1974-5, are now unarmed. The Ashtaboula class, which is still Navy-manned, has only two single 3-inch guns remaining.

Although virtually rebuilt in the 1960s, these ships are now over 35 years old and they are slow by modern standards. They will have to be replaced in the near future.

Below: The oiler *Ashtaboula* (AO-51) with the Ro-Ro cargo ship *Mercury* (TAKR-10) at Subic Bay in the Philippines.

AOE

Sacramento

Completed: 1964-70.
Names: AOE 1 *Sacramento;* AOE 2 *Camden;* AOE 3 *Seattle;* AOE 4 *Detroit.*
Displacement: 19,200t light; 53,600t full load.
Dimensions: 793 oa x 107 x 39ft (241.7 x 32.6 x 12m).
Propulsion: 2-shaft geared steam turbines; 100,000shp = 26kts.
Armament: 1 NATO Sea Sparrow launcher Mk 29 (1x8);
4 3-inch (76mm). Mk 33 (2x2).
Helicopters: 2 UH-46 Sea Knight.
Sensors: *Surveillance:* SPS-40, SPS-10.
Fire Control: 2 Mk 91.

The world's largest under-way replenishment vessels, the fast combat support ships of the Sacramento class are designed to supply a carrier battle group with all its basic needs. They combine the functions of fleet oilers (AO), ammunition ships (AE), stores ships (AF) and cargo ships (AK). They have exceptionally high speed for their type to enable them to keep pace with fleet units. The machinery installed in *Sacramento* and *Camden* is from the cancelled battleship *Kentucky* (BB 66).

Cargo capacity is 177,000 barrels of fuel oil, 2,150 tons of munitions, 250 tons of dry stores and 250 tons of refrigerated stores. The Sacramento

lass was one of the first two designs to employ the FAST automatic transfer ystem. There are four refuelling stations to port and two to starboard – an rrangement which reflects their primary mission in support of the arriers – and there are three constant-tension transfer stations for dry tores to port and four to starboard. Aft there is a large helicopter deck with three-bay hangar for VERTREP helicopters; each hangar bay is 47-52ft ong and 17-19ft wide (14.3-15.8 x 5.2-5.8m).

As completed, these ships each had four twin 3-inch (76mm) mounts, ogether with Mk 56 GFCS. The forward pair of mountings and the fire-ontrol systems were removed in the mid-1970s and have now been eplaced by a NATO Sea Sparrow launcher with twin Mk 91 fire-control ystems side by side atop the bridge. Two Phalanx CIWS guns are to be tted.

The Sacramento class proved very expensive, and a fifth ship planned for Y 1968 was not built. Instead the smaller and less costly Wichita-class AOR vas developed as an alternative. The requirement for a twelfth AOE/AOR-ype vessel to support the twelfth carrier battle group remains, however. A fth AOE was again planned for the FY 1980 Programme, but this, together vith another planned in FY 1984, did not materialise.

Below: The first combat support ship Camden (AOE-2). These ships were built to accompany the US Navy's carrier battle groups. They proved very costly and were eventually succeeded by the slower AOR type.

AOR

Wichita

Completed: 1969-75.
Names: AOR 1 *Wichita;* AOR 2 *Milwaukee;* AOR 3 *Kansas City;*
AOR 4 *Savannah;* AOR 5 *Wabash;* AOR 6 *Kalamazoo;*
AOR 7 *Roanoke.*
Displacement: 38,100t full load.
Dimensions: 659 oa x 96 x 33ft (206.9 x 29.3 x 10.2m).
Propulsion: 2-shaft geared steam turbines; 32,000shp = 20kts.
Armament: 1 NATO Sea Sparrow launcher Mk 29 (1x8) in AOR 3,7;
4 3-inch (76mm) Mk 33 (2x2) in AOR 1, 4, 6;
2/4 20mm (2/4x1) in AOR 2,7.
Helicopters: 2 UH-46 Sea Knights in AOR 2-3,5,7.
Sensors: *Surveillance:* SPS-10.
Fire Control: 2 Mk 91 in AOR 3,7.

The Wichita-class replenishment oilers, like the fast combat support ships of
the Sacramento class, are designed for the support of the carrier battle
groups. They are smaller vessels with much-reduced speed but have proved
to be very successful ships. They carry a similar quantity of fuel oil to the
larger AOEs but have only a limited capacity for provisions and munitions.
This is reflected in their rig; there are four fuelling stations to port and three
to starboard, but only two positions on either beam for the transfer of dry
stores. Cargo capacity is 160,000 barrels of fuel, 600 tons of munitions,
200 tons of dry stores and 100 tons of refrigerated stores.

AOR 1-6 were completed with two twin 3-inch (76mm) mountings above
the flight deck aft, together with the Mk 56 GFCS. The last ship, however,
was completed with a double helicopter hangar built around the funnel, and

all other ships are now being similarly fitted. The hangars are 62·3ft long and 19·21ft wide (18·19.2 × 5.8-6.4m). The guns are being replaced by a NATO Sea Sparrow launcher at the after end of the hangar, with a pair of Mk 91 fire control radars atop twin lattice masts forward of the funnel. An interim armament of 20mm guns has been fitted in some ships without 3-inch guns. All will eventually receive two Phalanx CIWS guns.

The Wichita class normally operates on only two boilers while maintenance is carried out on the third. The ships of the class can sustain 18 knots while operating in this mode.

Below: The replenishment oiler *Wichita* (AOR-1). Although slower than the AOEs these have proved to be very successful ships.

Bottom: *Wichita* underway. The twin 3-inch guns are being re-placed by a large double helicopter hangar and missile launchers.

Submarines

Ohio Class

Completed:	1979 onwards.
Names:	SSBN 726 *Ohio;* SSBN 727 *Michigan;* SSBN 728 *Florida;* SSBN 729 *Georgia;* SSBN 730 *Henry M Jackson;* SSBN 731 *Alabama;* SSBN 732 *Alaska;* SSBN 733 *Nevada;* SSBN 734 onwards not yet named.
Displacement:	16,600t surfaced; 18,700t submerged.
Dimensions:	560ft oa x 42ft x 35.5ft (170.7x12.8x10.8m).
Propulsion:	Single shaft nuclear, 60,000shp=30kts dived.
Armament:	24 Trident I (C-4) SLBM; 4 21in (533mm) torpedo tubes.
Sensors:	Sonar: BQQ 5 (passive only).

While the programme of upgrading the later Polaris SLBM submarines to carry Poseidon was under way in the early 1970s, development of an entirely new missile was started. This was to have a much longer range— 4,400 miles (7,100km)—which in turn necessitated a new and much larger submarine to carry it. The missile, Trident 1, is now in service on converted Lafayette class SSBNs, while the first of the submarines purpose-built for Trident, USS *Ohio*, joined the fleet in 1982. Initially Congress baulked at the immense cost of the new system—but then the Soviet Navy introduced its own long-range SLBM, the 4,200 mile (6,760km) SS-N-8, in the Delta class. This was followed in 1976 by the firing of the first of the increased

Submarines, both for strategic nuclear warfare and conventional warfare, represent a major part of the United States Navy's plans for an inventory of 600 deployable battle force warships, which include between 20 and 40 SSBNs and 100 SSNs for service through the 1990s. These vessels are described in detail in two companion 'Illustrated Guides' to Submarines and Sub-Hunters. However, a few representative types are described here.

---

range SS-N18s (4,846 miles, 7,800km). US reaction was to speed up the Trident programme, and the first of the Ohio class submarines was laid down on 10 April 1976. Eight are now in commission with a further sixteen building or currently planned. Trident II (D-5) will be fitted from the ninth of class onwards.

The eventual number of Trident-carrying SSBNs depends on two principal factors. The first is the outcome of the new round of Strategic Arms Limitation Talks (or Strategic Arms Reduction Talks) between the Reagan administration and the USSR, which will then, of course, have to be ratified by the US Congress. Any such agreement would presumably include, as in SALT-II proposals, the maximum numbers of SLBMs and launch platforms that each super-power was prepared to permit the other to possess. The other factor is the development of new types of long-range cruise missiles, some of which can be used in a strategic role even when launched from a standard 21in (533mm) submerged torpedo tube. This, and similar progress in other fields, may restrict the need for large numbers of SLBMs in huge and very expensive SSBNs. The great advantage, however, of the current generation of very long-range SLBMs is that they can be launched from American or Soviet home waters, thus making detection of the launch platform and destruction of either the submarine or the missiles launched from it extremely difficult, if not virtually impossible.

Below: Lowering a Trident 1 C-4 SLBM into a launch tube of USS *Ohio*, first of a projected class of 24 SSBNs, though the eventual total remains in doubt. By 1986 the unit cost of each boat had risen to $1,755 million.

SSBN

Lafayette Class/Franklin Class

Completed: 1962-1966.
Names: SSBN 616 to SSBN 659.
Displacement: 7,250t surfaced; 8,250t submerged.
Dimensions: 425ft oa x 33ft x 31.5ft (129.3 x 33 x 31.5m).
Propulsion: Single shaft nuclear; 15,000shp=30kt submerged.
Armament: 16 Poseidon C-3 SLBM (19 boats), 16 Trident D-4 SLBM 12 boats; four 21in (533mm) torpedo tubes (all).
Sensors: Sonar BQQ-2.

The 31 Lafayette class SSBNs were the definitive US submarines of the 1960s and 1970s. The first eight were originally fitted with Polaris A-2 missiles, while the remaining 23 had the improved Polaris A-3 with a range of 2,855 miles (4,594km) and three 200KT MRV warheads. The first five boats launched their missiles with compressed air, but the remainder use a rocket motor to produce a gas-steam mixture to eject the missiles from their tubes. All Lafayettes have now been fitted to take Poseidon C-3 SLBMs, which have a range of about 3,230 miles (5,200km) with ten 50KT MIRVs.

The Lafayettes are slightly enlarged and improved versions of the Ethan Allen design, and are almost indistinguishable from that class. The last 12 Lafayettes differ considerably from the earlier boats and are sometimes referred to as the Benjamin Franklin class. They have improved, quieter machinery and 28 more crewmen. Twelve of these are being refitted to take the larger three-stage Trident 1 C-4 SLBM, which has a range of about 4,400 miles (7,100km) and carries eight 100KT MIRVs. Although these SSBNs do not have the underwater performance of the SSNs, they have a respectable capability against surface ships or other submarines and are armed with conventional or wire-guided torpedoes and Subroc. Normally, however, they would attempt to evade detection or contact.

Daniel Webster (SSBN-626) of this class has been fitted with diving planes on a raised bow sonar instead of on the fin; although this has been successful, it has not been copied on other SSBNs.

Below: The Los Angeles class submarine, when submerged, is quieter, faster and more capable than earlier nuclear attack boats. Fourteen are authorised for FY87-91.

Above: USS Lafayette (SSBN-616) under way. Laid down in January 1961 and launched in May 1962, Lafayette was the first SSBN of this class commissioned, 23 April 1963.

Los Angeles Class

Completed: 1974 onwards.
Names: SSN 688 to SSN 777.
Displacement: 6,000t surfaced; 6,900t submerged.
Dimensions: 360ft oa x 31.75ft x 32.25ft (109.7 x 10.1 x 9.8m).
Propulsion: Single shaft nuclear; 35,000shp=30+kt submerged.
Armament: 4 21in (533mm) torpedo tubes; Subroc, Mk 48 torpedoes, Tomahawk (15 VLS tubes to be fitted from SSN-721 onwards).
Sensors: *Long range sonar:* BQQ-5 plus towed array.
Short range sonar: BQS-15.
Radar: BPS-15.

The first Los Angeles SSN entered service in 1976; thirty-six are now in commission and the eventual size of the class has yet to be decided. They are much larger than any previous SSN and have a higher submerged speed. They have the BQQ-5 sonar system and can operate Subroc, Sub-Harpoon and Tomahawk as well as conventional and wire-guided torpedoes. Thus, like all later US SSNs, although they are intended to hunt other submarines and to protect SSBNs they can also be used without modification to sink surface ships at long range with Sub-Harpoon. Further, Tomahawk will enable them to operate against strategic targets well inland.

The Los Angeles class is very sophisticated and each boat is an extremely potent fighting machine. With a production run of at least 44, it must be considered a very successful design. However, these boats are becoming very expensive: in 1976 the cost of each one was estimated at $221.25 million; the boat bought in 1979 cost $325.6 million; the two in 1981 cost $495.8 million each. Not even the USA can continue to spend money at that rate.

Nevertheless, the Reagan Administration has ordered a speeding up of the Los Angeles building programme, calling for two in 1982 and three per year thereafter. The Tomahawk missile programme is also being accelerated. Tomahawk has been fitted from SSN-719 (the twenty-second boat to be launched, in 1983) onward.

A design for a smaller and cheaper SSN, under consideration in 1980 as a result of Congressional pressure, appears to have been shelved. There are now plants to improve the Los Angeles boats—especially their sensors, weapon systems and control equipment—and fifteen Vertical Launch System (VLS) missile tubes are being fitted in the forward main ballast tank area for Tomahawk missiles, thus restoring the Mark 48 torpedo load to its original figure.

Right: *Philadelphia* **on pre-commissioning trials during 1977.**

Below: USS Philadelphia (SSN-690). The unit cost of each Los Angeles, the largest SSNs built, is about $500 million.

Weapons and Sensors

Carrier-Borne Fixed-Wing Aircraft

F-14A Tomcat
In service: 1972.
Weight: 72,000lb (32,727kg) max.
Dimensions: 62 x 38 (swept) x 16ft (18.9 x 11.6 x 4.9m).
Fleet Air Defence fighter with AWG-9 missile-control system and six Phoenix AAMs. Two 12-plane squadrons in later CVs.

F-4J Phantom
In service: 1966
Weight: 54,600lb (24,818kg) max.
Dimensions: 58 x 38 x 16ft (17.8 x 11.7 x 5m).
All-weather multi-purpose fighter with Sparrow and Sidewinder AAMs. Two 12-plane squadrons in earlier CVs. To be replaced by F/A-18 Hornet in mid-1980s.

Below: The A-6 Intruder has been the standard all-weather attack aircraft aboard US carriers since the mid-1960s.

Most US Navy weapons systems remain in service for a considerable number of years, and after that time are generally replaced by systems which represent a "quantum jump" in terms of their technology. Existing equipment therefore receives frequent updates to improve performance and reliability. This applies particularly to electronics and avionics, and few US ships emerge from even routine refits without modifications which facilitate the collection, analysis and transfer of action data.

A-7E Corsair

In service: 1969
Weight: 42,000lb (19,090kg) max.
Dimensions: 46 x 39 x 16ft (14.1 x 11.8 x 4.9m).
Light attack aircraft with limited all-weather and night capability, 16,000lb (7,270kg) of ordnance. Two 12-plane squadrons in all CVs. To be replaced by F/A-18 Hornet in mid-1980s.

A-6E Intruder

In service: 1970.
Weight: 60,400lb (27,455kg) max.
Dimensions: 55 x 53 x 16ft (16.7 x 16.2 x 4.9m).
All-weather and night attack aircraft. 14,000lb (6,364kg) of ordnance. One 10-plane squadron + 4 KA-6D tankers in all CVs.

Below: Ground crew prepare an A-7 Corsair on the flight deck of *America* (CV-66). Two squadrons operate from each carrier.

E-2C Hawkeye
In service: 1973.
Weight: 51,570lb (23,440kg) max.
Dimensions: 58 x 81 x 18ft (17.6 x 24.6 x 5.6m).
Airborne Early Warning (AEW) aircraft. 24ft (7.3m) diameter saucer-shaped radome for APS-125 UHF radar. Four-plane detachment in all CVs.

EA-6B Prowler
In service: 1971.
Weight: 58,500lb (26,590kg) max.
Dimensions: 59 x 53 x 16ft (18.1 x 16.2 x 5m).
ECM variant of Intruder. Four-plane squadron in all CVs.

S-3A Viking
In service: 1974.
Weight: 52,540lb (23,882kg) max.
Dimensions: 53 x 69 x 23ft (16.3 x 20.9 x 6.9m).
ASW aircraft with onboard AYK-30 digital computer for processing sonobuoy data, four Mk 46 torpedoes, and 3,000lb other ordnance. One 10-plane squadron in all CVs except Midway class.

Above right: An E-2C Hawkeye AEW aircraft comes in to land.

Right: The S-3A Viking is a sophisticated ASW aircraft.

Surveillance Radars
SPS-48
In service: 1965 (first operational installation).
Long-range (230nm, 426km) 3-D radar used to provide target data for Terrier/Standard ER missile in CGs and for aircraft control in CVs. Large square planar antenna.

SPS-30
In service: 1962.
Long-range 3-D radar used for aircraft control in older CVs. Large solid dish antenna with prominent feed-horn. Being replaced by SPS-48.

Right: The SPS-48 is the standard 3-D radar on US cruisers.

Below: Air detection and tracking consoles on *Mount Whitney*.

SPS-39/52

In service: 1960/1966.

3-D radar used to provide target data for Tartar/Standard MR missile in DDGs and FFGs. Rectangular planar antenna.

SPS-49

In service: 1976.

Long-range air search radar. In FFG-7 and to be retro-fitted to all major classes in place of SPS-37/37A/43/43A. Elliptical lattice antenna.

SPS-37A/43A

In service: 1961.

Long-range (300nm, 556km) air search radar in CVs. 13-metre (42.6ft) rectangular lattice antenna.

Below: Two frigates of the Brooke (foreground) and Knox classes displaying typical small-ship radar arrays. The square planar antenna is an SPS-52, while the Knox has the SPS-40 air search antenna. Both ships have the SPS-10 surface radar.

SPS-37/43

In service: 1960/1961.

Long-range (230nm, 426km) air search radar in CGs and some DDs and DDGs. Rectangular mattress antenna.

SPS-40

In service: 1962.

Medium-range (150-80nm, 278-334-km)) air search radar in DDs, FFs, some DDGs, and amphibious vessels. Elliptical lattice antenna with feed-horn above.

SPS-55

In service: 1975.

Surface search radar. Has replaced SPS-10 in new construction.

SPS-10

In service: 1953.

Surface search radar. Standard on all but most recent units. To be upgraded to SPS-67.

Surface-to-Air Missiles

Standard SM-1ER (RIM-67A)
In service:	1970.
Length:	27ft (8.23m).
Range:	35nm (65km).
Fire Control:	SPG-55 with Mk 76 MFCS.
Guidance:	Semi-active homing.
Remarks:	Terrier replacement on CGs. Twin launcher. Mk 10 (40-60 missiles–80 in CGN 9).

Standard SM-1MR (RIM-66B)
In service:	1970.
Length:	15ft (4.57m).
Range:	15nm (27.8km).
Fire Control:	SPG-51 with Mk 74 MFCS.
Guidance:	Semi-active homing.
Remarks:	Same missile as above but without booster. Tartar replacement on DDGs, FFGs and new CGNs. Twin launcher Mk 11 (42 missiles), single launcher Mk 13 (40 missiles), single launcher Mk 22 (16 missiles) or twin launcher Mk 26 (24-44 missiles).

NATO Sea Sparrow (RIM-7H)
In service:	1977.
Length:	12ft (3.65m).
Range:	8nm (14.8km).
Fire Control:	Mk 91.
Guidance:	Continuous Wave (CW) semi-active homing.
Remarks:	Improved Point Defense Missile System (IPDMS) in CVs, Spruance-class DDs and large replenishment vessels. High performance version of Sparrow missile with folding fins and specially designed lightweight 8-round box launcher (Mk 29). Manual reloading. Automatic tracking.

Sea Sparrow (RIM-7E)
In service:	1969.
Length:	12ft (3.65m).
Range:	5nm (9.27km).
Fire Control:	Mk 115.
Guidance:	Continuous Wave (CW) semi-active homing.
Remarks:	Basic Point Defense Missile System (BPDMS) in CVs and Knox-class FFs. Fired from modified ASROC launcher (Mk 25) on modified 3-inch (76mm) gun carriage. Mk 115 illuminator manually trained on target.

Above right: A Standard SM-1 medium-range (MR) missile leaves the forward launcher of a cruiser of the California class. The SM-1 has now replaced the Tartar missile on destroyers and frigates fitted with the twin-arm Mk 11 launcher or the single-arm Mk 13 and Mk 22 launchers. It is also fired from the twin-arm Mk 26 or the single Mk 13 launcher aboard latest CGNs.

Right: An RIM-7E Sea Sparrow missile is fired from one of three Mk 25 launchers aboard *Enterprise* (CVN-65). The RIM-7E was adapted from the air-launched Sparrow missile and forms the basis of the US Navy's Basic Point Defense Missile System (BPDMS). It is fired from a modified ASROC launcher and is now being superseded by the RIM-7H version.

ASW Weapons and Sensors

LAMPS (Light Airborne Multi-Purpose System)
In service: 1971.
Manned anti-submarine helicopters used to localise and attack submarine contacts detected by shipboard sonar. Fitted with surface search radar, MAD and sonobuoys. Current LAMPS I is SH-2F Seasprite. Will be replaced by SH-60B Seahawk (LAMPS III) in mid-1980s.

ASROC (RUR-5A)
In service: 1961.
Length: 15ft (4.6m).
Range: 6nm (11.1km).
Payload: Mk 46 homing torpedo or nuclear depth bomb Mk 17.
Fire Control: Mk 114/Mk 116.
Anti-submarine rocket fitted in all major surface units up to FFG 7. Fired from octuple Mk 16 launcher or Mk 10/Mk 26 SAM launchers. Cannot be guided in flight. Will be phased out in late 1980s.

Mk 46 Torpedo
In service: 1967.
Length: 8.5ft (2.6m)
Diameter: 12.75in (324mm).
Guidance: active/passive acoustic homing.
Fired from triple trainable or single fixed Mk 32 tubes on all surface warships. Normal payload of ASROC missile. NEARTIP update.

SQS-26/53
In service: 1962/1975.
Large LF bow sonar. Simultaneous active/passive operation in a variety of modes (incl. bottom bounce, convergence zone). Detection ranges out to first convergence zone (25-35nm, 46.3-65km). Fitted in most FFs and all major surface units since mid-1960s. SQS-53 has solid-state electronics and digital interface with Mk 116 UFCS.

SQS-23
In service: 1958.
Predecessor of above. LF sonar with detection ranges of 6nm (11.1km) approx. In all major surface warships built late 1950s/early 1960s. To be upgraded to SQQ-23 status with active/passive operation.

SQS-56
In service: 1977.
Austere MF hull sonar designed for FFG 7. Latest technology but modest range.

SQS-35
In service: 1968.
Independent MF variable depth sonar fitted in stern counter of Knox-class FFs. SQR-18 passive array (in service 1978) can be streamed from towed body.

Top right: LAMPS helicopters were introduced in the 1970s and are standard on antisubmarine destroyers and frigates.

Centre: An ASROC missile launched from the frigate _Brooke_ (FFG-1). ASROC is fitted in all except the latest escorts.

Right: A lightweight Mk 46 antisubmarine torpedo is launched from the standard triple Mk 32 tubes fitted in most US escorts.

Anti-Ship Missiles, and Guns

Tomahawk (BGM-109)

In service: 1983 (scheduled).
Length: 20.25ft (6.2m).
Range: 300-500nm (556-926.6km).
Guidance: active radar homing.
Anti-Ship (T-ASM) and Land Attack (T-LAM, range 2,000nm, 3,700km) versions. Evaluation in *Merrill* (DD 976). To be fitted to major surface units.

Harpoon (RBM-84)

In service: 1977.
Length: 15ft (4.6m).
Range: 60nm (111km).
Guidance: active radar homing.
Fired from lightweight canisters fixed to quadruple ramps on CGs and latest DDs, and from a variety of launchers (Mk 11, Mk 13, Mk 16 and Mk 26) in other ships. LAMPS helicopter provides relay beyond horizon range.

5-inch/54 cal. Mk 45 (single)

In service: 1974.
Fire Control: SPG-60, SPQ-9 with Mk 86 GFCS.
Lightweight D-P gun with modest performance but good reliability and low manning requirements.

5-inch/54 cal. Mk 42 (single)

In service: 1953.
Fire Control: SPG-53 with Mk 68 GFCS.
High-performance D-P gun. Complex and not always reliable.

76 mm/62 cal. Mk 75 (single)

In service: 1977.
Fire Control: Mk 92 GFCS.
Lightweight high-performance gun manufactured under licence from OTO-Melara for FFG-7 and PHM.

3-inch/50 cal. Mk 33 (twin)

In service: 1944.
Fire Control: Mk 35 radar with Mk 56 GFCS.
Being removed from older CGs and DDs because of maintenance problems but still fitted in some amphibious vessels and auxiliaries. Later installations have aluminium or GRP gun-shield.

20 mm/76 cal. Mk 15 (6 barrels)

In service: 1980.
Fire Control: Local radar.
Phalanx Close-In Weapon System (CIWS). 3,000rpm. To be fitted as standard "last-ditch" anti-missile weapon in 250 warships. Three to be fitted in CVs, two in all other major surface units, including amphibious vessels.

Top right: The first launch of an air-launched AGM-109 Tomahawk missile from an A-6 Intruder in 1976. Similar ship-launched variants are to be fitted to major surface units.

Centre: A 5-inch/54 cal. Mk 42 aboard the frigate *Lockwood* (FF-1064). Modifications have been made to improve the reliability of the gun, which has proved fragile in operation.

Right: Two twin 3-inch/50 cal. guns aboard an auxiliary vessel. Some installations have an aluminium or GRP gunshield.

Section Three

AIR WEAPONS AND EQUIPMENT

Contents of Section Three

Introduction

THIS book gives an up-to-date appraisal of the fixed-wing aircraft of today's United States Air Force. It is not concerned with helicopters, which are covered in a companion volume—*An Illustrated Guide to Military Helicopters*—nor with any kind of missile other than those fired or launched from aircraft. ICBMs (intercontinental ballistic missiles) were in th 1950s assigned wholly to th USAF, after a bitter battle Washington against the Arm and today a significant part the total Air Force budget go to the support of Strategic A Command's Minuteman ICB force.

For the record, this force both numerically, and in the siz

Above: In many respects the F-16 Fighting Falcon epitomises the US Air Force at its best. It is an advanced technology warplane which has evolved from being a small demonstrator into a brilliantly capable multi-role fighter considered by many to be the world's No. 1. It serves in various guises with the USAF and also to many of America's NATO allies and other friends (over 1,500 aircraft in total). The version shown is an F-1B two-seat trainer.

and payload of the missiles, puny compared with the terrifying ICBM capability deployed by the Strategic Rocket Forces of the Soviet Union. While the Soviet rockets have grown in scale, accuracy, numbers and lethality with every week that passes, the

USAF for a long time had no funds to buy any *new* missiles at all; the Minuteman force was fully deployed as long ago as April 1967. For many years funds were provided for a new ICBM, called M-X (Missile-X). Startling amounts were frittered away on studies of how it could be best deployed so that the missiles would not be destroyed by the increasingly accurate Soviet ICBMs.

However, after a vast amount of expenditure, consideration

of numerous basing concepts — and much political wrangling — it was finally decided to deploy 100 MX (now named 'Peacekeeper') in former Minuteman silos near FE Warren AFB in Wyoming. At the same time the Minuteman force is being updated and the aging force of Titan IIs is being retired, the last being due for deactivation in 1987.

Design and development of a small, single warhead ICBM (nicknamed 'Midgetman') and prototypes of the mobile launchers are already running. The missile will weigh less than 30,000lb (13,608kg).

Though the American aerospace industry can in general produce better aircraft and supporting hardware than any other country, and certainly can do it quicker, the price is a severe deterrent to any US administration. Even that of President Reagan, which has been trying to rectify the deferred and negative decisions of the 1970s, has had to look for ways to cut the defence budget, despite large increases in the early days of the Administration. Several commentators have said that this will inevitably lead to actual cuts in 'total obligational authority' of twice the net cuts. meaning

Below: The two competitive designs for the USAF's Small ICBM hard mobile launcher.

Right: Test firing of the Peacekeeper launch canister using a simulated missile.

that major programmes will have to go, including some aircraft projects.

In the quality of its hardware, and the skill, dedication and professionalism of its people, the USAF has never been so good as today, but in its strength to preserve world peace the picture is rather bleak. Abandonment of the nuclear tripwire policy of the 1955-65 era meant that there had to be immensely powerful forces ready to deter aggression anywhere. As these forces have shrunk, so has the President tried to muster a Rapid Deployment Force intended to make a small but effective sharp cutting edge available within 24 hours almost anywhere. Such a force is ill-adapted to counter either the colossal manpower and firepower of the Soviet Union or the religious fanatics and urban terrorists who have chosen to prey upon American lives and property in recent years. Moreover, for any really large force the USAF would be hard-pressed to provide sufficient airlift. Even if the C-5A did not have to be re-winged, the need for global airlift over intercontinental distances, possibly terminating at austere airstrips cannot at present be met, and KC-10s and C-17s cannot be procured in anything approaching the necessary numbers.

Improving SAC

Apart from a very small force of some 50 FB-111A bombers, the entire winged strength of Strategic Air Command continues to reside in the remaining B-52G and H bombers, plus a

Below: Dummy MX, now called Peacekeeper. The first 50 will be installed in Minuteman silos; other basing modes are being examined.

Above: Artist's impression of the C-17, 210 of which are planned for Military Airlift Command. First flight should be in 1989; IOC 1992.

Below: Salvo launch of two Minuteman III ICBMs. Though production was complete in 1977, the force is continually being updated.

Office of the Secretary of The Air Force

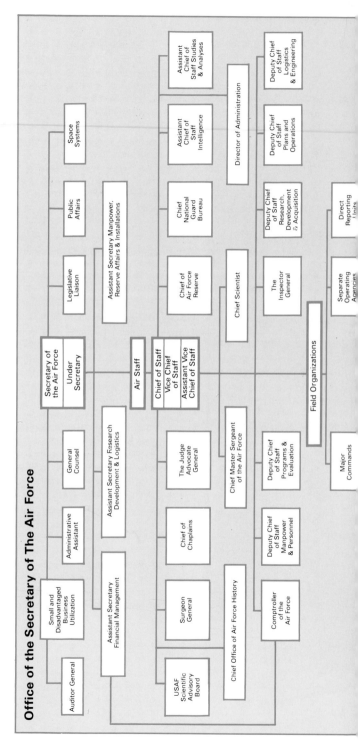

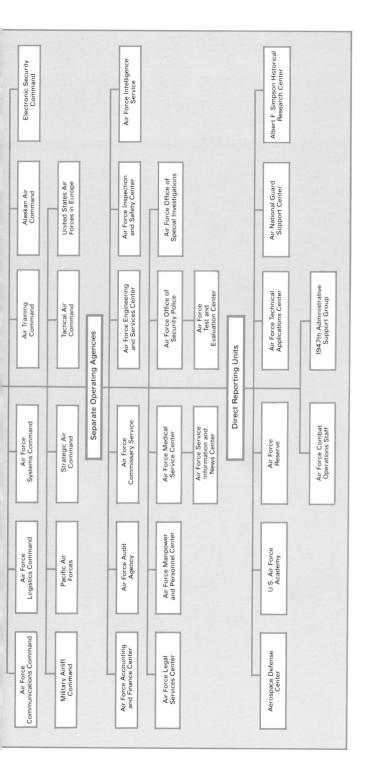

few sharply differing B-52Ds, which are now being withdrawn from the active inventory. The need for a modern long-range deterrent aircraft has been self-evident for 20 years, and the only encouragement that can be drawn from the fact that none has been provided is that today the B-70 (RS-70) would not be the optimum aircraft, just as the

B-1 will not be the optimum in 1990. So much time has gone by that any B-1 is better than nothing, and the B-1B, as it enters the inventory in the late 1980s, will restore credibility to the deterrent that has kept the peace for so long. For the more distant future a 'stealth' bomber has been under study for many years. It has not

Below: A 25-year-old KC-135A refuels a B-1 prototype, with an F-15A from 57th Tac Trg Wing in attendance.

Right: Another old-timer, a B-52G strategic bomber being tested in the maritime support role.

Far left: Plans for a Rapid Deployment Force even involve the use of the KC-135 tankers of SAC as carriers of infantry and other ground forces.

Left: This is the best illustration (from Boeing) yet published of the kind of bomber being planned under 'Stealth Technology'.

Above: Apart from CSIRS (see text below) the costly SR-71 is the only USAF recon platform intended for manned overflights.

reached the stage at which it can appear in a book such as this, but in the long term it could be very important indeed, if the US has the will to produce it.

The word 'stealth' has come to mean an aircraft offering minimal signatures to defensive detection systems. Stealth characteristics can be achieved by a combination of aircraft shape, exterior surface quality, materials and several other factors, most importantly the EW (electronic warfare) sub-systems carried on board the aircraft. Surviving in hostile air-space by high flight speed or altitude is no longer viable but, after prolonged effort, stealth technology has reached the point at which it dominates the design of offensive aircraft, not excepting cruise missiles. The USAF is now funding at an increasing rate an ATB (Advanced Tech-

Left: Though the Space Shuttle is a NASA programme—and NASA is careful to maintain its civilian status—the Air Force is one of the chief customers for operational flights. A USAF Space Shuttle launch facility has been built at the Vandenburg AFB in California and several highly classified missions had been undertaken up to the time of the loss of the *Challenger* in February 1986, which has resulted in major delays to both civil and military programmes.

nology Bomber) which it is hoped will supplement the B-1B in the SAC inventory from about 1992. Northrop's appointment as prime contractor generated slightly misleading speculation that the ATB would be a YB-49 type of flying wing. The California company is teamed with Boeing and Vought, with GE providing the vitally important 'zero signature' propulsion.

In the much shorter term Lockheed, which is supplying the TR-1 reconnaissance aircraft designed to non-stealth technology, has for some time been using stealth technology in a relatively small tactical platform called CSIRS (Covert Survivable In-weather Recon/Strike). This system entered USAF service in 1983 and utilizes a section of the advanced aerodynamics of the SR-71 and GTD-21 RPV; the CSIRS tries to avoid being shot down on multi-sensor recon-naissance and precision attack missions by a combination of high performance and as much stealth technology as could be incorporated in the timescale, for the available budget. It is planned to deploy 20 CSIRS, with possibly more to follow of a more advanced derived type, but the work is largely classified and again could not be included here as a regular USAF type.

At a totally different level, another machine not included is the Piper Enforcer. Unbelievably, ▶

Below: Largest of the known types of Air Force satellites, the Type 467 Big Bird series each weigh about 25,000 lb (11.34 t) and have been launched since June 1971.

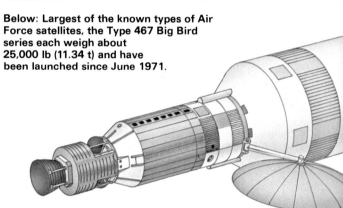

▶ this is derived from the P-51 Mustang, first flown to British order in 1940 and subsequently one of the best fighter/bomber aircraft of World War II and the Korean war. During the Vietnam war it often came into discussion, and Cavalier Aircraft sold almost new-build P-51s to the Air Force and Army, though only in small numbers for training and evaluation. Piper, a leading general aviation builder, was asked to produce a largely redesigned Mustang with a turboprop engine to meet a possible need for a light close-support attack aircraft. Piper announced the start of flight testing of the first Enforcer on 29 April 1971, the chosen

engine being the Lycoming T55 Subsequently Piper made no further announcement, and many observers were surprised when in 1981 the company was awarded a three-year contract for some $2 million, to fly two further Enforcers with many new features. These completed their test programme in August 1984 and were then placed in storage; the project seems to have ended. That there must be a place for a very small, agile, propeller or fan-engined tactical aircraft, pulling 7g turns at about 300 knots and able to kill tanks and other battlefield targets, appear indisputable. The wisdom of basing it on even a redesigned

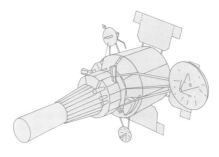

Above: Integrated Missile Early-Warning Satellite uses infra-red sensors to detect ICBM launches.

Left: This NKC-135A has served in different configurations as an airborne laser laboratory.

Below: Though it does not approach the Soviet space effort US surveillance continues: Landsat picture of the Plesetsk Cosmodrome.

Mustang is highly questionable.

Today's 'Mustang', of course, is the F-16, and this is perhaps the brightest spot in the entire Air Force inventory. Out of a very limited Light Weight Fighter programme, whose main objective was to see if a useful fighter could be made smaller and cheaper than the F-15, has come a tactical aircraft whose limitations are already hard to probe and are being pushed wider all the time. Perhaps the single event that did most to convert the doubters—whose opinion of the F-16 rested on supposed inadequate avionics, so that it could not do a real job in the bad weather of northern Europe—

was the RAF's annual tac-bombing contest held in mid-1981. A team of seven F-16s from the 388th TFW not only won the contest, beating such specialized attack systems as the Jaguar, Buccaneer and F-111F, but set a remarkable new record in scoring 7,831 of the possible 8,000 points. The USAF can take comfort in the certainty that this aircraft will continue to develop for at least the next 20 years, and will probably be the most numerous aircraft in the inventory for most of that time.

Almost the only shortcoming of the F-16, and it is a shortcoming of every other aeroplane in the USAF, is that it is tied to ▶

▶ airfields whose precise position is known to potential enemies. Those potential enemies having the capability to do so, such as the Soviet Union, could wipe out those bases in minutes. It is simply a matter of everyday fact that, should it choose to do so, the Soviet Union could suddenly and totally destroy every airfield used by all the air forces of NATO, including every operating base of the USAF. It would then be too late to rectify the folly of not deploying strong forces of V/STOL aircraft dispersed so completely through the countryside—if possible at locations offering natural ski jumps—that no amount of satellite recon-

Below: Almost a billion dollars invested in tactical airpower could vanish in a split second if a Soviet ICBM was launched at Langley's 1st Tac Ftr Wing.

aissance could find them, and the task of destroying them by missiles would be uneconomic.

Since 1960 the USAF's position on V/STOL has been variously negative, non-existent and ridiculous. The fact that the only V/STOL actually deployed (in the West) has been of British origin has served to warp and diminish USAF interest in the only survivable form of modern airpower.

Billions spent on B-1B, stealth aircraft and even the agile F-16 will be wasted if at 11 tomorrow morning someone presses a button and sends the whole lot up in fireballs as they stand on their airfield ramps. There would then no longer be any USAF, except perhaps for the planning staffs in the Pentagon and at Air Force Systems Command, who would be left to ponder on where they went wrong . . . .

Beech King Air

VC-6B

Origin: Beech Aircraft Corporation, Wichita, Kansas.
Type: VIP liaison transport.
Engines: Two 580ehp P&WC PT6A-21 turboprops.
Dimensions: Span 50ft 3in (15.32m); length 35ft 6in (10.82m); wing area 293.94sq ft (27.31m²).
Weights: Empty 5,778lb (2.621kg); loaded 9,650lb (4,377kg).
Performance: Maximum cruising speed 256mph (412km/h) at 12,000ft (3,660m); max rate of climb 1,995ft (596m)/min; service ceiling 28,100ft (8,565m); range with max fuel at max cruising speed with allowances 1,384 miles (2,227km) at 21,000ft (6,400m) at 249mph (401km/h); typical field length, 3,500ft (1,067m).
Armament: None.
History: First flight (company prototype) 20 January 1964; VC-6A delivered to Air Force February 1966.

Development: The Model 90 King Air was essentially a Queen Air fitted with PT6 turboprop engines. With the B90 model the span was increased and gross weight raised considerably to take advantage of the power available. Large numbers of the original A90 series were bought by the Army, for many duties, but a single B90 was bought for the Air Force to serve as a VIP transport--a rare case of a single-aircraft buy of an off-the-shelf type. Originally designated VC-6A, it was later upgraded to VC-6B.

Beech Super King Air

C-12A, VC-12A

Origin: Beech Aircraft Corporation, Wichita, Kansas.
Type: Utility, VIP and mixed passenger/cargo transport.
Engines: Two 801ehp P&WC PT6A-38 turboprops.
Dimensions: Span 54ft 6in (16.61m); length 43ft 9in (13.34m); wing area 303sq ft (28.15m²).
Weights: Empty 7,800lb (3,538kg); loaded 12,500lb (5,670kg).
Performance: Maximum cruising speed, 272mph (437km/h) at 30,000ft (9,144m); service ceiling, 31,000ft (9,450m); range at maximum cruising speed, 1,824 miles (2,935km); TO/landing distances, about 2,800ft (850m).
Armament: None.
History: First flight (company prototype) 27 October 1972; first military contract, August 1974.

Development: For many years the top end of the Beechcraft range, and a Cadillac among propeller-driven executive aircraft, the T-tailed Super King Air 200 has found wide acceptance among all the US armed forces. The Air Force purchased 30 of the initial military model, the C-12A, with engines of lower power than commercial and later military variants, resulting in reduced performance. Apart from the lower-powered engines the C-12A was basically an off-the-shelf aircraft for service in various liaison and transport roles. The cockpit is laid out for two-pilot operation, though the right seat may be occupied by a passenger. The main cabin is usually equipped for eight passengers, though other arrangements are in use, and conversion to cargo operation is quick and simple. Avionics are even more comprehensive than usual for a light twin, and provision is made in the baggage area in the rear fuselage for storing survival gear. The interior is fully pressurized and air-conditioned, and the wing and tail are deiced by

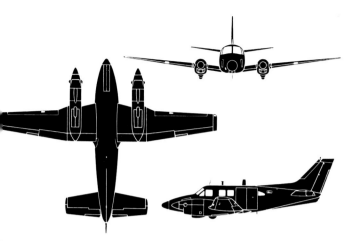

Above: The Beech VC-6B is a USAF B90 (now C90) with small changes.

standard with small modifications. Tail number is 66-7943 and the aircraft serves with the 89th Military Airlift Group at Andrews AFB, near Washington, DC, as a unit of the 1254th Special Air Missions Squadron. Unlike previous King Air models the B90 is pressurized, and of course the VC-6B is fully equipped for flight in bad weather, by night or in severe icing conditions.

Above: A USAF VC-12A in company with a US Army C12-A Huron (rear). Both are variants of pressurised Super King Air.

pneumatic boots. Aircraft styled VC-12A are equipped for VIP duties, with the 89th Military Airlift Group at Andrews AFB, Maryland, adjacent to DC. Other C-12As are assigned to overseas HQs or embassies; for example at Ramstein AB, HQ of USAFE.

Beech has always been the top General Aviation company for military contracts. It has played a major role in missile and space programmes, and is also one of the largest producers of RPVs (remotely piloted vehicles) and target drones, current types including the Mach 3 AQM-37A and MQM-107 Streaker family. Beech also makes airframes for Bell OH-58 Kiowa and JetRanger helicopters and portions of UH-1 Iroquois helicopters under subcontract to Bell Helicopter Textron.

Boeing B-52 Stratofortress

B-52D, G and H

Origin: Boeing Airplane Company (from May 1961 The Boeing Company)
Seattle, Washington.

Type: Heavy bomber and missile platform.

Engines: (D) eight 12,100lb (5,489kg) thrust P&WA J57-19W or 29W
turbojets, (G) eight 13,750lb (6,237kg) thrust P&WA J57-43W or -43W
turbojets, (H) eight 17,000lb (7,711kg) thrust P&WA TF33-1 or -
turbofans.

Dimensions: Span 185ft 0in (56.39m); length (D, and G/H as built) 157ft
7in (48.0m), (G/H modified) 160ft 11in (49.05m); height (D) 48ft 4½in
(14.7m), (G/H) 40ft 8in (12.4m); wing area 4,000sq ft (371.6m²).

Weights: Empty (D) about 175,000lb (79,380kg), (G/H) about 195,000l
(88,450kg); loaded (D) about 470,000lb (213,200kg), (G) 505,000l
(229,000kg), (H) 505,000 at takeoff, inflight refuel to 566,000l
(256,738kg).

Performance: Maximum speed (true airspeed, clean), (D) 575mp
(925km/h), (G/H) 595mph (957km/h); penetration speed at low altitud
(all) about 405mph (652km/h, Mach 0.53); service ceiling (D) 45,000ft
(13.7km), (G) 46,000ft (14.0km), (H) 47,000ft (14.3km); range (max fue
no external bombs/missiles, optimum hi-alt cruise) (D) 7,370 mile
(11,861km), (G) 8,406 miles (13,528km), (H) 10,130 iles (16,303km
takeoff run, (D) 11,100ft (3,383m), (G) 10,000ft (3,050m), (H) 9,500ft
(2895m).

Armament: (D) four 0.5in (12.7mm) guns in occupied tail turret, MD-
system, plus 84 bombs of nominal 500lb (227kg) in bomb bay plus 24 c
nominal 750lb (340kg) on wing pylons, total 60,000lb (27,215kg); (G) fou
0.5in (12.7mm) guns in remote-control tail turret, ASG-15 system, plus
nuclear bombs or up to 20 SRAM, ALCM or mix (eight on internal dispense
plus 12 on wing plyons); (H) single 20mm six-barrel gun in remote-contro
tail turret, ASG-21 system, plus bombload as G.

History: First flight 15 April 1952; later, see text.

Above: B-52H No 60-0062 was used for SRAM compatibility testing.

Development: Destined to be the longest-lived aircraft in all aviation history, the B-52 was designed to the very limits of the state of the art in 1948-49 to meet the demands of SAC for a long-range bomber and yet achieve the high performance possible with jet propulsion. The two prototypes had tandem pilot positions and were notable for their great size and fuel capacity, four double engine pods and four twin-wheel landing ▶

Left: The B-52G is not only the most numerous of all B-52 variants but also the most consistently updated model. At present it is the only sub-type to be armed with the AGM-86B cruise missile.

Below: The monster drag chute, usually of 32ft (9.75m) size, is not often used. This aircraft is a B-52H, photographed in 1981 with all avionic updates including ALQ-153 on the fin.

341

▶ trucks which could be slewed to crab the aircraft on to the runway in a crosswind landing. The B-52A changed to a side-by-side pilot cockpit in the nose and entered service in August 1954, becoming operational in June 1955. Subsequently 744 aircraft were built in eight major types, all of which have been withdrawn except the B-52D, G and H.

The B-52D fleet numbered 170 (55-068/-117, 56-580/-630 built at Seattle and 55-049/-067, 55-673/-680 and 56-657/-698 built at Wichita) delivered at 20 per month alongside the same rate for KC-135 tankers in support. The B-52G was the most numerous variant, 193 being delivered from early 1959 (57-6468/-6520, 58-158/-258 and 59-2564/-2602, all from Wichita), introducing a wet (integral-tank) wing which increased internal fuel from 35,550 to 46,575 US gal and also featured shaft-driven

Top: B-52G No. 59-2565 in the current colour scheme.

Right: Totally unlike the cockpits of early versions, the B-52G and H flight decks are dominated by EVS (TV and infra-red) displays.

Below: These B-52H bombers are the newest of the entire family, already at more than double the original design structure life.

▶generators, roll control by spoilers only, powered tail controls, injection water in the leading edge, a short vertical tail, rear gunner moved to the main pressurized crew compartment and an inner wing stressed for a large pylon on each side. The final model, the B-52H, numbered 102 (60-001/-062 and 61-001/-040), and was essentially a G with the new TF33 fan engine and a new tail gun.

During the Vietnam war the B-52D was structurally rebuilt for HDB (high-density bombing) with conventional bombs, never considered in the original design. The wings were given inboard pylons of great length for four tandem triplets of bombs on each side, and as noted in the data 108 bombs could be carried in all with a true weight not the 'book value' given but closer to 89,100lb (40,400kg). Another far-reaching and costly series of structural modifications was needed on all models to permit sustained operations at low level, to keep as far as possible under hostile radars, again not previously considered. The newest models, the G and H were given a stability

Right: Newest of the B-52s, the B-52H combines the high-capacity wet wing of the B-52G with the economical TF33 turbofan engine.

Below: Aircrews 'scramble' toward a line-up of G models during the 1979 Global Shield exercises.

Above: A live drop of a SRAM from a B-52H, showing the point of maximum fall at which the first-pulse rocket motor ignites.

Above: A live drop of an AGM-86A cruise missile, from a special test NB-52G in 1976. The production ALCM is longer.

Below: Taken in May 1979, this picture shows one of the B-52Gs used for the fly-off ALCM competition; the AGM-86Bs are dummies

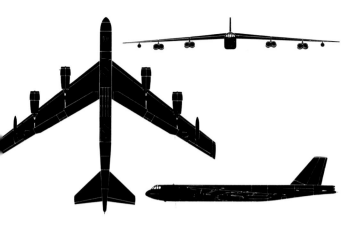

Above: Three-view of Boeing B-52H, without EVS blisters.

ugmentation system from 1969 to improve comfort and airframe life in
urbulent dense air. From 1972 these aircraft were outfitted to carry the
RAM (Short-Range Attack Missile), some 1,300 of which are still with the
AC Bomb Wings. Next came the EVS (Electro-optical Viewing System)
vhich added twin chin bulges. The Phase VI ECM (electronic counter-
neasures) cost $362.5 million from 1973. Quick Start added cartridge
ngine starters to the G and H for a quick getaway to escape missile attack.
lext came a new threat-warning system, a satellite link and 'smart noise'
ammers to thwart enemy radars. From 1980 the venerable D-force was
pdated by a $126.3 million digital nav/bombing system. Further major
hanges to the G and H include the OAS (offensive avionics system) which is
ow in progress costing $1,662 million. The equally big CMI (cruise-missile
iterface) will eventually fit the G-force for 12 AGM-86B missiles on the
ylons, the first wing becoming operational in December 1982. In the late
980s it is proposed to carry out further modifications to fit a Common
trategic Rotary Launcher (CSRL), which can carry SRAMs, ALCMs,
dvanced cruise missiles or free-fall nuclear bombs.

The last B-52D was retired in late 1983, leaving some 265 B-52Gs and
Is in SAC's active inventory, equipping 15 Bomb Wings, all with home
ases in the continental USA. Large number are also in storage.

Boeing C-135 family

Origin: Boeing Airplane Company (from May 1961 The Boeing Company) Seattle, Washington.
Type: Tankers, transports, EW, Elint, command-post and rsearch aircraft
Engines: (A and derivatives) four 13,750lb (6,273kg) thrust P&WA J57 59W or -43WB turbojets, (B and derivatives) four 18,000lb (8165kg) thrust P&WA TF33-3 turbofans, (RE) four 22,000lb (9,979kg) thrus CFM56-1B11 turbofans.
Dimensions: Span (basic) 130ft 10in (39.88m); length (basic) 134ft 6in (40.99m); height (basic) 38ft 4in (11.68m), (tall fin) 41 1ft 8in (12.69m wing area 2,433sq ft (226m²).
Weights: empty (KC-135A basic) 98,466lb (44,664kg), (KC, operating weight) 106,306lb (48,220kg), (C-135B) 102,300lb (46,403kg); loaded (KC, original) 297,000lb (134,719kg), (KC, later max) 316,000lb (143,338kg), (C-135B) 275,000lb (124,740kg) (typical of special variants).
Performance: Maximum speed (all) about 580mph (933km/h); typica high-speed cruise, 532mph (856km/h) at 35,000ft (10.7km); initial climb (J57, typical) 1,290ft (393m)/min, (TF33) 4,900ft (1,494m)/min; service ceiling (KC, full load) 36,000ft (10.9km), (C-135B) 44,000ft (13.4km); mission radius (KC) 3,450 miles (5,552km) to offload 24,000lb (10,886kg transfer fuel, 1,150 miles (1,950km) to offload 120,000lb (54,432kg); field length (KC, ISA+17°C) 13,700ft (4,176m).
Armament: None.
History: First flight 31 August 1956, variants see text.

Development: Boeing risked more than the company's net worth to build a prototype jetliner, first flown in July 1954. An important factor behind the gamble was the belief the USAF would buy a jet tanker/transport to replace the Boeing KC-97 family, and this belief was justified by the announcement of an initial order for 29 only three weeks after the company prototype flew, and long before it had done any inflight refuelling tests. The KC-135A Stratotanker differed only in minor respects from the original prototype whereas the civil 707 developed in a parellel programme was a totally fresh design with a wider fuselage, airframe of 2024 alloy designed on fail-safe principles and totally revised systems. The KC-135A was thus a rapid programme and deliveries began on 30 April 1957, building up to a frantic 20 per month and eventually reaching 732 aircraft.

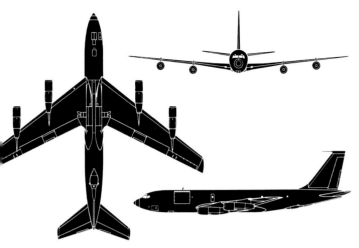

Above: Three-view of KC-135B (TF33 turbofan engines).

Above: The EC-135C (14 aircraft) are airborne command posts used by SAC to command all deterrent operations backing up the E-4 fleet. Powered by fan engines and retaining the boom, they have blade, wire, saddle and ventral trailing-wire aerials, plus HF probes on the wingtips.

Left: The 1956-built third KC-135 seen in the 1960s as a KC-135R, with rebuilt front and rear fuselage. In 1971 it became the sole RC-135T.

▶ The basic KC-135A has a windowless main fuselage with 80 tip-up troop or ground-crew seats and a cargo floor with tiedown fittings. Fuel is carried in 12 wing tanks and nine in the fuselage, only one of the latter being above the main floor (at the extreme tail). All but 1,000 US gal (3,785 lit) may be used as transfer fuel, pumped out via a Boeing high-speed extensible boom steered by a boom operator lying prone in the bottom of the rear fuselage. Only one receiver aircraft can be refuelled at a time, keeping station by watching rows of lights along the underside of the forward fuselage. The original short fin was later superseded by a tall fin and powered rudder, and many tankers were given an ARR (air refuelling receiver) boom receptacle. The KC force numbers 615 active aircraft in 35 squadrons, including 80 aircraft in Reserve units. The 100th ARW (Air Refueling Wing) at Beale AFB exclusively uses the KC-135Q with special avionics and JP-7 fuel for the SR-71 aircraft.

MATS, now MAC, bought 15 C-135A and 30 C-135B Stratolifter transports, the Bs with fan engines with reversers and much sprightlier performance with less noise and smoke. These remained windowless but had the refuelling boom removed (though retaining the operator's blister) and were equipped for 126 troops or 89,000lb (40,370kg) cargo loaded through a large door forward on the left side. In MATS these aircraft were soon replaced by the C-141. The final new-build versions were the four RC-135A survey/mapping aircraft for MATS and ten RC-135B for strategic reconnaissance. Thus, total C-135 production for the USAF numbered 808, completed in February 1965.

Since then the family has swelled by modification to become perhaps the most diverse in aviation history, the following all being USAF variants: EC-135A, radio link (SAC post-attack command control system); EC-135B, AF Systems Command, ex-RIA (Range Instrumented Aircraft) mainly twice-rebuilt; EC-135C, SAC command posts; EC-135G, ICBM launch and radio link (with boom); EC-135H, airborne command posts; EC-135J, airborne command posts (Pacaf); EC-135K, airborne command posts (TAC); EC-135L, special SAC relay platforms; EC-135N, now C-135N, Apollo range, four with A-LOTS pod tracker; EC-135P, communications/command posts; KC-135A, original designation retained for SAC relay links; KC-135R, also RC-135R, special recon/EW rebuilds; NC-135A, USAF, NASA and AEC above-ground nuclear-test and other radiation studies; NKC-135A, Systems Command fleet for ECM/ECCM, laser, ionosphere, missile vulnerability, icing, comsat, weightless, boom and other research; RC-135B and C, recon aircraft with SLAR cheeks and other sensors; RC-135D, different SLARs and thimble noses; RC-135E, glassfibre forward fuselage and inboard wing pods; RC-135M, numerous electronic installations, fan engines; RC-135S,

Below: A standard KC-135A refuels two F-4Es and an F-4D over SE Asia. It has the tall fin and powered rudder (a modification).

Above: This RC-135V is unlike most of the seven of this type in having HF wingtip probes as well as SLAR cheeks and ventral blades.

Above: The HF probes above the wingtips show clearly on this EC-135J of Pacaf, as well as the black saddle dome.

most M installations plus many others; RC-135T, single special SAC aircraft; RC-135U, special sensors and aerials cover almost entire airframe, including SLAR cheeks, extended tailcone and various chin, dorsal, ventral and fin aerials; RC-135V, rebuild of seven Cs and one U with nose thimble, wire aerials and ventral blades; RC-135W, latest recon model mostly rebuilt from M with SLAR sheeks added; WC-135B, standard MAC weather platforms.

Below: One of the 56 tankers modified to KC-135Q configuration, with special provisions for JP-7 (SR-71) fuel and grey Corogard finish.

Boeing VC-137

VC-137B, C

Origin: The Boeing Company, Seattle, Washington.
Type: Special missions transport.
Engines: Four 18,000lb (8,165kg) thrust P&WA JT3D-3 turbofans.
Dimensions: Span (B) 130ft 10in (39.87m), (C) 145ft 9in (44.42m);
length (B) 144ft 6in (44.04m), (C) 152ft 11in (46.61m); wing area (B)
2,433sq ft (226m²), (C) 3,010sq ft (279.64m²).
Weights: Empty (B) about 124,000lb (56,250kg), (C) about 140,500lb
(63,730kg); loaded (B) 258,000lb (117,025kg), (C) 322,000lb (146,059kg).
Performance: Maximum speed (B) 623mph (1002km/h), (C) 627mph
(1010km/h); maximum cruise, (B) 618mph (995km/h) (C) 600mph
(966km/h); initial climb (B) 5,050ft (1539m)/min, (C) 3,550ft (1,082m)/min;
service ceiling (B) 42,000ft (12.8km), (C) 38,500ft (11.73km); range,
maximum payload, (B) 4,235 miles (6,820km), (C), 6,160 miles (9915km).
Armament: None.
History: First flight (civil-120B) 22 June 1960, (-320B) 31 January 1962.

Development: These aircraft bear no direct relationship to the prolific C135
family but were commercial airliners (hence the civil engine designation)
bought off-the-shelf but specially furnished for the MAC 89th Military Airlift
Group, based at Andrews AFB, Maryland, to fly the President and other
senior executive officials. All have rear cabins with regular airline seating but

Boeing T-43

T-43A

Origin: The Boeing Company, Seattle, Washington.
Type: Navigator trainer.
Engines: Two 14,500lb (6,577kg) thrust P&WA JT8D-9 turbofans.
Dimensions: Span 93ft 0in (28.35m); length 100ft 0in (30.48m); wing
area 980 sq ft (91.05m²).
Weights: Empty 64,090lb (29,071kg); loaded 115,500lb (52,391kg).
Performance: Maximum cruising speed 562mph (904km/h); normal
cruising speed, about 464mph (747km/h) at 35,000ft (10.67km); range
with MIL-C-5011A reserves, 2,995 miles (4,820km).
Armament: None.
History: First flight (737-100) 9 April 1967, (T-43A) 10 April 1973.

Development: Vietnam experience revealed a serious deficiency of
facilities for training modern navigators, the only aircraft for this purpose
being 77 T-29 piston-engined machines based on the immediate post-war
Convair-Liner. In May 1971 the Air Force announced an $87.1 million order
for 19 off-the-shelf Boeing 737-200s, with an option (not taken up) for a
further ten. The 19 aircraft were delivered in the 12 months from June
1973, and all have since operated with the 323rd Flying Training Wing at
Mather AFB, California. Numerous change orders were issued to the basic
737-200, though engines and equipment items are treated as commercial
(there is no military designation for the JT8D). There is only a single door and
nine windows along each side of the cabin, the floor is strengthened to carry
heavy avionics consoles and operating desks, there are additional avionics
aerials, and an 800 US-gal (3027 lit) auxiliary fuel tank is installed in the aft
cargo compartment. In addition to the two pilots and supernumerary there
are stations for 12 pupil navigators, four advanced trainees and three
instructors. Training is given under all weather conditions and at all heights
with equipment which is often modified to reflect that in operational types.

Above: Air Force One is strictly so-called only when the US President is aboard; at all other times it is just an immaculately polished VC-137C which uses regular USAF callsigns.

special midships HQ/conference section and a forward communications centre with special avionics in contact with stations on land, sea, in the air and in space. There are special security provisions. The two VC-137Bs were bought as early 707-153s with JT3C-6 engines and were redesignated on fitting turbofan engines. The first VC-137CC (62-6000), a much larger aircraft equivalent to a 707-320B, was the original Presidential Air Force One. It is now back-up to today's Air Force One, 72-7000.

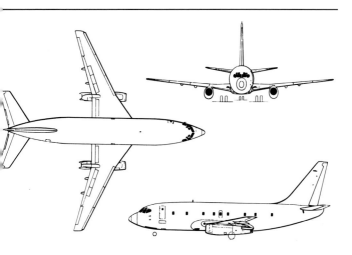

Above: Standard configuration of the T-43A.

Below: All specialist USAF navigators have trained on the T-43A.

Boeing E-3 Sentry

E-3A

Origin: Boeing Aerospace Company, Kent, Washington.
Type: Airborne Warning and Control System (AWACS) platform.
Engines: Four 21,000lb (952kg) thrust P&WA TF33-100/100A turbofans.
Dimensions: Span 145ft 9in (44,42m), length 152ft 11in (46.61m), height 41ft 4in (12.6m) (over fin); wing area 3,050sq ft (283.4m²).
Weights: Empty, not disclosed but about 162,000lb (73,480kg), loaded 325,00lb (147,400kg).
Performance: Maximum speed 530mph (853km/h); normal operating speed, about 350mph (563km/h); service ceiling, over 29,000ft (8.85km); endurance on station 1,000 miles (1,609km) from base, 6h.
Armament: None.
History: First flight (EC-137D) 5 February 1972, (E-3A) 31 October 1975; service delivery (E-3A) 24 March 1977.

Development: The USAF had been one of the pioneers of overland surveillance platforms, mainly using EC-121 Warning Stars (based on the Super Constellation, and continuing in unpublicized service until almost 1980). During the 1960s radar technology had reached the point at which, with greater power and rapid digital processing, an OTH (over the horizon) capability could be achieved, plus clear vision looking almost straight down to detect and follow high-speed aircraft flying only just above the Earth's surface. One vital ingredient was the pulse-doppler kind of radar, in which

Right: The first flight-cleared Westinghouse APY-1 radar was tested in this EC-137D (converted 707).

Below: Another photograph of the original EC-137D which from 1972 completed most of the AWACS test programme with the exception of inflight refuelling.

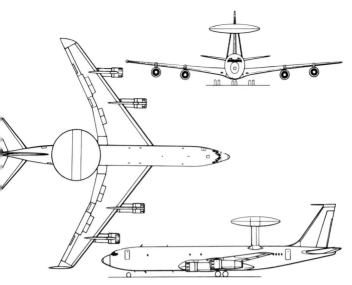

Above: Three view of the production E-3A (rotodome parked).

355

▶the 'doppler shift' in received frequency caused by relative motion between the target and the radar can be used to separate out all reflections except those from genuine moving targets. Very clever signal processing is needed to eliminate returns from such false 'moving targets' as leaves violently distributed by wind, and the most difficult of all is the motion of the sea surface and blown spray in an ocean gale. For this reason even more clever radars are needed for the overwater mission, and the USAF did not attempt to accomplish it until quite recently.

Right: Takeoff of an EC-137D test aircraft, with rotodome revolving. Below: E-3A Sentries of the USAF 963rd AWAC Squadron at Tinker AFB, Oklahoma. This is a unit of the 552nd AWAC Wing of TAC.

▶ While Hughes and Westinghouse fought to develop the new ODR (overland downlock radar), Boeing was awarded a prime contract on 8 July 1970 for the AWACS (Airborne Warning And Control System). Their proposal was based on the commercial 707-320; to give enhanced on-station endurance it was to be powered by eight TF34 engines, but to cut costs this was abandoned and the original engines retained thought driviIng high-power electric generators. The aerial for the main radar, back-to-back with an IFF (identification friend or foe) aerial and communications aerials, is mounted on a pylon above the rear fuselage and streamlined by adding two D-shaped radomes of glassfibre sandwich which turn the girdler-like aerial array into a deep circular rotordome of 30ft (9.14m) diameter. This turns very slowly to keep the bearings lubricated; when on-station it rotates at 6rpm (once every ten seconds) and the searchlight-like beam is electronically scanned under computer control to sweep from the ground up to the sky and space, picking out every kind of moving target and processing the resulting signals at the rate of 710,000 complete 'words' per second. The rival radars were flown in two EC-137D aircraft rebuilt from existing 707s, and the winning Westinghouse APY-1 radar was built into the first E-3A in 1975. The first E-3A force was built up in TAC, to support quick-reaction deployment and tactical operation by all TAC units. The 552nd AWAC Wing received its first E-3A at Tinker AFB, Oklahoma, on 24 March 1977, and went on operational duty a year later. Subsequently the 552nd have operated in many parts of the world. It was augmented from 1979 by NORAD (North American Air Defense) personnel whose mission is the surveillance of all North American airspace and the control of NORAD forces over the Continental USA.

From the 22nd aircraft in 1981 an overwater capability has been incorporated, and from No 24 the systems are to an upgraded standard linked into the JTIDS (Joint TActical Information Distribution System) shared by all US services as well as NATO forces which use 18 similar aircraft. The USAF total fleet is 34 aircraft: the first 24 E-3As are now being uprated to E-3B and the last 10 to E-3C standards.

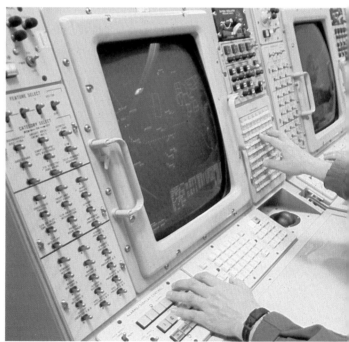

Above: A recent portrait of an E-3A Sentry of the TAC 552nd AWAC Wing, taken from the boomer's position of a KC-135A tanker. The Sentry's inflight-refuelling receptacle can be seen open, ready to receive the high-speed boom of the tanker. Normal endurance on station 1,000 miles (1,610km) from base is six hours, without an inflight refuelling.

Left: Of a normal complement of 17, only four are needed to fly the E-3A. The rest are AWACS specialists; their number can vary between about 12 and 15 according to the demands of the mission and tactical situation. Most, including those pictured, sit at MPCs (multi-purpose consoles), nine of which are installed in the standard AWACS configuration, along with two auxiliary displays.

Boeing E-4 AABNCP

E-4B

Origin: Boeing Aerospace Company, Kent, Washington.
Type: Advanced airborne command post.
Engines: Four 52,500lb (23,814kg) thrust General Electric F103-10C turbofans.
Dimensions: Span 195ft 8in (59.64m); length 231ft 10in (70.66m); wing area 5,500 sq ft (511m²).
Weights: Empty, not disclosed but about 410,000lb (186 tonnes); loaded 820,000lb (371,945kg).
Performance: Maximum speed, 700,000lb (317,515kg) at 30,000ft (9,144m), 602mph (969km/h); typical cruising speed, 583mph (939km/h) at 35,000ft (10,670m); maximum range with full tanks, 7,100 miles (11,426km); takeoff field length, ISA, 10,400ft (317m); cruise ceiling 45,000ft (13,715m).
Armament: None.
History: First flight (747 prototype) 9 February 1969, (E-4A) 13 June 1973.

Development: This unique variant of the commercial 747 transport is being procured in small numbers to replace the various EC-135 airborne command posts of the US National Military Command System and SAC

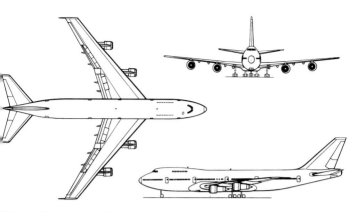

Above: Three-view of original E-4A with F105 (JT9D) engines.

Left: This profile depicts the first 747 to be brought up to E-4A standard, with Pratt & Whitney F105 (JT9D) engines. The same aircraft, USAF 75-0125, is shown overleaf completely updated to E-4B standard.

Below: A production E-4A, USAF 80-1676, operating with SAC prior to being brought up to E-4B standard. These aircraft have the same livery as Air Force One.

▶Under the 481B AABNCP (Advanced Airborne National Command Post) programme the Air Force Electronic Systems Division awarded Boeing a contract in February 1973 for the first two unequipped aircraft, designated E-4A and powered by JT9D engines, to which a third aircraft was added in July 1973. E-Systems won the contract to instal interim equipment in these three E-4A aircraft, the first of which was delivered to Andrews AFB in December 1974. The next two were delivered in 1975.

The third E-4A differed in being powered by the GE F103 engine, and this was made standard and subsequently retrofitted to the first two aircraft. In December 1973 a fourth aircraft was contracted for, and this was fitted with more advanced equipment resulting in the designation E-4B. All AABNCP aircraft have been brought up to the same standard and are designated E-4B. The first E-4B (75-0125), the fourth in the E-4 series, was delivered on 21 December 1979. The E-4B has accommodation for a larger battle staff on its 4,620 sq ft (429.2m²) main deck, which is divided into six operating areas: the National Command Authorities area, conference room briefing room, battle staff, communications control centre and rest area. The flight deck includes a special navigation station (not in 747s) and crew rest area,

Above: Takeoff of 80-1676 in original E-4A configuration.

The first E-4B, 75-0125 after further reconstruction, was redelivered to the Air Force in December 1979. It has the SHF 'doghouse' communications blister.

essential for air-refuelled missions lasting up to 72 hours. Lobe areas under the main deck house technical controls and stores for on-board maintenance.

One of the world's most costly military aircraft types, the E-4B is designed for unique capabilities. Its extraordinary avionics, mainly communications but including many other types of system, were created by a team including Electrospace Systems, Collins, Rockwell, RCA and Burroughes, co-ordinated by E-Systems and Boeing. Each engine drives two 150kVA alternators, and a large air-conditioning system (separate from that for the main cabin) is provided to cool the avionics compartments. Nuclear thermal shielding is extensive, and among the communications are an LF/VLF using a wire aerial trailed several miles behind the aircraft, and an SHF (super high frequency) system whose aerials are housed in the dorsal blister that was absent from the E-4A. Since November 1975 the sole operational management for the AABNCP force has been vested in SAC, and the main base is Offutt AFB, Nebraska, which is also home to the 55th Strategic Recon Wing, user of the EC-135 command posts. All four aircraft of the E-4B fleet are now in service and their Electro-Magentic Pulse (EMP)-protected electronic system represent a vital and unique C^3 capability for the USA.

Above: Inflight refuelling of an E-4A (probably 0125).

Cessna O-2 Skymaster

Model 337, O-2A

Origin: Cessna Aircraft Company, Wichita, Kansas.
Type: Forward air control and reconnaissance.
Engines: Tandem 210hp Continental IO-360C six-cylinder.
Dimensions: Span 38ft 2in (11.63m); length 29ft 9in (9.07m); wing area 202.5sq ft (18.8m^2).
Weights: Empty 2,848lb (11,292kg); loaded (max) 5,400lb (2,448kg).
Performance: Maximum speed 200mph (322km/h); cruising speed 144mph (232km/h); initial climb 1,180ft (360m)/min; service ceiling 18,000ft (5,490m); takeoff or landing over 50ft (15m), 1,675ft (510m); range with max fuel, 1,325 miles (2,132km).
Armament: Can carry underwing 7.62mm Minigun pod, light rockets or other light ordnance.
History: First flight (337 prototype) 28 February 1961, (0-2A) early 1967.

Development: The USAF placed a contract with Cessna for a military version of the Model 337 Skymaster 'push/pull' twin to supplement and then replace the single-engined O-1. Features included side-by-side dual controls for pilot and observer (the latter having extra windows low on the right side), four underwing pylons for flares or many other loads, and extensive navaids and communications systems. By 1971 a total of over 350 had been delivered, plus some 160 0-2B spy-war aircraft. Today large numbers of O-2A serve in utility and FAC rfoles with TAC's 24th CW at Howard AFB, Canal Zone, 507th TACW at Shaw AFB, SC, and 602nd TACW at Bergstrom, Texas; USAFE's 601st TCW at Sembach; Alaska's 25th TASS at Eielson AFB; and in the following ANG units: 105th TASW, White Plains, NY; 110th TASG, Battle Creek, Mich; 111th TASG, Willow Grove, Pa; 115th TASW, Traux Field, Wis; 163rd TASG, Ontario, Calif; and 182nd TASG, Peoria, III.

Cessna T-41

Model 172, T-41A Mescalero, T-41C.

Origin: Cessna Aircraft Company, Wichita, Kansas.
Type: Primary pilot trainer.
Engine: (A) one 150hp Lycoming O-320-E2D, (C) 210hp Continental IO-360-D.
Weights: Empty (A) 1,363lb (618kg); loaded (A) 2,300lb (1,043kg).
Performance: Maximum speed (A) 144mph (232km/h), (C) 153mph (246km/h); maximu mcruising speed (A) 138mph (22km/h), (C) 145mph (233km/h); initial climb (A) 645ft (196m)/min, (C) 880ft (268m)/min; service ceiling (A) 13,100ft (3,995m), (C) 17,000ft (5,180m)
Armament: None
History: First flight (civil 172) 1955, (T-41A) August 1964.

Development: The high cost of pupil wastage (failure) in all-jet training prompted the Air Force to reconsider its policy, and in July 1964, after two years of study, the decision was taken to introduce a light piston-engined machine for initial training, to weed out pupils with an initial 30h at relatively low cost. The Model 172 was picked off-the-shelf, and 170 were ordered as the T-41A Mescalero, total orders to date being 237 (the last in 1973). Joint civil/military serials are carried, without national insignia, and the USAF aircraft are operated by eight civilian contract schools located near USAF undergraduate pilot schools. In addition 52 more powerful T-41Cs were purchased for cadet training at the Air Force Academy at Colorado Springs. These resemble the civil 172E but have fixed-pitch propellers.

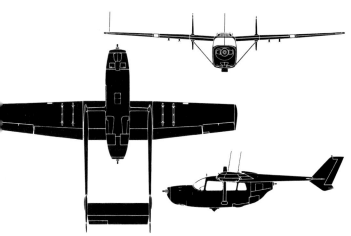

Above: Three-view of standard Cessna O-2A.

Below: The first of the 160 O-2B psychological-warfare aircraft.

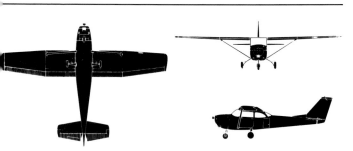

Above: Three-view of standard T-41A Mescalero.

Below: The civil and USAF numbers are repetitive.

Cessna T-37

Model 318, T-37B, A-37B Dragonfly

Origin: Cessna Aircraft Company, Wichita, Kansas.
Type: T-37, primary trainer; A-37, light attack.
Engines: (T) two 1,025lb (465kg) thrust Teledyne CAE J69-25 turbojets, (A) two 2,850lb (1293kg) thrust General Electric J85-17A turbojets.
Dimensions: Span (T) 33ft 9.3in (10.3m), (A, over tanks) 35ft 10.5in (10.93m); length (T) 29ft 3in (8.92m), (A, excl refuelling probe) 28ft 3.25in (8.62m); wing area 183.9 sq ft (17.09m²).
Weights: Empty (T) 3,870lb (1,755kg), (A) 6,211lb (2,817kg); loaded (T) 6,600lb (2,993kg) (A) 14,000lb (6,350kg).
Performance: Maximum speed (T) 426mph (685km/h), (A) 507mph (816km/h); normal cruising speed (T) 380mph (612km/h), (A, clean 489mph (787km/h); initial climb (T) 3,020ft (920m)/min, (A) 6,990ft (2130m)/min; service ceiling (T) 35,100ft (10,700m), (A) 41,765ft (12,730m); range (T, 5% reserves, 25,000ft/7,620m cruise) 604 miles (972km), (A, max fuel, four drop tanks) 1,012 miles (1628km), (A, max payload including 4,100lb/1860kg ordnance) 460 miles (740km).
Armament: (T) None, (A) GAU-2B/A7.62mm Minigun in fuselage, eight underwing pylons (four inners 870lb/394kg each, next 600lb/272kg and outers 500lb/227kg) for large number of weapons, pods, dispensers, clusters, launchers or recon/EW equipment.
History: First flight (T) 12 October 1954, (A) 22 October 1963.

Above: Three-view of A-37B Dragonfly with bombs and tanks.

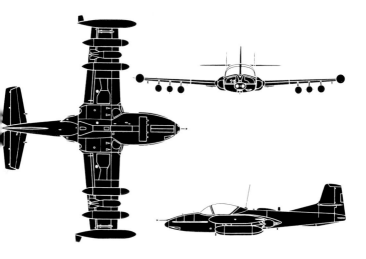

Left: As described overleaf, the A-37B equips squadrons in both the AF Reserve and the Air National Guard. It is an excellent low-cost attack training type.

Below: Though the A-37B (rear) is twice as heavy as the T-37A (foreground) its more powerful engines give it a somewhat better flight performance.

▶**Development:** After prolonged study the Air Force decided in 1952 to adopt a jet primary pilot trainer, and after a design competition the Cessna Model 318 was selected. Features included all-metal stressed-skin construction, side-by-side seating in a cockpit with ejection seats and a single broad clamshell canopy, two small engines in the wing roots with nozzles at the trailing edge, fixed tailplane half-way up the fin, manual controls with electric trim, hydraulic slotted flaps and hydraulic tricycle landing gear of exceptional track but short length, placing the parked aircraft low on the ground. The introduction was delayed by numerous trivial modifications and even when service use began in 1957 pupils were first trained on the T-34. Altogether 534 T-37As were built, but all were brought up to the standard of the T-37B, of 1959, which had more powerful J69 engines, improved radio, navaids and revised instrument panel. After 41 had been converted to A-37As further T-37As were bought in 1957 to bring the total of this model to 447. They serve in roughly equal numbers with the advanced T-38A at all the USAF's pilot schools: 12th Flying Training Wing at Randolph; 14th at Columbus (Miss); 47th at Laughlin; 64th at Reese; 71st at Vance; 80th at Sheppard and 82nd at Williams.

The A-37 was derived to meet a need in the early 1960s for a light attack aircraft to fly Co-In (counter-insurgent) missions. Cessna had previously produced two T-37C armed trainers (many of this model were later supplied to Foreign Aid recipients, including South Vietnam in the 1960s),

d later these aircraft were then rebuilt as AT-37 prototypes esignation YAT-37D) with much more powerful engines and airframes stressed for increased weights which, in stages, were raised to 14,000lb ,350kg). No fewer than eight underwing pylons plus wingtip tanks were lded, giving a great weapon-carrying capability whilst offering performance gnificantly higher than that of the trainer. Redesignated A-37A, a squadron nverted from T-37Bs on the production line was evaluated in Vietnam in)67. Altogether 39 A-37As were built by converting T-37Bs on the line, llowed by 511 of the regular USAF production model with full-rated J85 igines, 6g structure, flight-refuelling probe, greater internal tankage and her changes. The A-37 Dragonfly proved valuable in south-east Asia, nere many were left in South Vietnamese hands after the US withdrawal. ter the end of the US involvement the A-37B was withdrawn from regular SAF service but it continues to equip a Reserve wing and two Air National uard groups. The AFR's 434th TFW flies the A-37B at Grissom AFB, unker Hill, Indiana, and the ANG units are the 174th TFG (Syracuse, NY) d the 175th (Baltimore, Md).

elow: Quite apart from the impressive array of tanks and bombs e A-37B Dragonfly bristles with communications and other ission avionic aerials not present on the T-37A trainer.

de Havilland Canada C-7

DHC-4 C-7A, C-7B

Origin: The de Havilland Aircraft of Canada, Toronto.
Type: STOL tactical transport.
Engines: Two 1,450hp Pratt & Whitney R-2000-7M2 Twin Wasp 1
cylinder.
Weights: Empty (A) 16,795lb (7,618kg), (B) 18,260lb (8,283kg); loade
(A) 26,000lb (11,794kg), (B) 31,300lb (14,198kg).
Performance: Maximum speed 216mph 9348km/h); typical cruisin
speed, 182mph (293km/h); initial climb 1,355ft (413m)/min; servic
ceiling, (A) 27,700ft (8,443m), (B) 24,800ft (7,559m); range (B) from 24
miles (389km) with max payload of 8,40lb (3,964kg) to 1,307 mile
(2,103km) with maximum fuel; takeoff or landing over 50ft (15m), abo
1,200ft (366m).
Armament: None.
History: First flight 30 July 1958; service delivery (US Army inventor
January 1961.

Fairchild C-123 Provider

C-123K

Origin: Fairchild Engine and Airplane Corporation, Hagerstown, Md (no
Fairchild Republic Company, Farmingdale, NY).
Type: Tactical airlift transport.
Engines: Two 2,500hp Pratt & Whitney R-2800-99W Double Wasp 1
cylinder plus two 2,850lb (1,293kg) thrust GE J85-17 auxiliary turbojets
Dimensions: Span 110ft 0in (33.53m); length 76ft 3in (23.92m); win
area 1,223sq ft (113.6m²).
Weights: Empty 35,366lb (16,042kg), loaded 60,000lb (27,216kg).
Performance: Maximum speed (with jets) 228mph (367km/h); maximu
cruising speed, 173mph (278km/h); initial climb (no jets) 1,150ft (351m)/mi
service ceiling 29,000ft (8,839m); range with maximum payload
15,000lb (6,804kg), 1,035 miles (1,666km).
Armament: None.
History: First flight (XC-123) 14 October 1949, (K) 27 May 1966.

Development: The history of this tactical transport goes back to Cha
Aircraft, of Trenton, NJ. Here the largest of a series of advanced stresse
skin transports and gliders (including a four-jet transport) was designed
M. Stoukoff in 1949, won an Air Force order for 300 but fell down wh
Kaiser-Frazer failed to build them. Fairchild stepped in, bought Chase a
delivered the 300 on schedule. So good were these machines that they we
updated in many ways, the final C-123K model having underwing-jet pod
Typical loads include trucks, artillery, 61 troops or 50 litter (stretche
patients with six sitting wounded and six attendants. The last units to
equipped with the C-123K were two AFRES units, 302nd TAW (Rickenbak
AFB, Ohio), and 439th (Westover AFB, Mass); only a few remain in servic

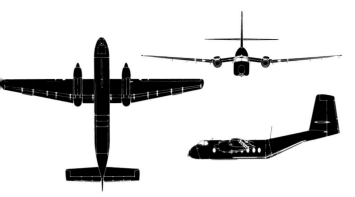

Above: Three-view of C-7A Caribou (without radar).

Development: A specialized STOL (short takeoff and landing) transport aimed mainly at the military market, the piston-engined Caribou has a fairly small interior roughly with the capacity and load capability of a C-47 (DC-3) but with a full-section rear loading ramp which can also be used for air dropping. Features include high-lift flaps, manual controls from a dual cockpit, nose radar and pneumatic boot deicers on all leading edges. The US Army purchased 159 of which the final 103 were to a later standard with increased weight. Normal loads included 32 troops or two Jeeps or similar small vehicles. In 1967, at the height of their involvement in Vietnam, a political decision transferred these aircraft to the Air Force. The last C-7 unit was the ANG's 135th TAG, but a few are still flying.

Left: A radar-equipped C-7A serving with the AF Reserves.

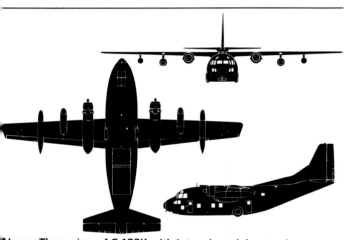

Above: Three-view of C-123K with jet pods and drop tanks.

Below: A recent picture of a C-123K, AF No 64-669.

Fairchild A-10 Thunderbolt II

A-10A, A-10/T, A-10/NAW

Origin: Fairchild Republic Company, Farmingdale, NY.

Type: Close-support attack aircraft.

Engines: Two 9,065lb (4,112kg) thrust General Electric TF34-100 turbofans

Dimensions: Span 57ft 6in (17.53m); length 53ft 4in (16.26m); heigh (regular) 14ft 8in (4.47m), (NAW) 15ft 4in (4.67m); wing area 506sq f (47m²).

Weights: Empty 21,519lb (9761kg); forward airstrip weight (no fuel bu four Mk 82 bombs and 750 rounds) 32,730lb (14,846kg); maximum 50,000lb (22,680kg). Operating weight empty, 24,918lb (11,302kg) (NAW) 28,630lb (12,986kg).

Performance: Maximum speed, (max weight, A-10A) 423mph (681km/h), (NAW) 420mph (676km/h); cruising speed at sea level (both) 345mph (555km/h); stabilized speed below 8,000ft (2,440m) in 45° dive at weigh 35,125lb (15,932kg), 299mph (481km/h); maximum climb at basic desigr weight of 31,790lb (14,420kg), 6,000ft (1,828m)/min; service ceiling, no stated; takeoff run to 50ft (15m) at maximum weight, 4,000ft (1,220m) operating radius in CAS mission with 1.8 hour loiter and reserves, 288 miles (463km); radius for single deep strike penetration, 620 miles (1,000km) ferry range with allowances, 2,542 miles (4091km).

Armament: One GAU-8/A Avenger 30mm seven-barrel gun with 1,174 rounds, total external ordnance load of 16,000lb (7,257kg) hung on 11 pylons, three side-by-side on body and four under each wing; severa hundred combinations of stores up to individual weight of 5,000lb (2,268kg) with maximum total weight 14,638lb (6,640kg) with full interna fuel.

History: First flight (YA-10A) 10 May 1972; (production A-10A) 21 October 1975, (NAW) 4 May 1979.

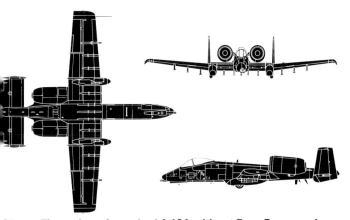

Above: Three-view of standard A-10A without Pave Penny pod.

Below left: Condensation vapour shimmers above the wings and streams from the downturned tips as an A-10A of the 354th TFW pulls round in a tight turn above the forests of South Carolina. The white missiles under the wing are AGM-65A Maverick precision guidance weapons (normally six carried).

Below: An unusual shot of an A-10A peeling off taken from the right-hand seat of an A-37B. Clean manoeuvrability is good.

Bottom: With a straight-wing aircraft as big as a small airliner, and very much slower, it might be thought A-10 pilots felt second-class citizens. These noses quash such an idea stone dead!

373

► **Development:** After prolonged study of lightweight Co-In and light armed reconnaissance aircraft the Air Force in 1967 initiated the A-X programme for a new-generation CAS (close air support) aircraft. It had never had such an aircraft, this mission being previously flown by fighters, bombers, attack and even FAC platforms, including such diverse types as the F-105 and A-1. Emphasis in A-X was not on speed but on lethality against surface targets (especially armour), survivability against ground fire (not including SAMs), heavy ordnance load and long mission endurance. Low priority was paid to advanced nav/attack avionics, the fit being officially described as 'austere'. After a major competition the Northrop A-9A and Fairchild A-10A were pitted against each other in a flyoff contest throughout 1972, after which the A-10A was announced the Air Force's choice on 18 January 1973. Including six DT&E (development, test and evaluation) aircraft the planned force was to number 733, to be deployed in TAC wings in the USA and Europe, and also to a growing number of AFR and ANG squadrons.

Right: Seen over the desert in 1981, the N/AW (Night/Adverse Weather) A-10A is a company-sponsored two-seater with radar in the left gear pod, FLIR in the right and external laser and TV.

The original A-10A was a basically simple single-seater, larger than most tactical attack aircraft and carefully designed as a compromise between capability, survivability and low cost. As an example of the latter many of the major parts, including flaps, main landing gears and movable tail surfaces, are interchangeable left/right, and systems and engineering features were designed with duplication and redundancy to survive parts being shot away. The unusual engine location minimizes infra-red signature and makes it almost simple to fly with one engine inoperative or even shot off. Weapon pylons were added from tip to tip, but the chief tank-killing ordnance is the gun, the most powerful (in terms of muzzle horsepower) ever mounted in an aircraft, firing milk-bottle-size rounds at rates hydraulically controlled at 2,100 or 4,200 shots/min. The gun is mounted 2° nose-down and offset to the left so that the firing barrel is always on the centreline (the nose landing gear being offset to the right).

The basic aircraft has a HUD (head-up display), good communications fit ▶

Left: An A-10A demonstrates its agility in a pull-up at very low level over a column of USA M60 battle tanks. The long store under the right wing is a Westinghouse ALQ-119 ECM pod.

Below: Taken during early evaluation trials with one of the YA-10A prototypes, this photograph shows ammunition being made up into belts. This aircraft has only a small gun of 20mm size.

▶ and both Tacan and an inertial system, as well as ECM and radar homing and warning. Deliveries to the 354th TFW at Myrtle Beach, South Carolina began in 1977, and over 500 have since been received by units in TAC, USAFE (including the 81st TFW in England and 601 TCW at Sembach) and various other commands including the Reserve and ANG. Though relatively slow and ungainly the 'Thud-II' has won over any pilot who might have looked askance at it, and has demonstrated in its first 100,000 hours the ability to do a major job under increasingly hazardous conditions and at the lowest height normally practised by any jet aircraft. Nevertheless attrition at 9 aircraft per 100,000 hours in 1981 was double expectation, resulting in an

Below: A beautiful portrait at dusk of a Maverick-armed A-10A of the 354th TFW. There seems no doubt that, in the long term, this model will be updated for all-weather use with more sensors.

increase in the overall programme to 825 to sustain the desired force to the mid-1990s. Significantly, half the 60 aircraft in the FY81 budget were two-seaters, which though priced $600,000 higher are expected to effect savings by reducing the demand for chase aircraft.

In 1979 Fairchild flew a company-funded NAW (night/adverse weather) demonstrator with augmented avionics and a rear cockpit for a WSO seated at a higher level and with good forward view. Both the regular and NAW aircraft can carry a Pave Penny laser seeker pod under the nose, vital for laser-guilded munitions, and the NAW also has a Ferranti laser ranger, FLIR (forward-looking infra-red), GE low-light TV and many other items including a Westinghouse multimode radar with WSO display. It is probable that during the rest of the decade A-10As will be brought at least close to the NAW standard, while the two-seat NAW might be procured alongside or in place of future buys of the basic A-10A.

General Dynamics F-16 Fighting Falcon

F-16A, B

Origin: General Dynamics Corporation, Fort Worth, Texas.

Type: Multi-role fighter (B) operational fighter/trainer.

Engine: One 23,840lb (10,814kg) thrust Pratt & Whitney F100-200 afterburning turbofan.

Dimensions: Span 31ft 0in (9.449m) 32ft 10in/1.01m over missile fins) length (both versions, excl probe) 47ft 7.7in (14.52m); wing area 300.0 sq ft (27.87m²).

Weights: Empty (A) 15,137lb (6,866kg), (B) 15,778lb (7,157kg); loaded (AAMs only) (A) 23,357lb (10,594kg), (B) 22,814lb (10,348kg), (max external load) (both) 35,400lb (16,057kg). (Block 25 on) 37,500lb (17,010kg).

Performance: Maximum speed (both, AAMs only) 1,350mph (2,173km/h Mach 2.05) at 40,000ft (12.19km); maximum at SL, 915mph (1,472km/h Mach 1.2); initial climb (AAMs only) 50,000ft (15.24km)/min; service ceiling, over 50,000ft (15.24km); tactical radius (A, six Mk 82, internal fuel HI-LO-HI) 340 miles (547km); ferry range, 2,415 miles (3,890km).

Armament: One M61A-1 20mm gun with 500/515 rounds, centreline pylon for 300 US gal (m1,136lit) drop tank or 2,200lb (998kg) bomb inboard wing pylons for 3,500lb (1,587kg) each, middle wing pylons for 2,500lb (1,134kg) each (being uprated under MSIP-1 to 3,500lb), outer wing pylons for 250lb (113.4kg), all ratings being at 9 g.

History: First flight (YF) 20 January 1974, (production F-16A) 7 August 1978; service delivery (A) 17 August 1978.

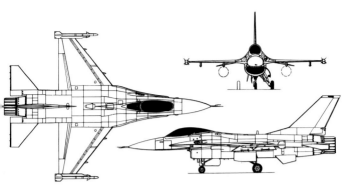

Above: Three-view of standard F-16A-GD-15.

Development: The Fighting Falcon originated through a belief by the Air Force that there might be a more cost/effective fighter than the outstanding but necessarily expensive F-15. In a Lightweight Fighter (LWF) programme of 1972 it sought bids from many design teams, picked GD's Model 401 and ▶

Left: An F-16B two-seater of the 388th TFW, Hill AFB. The AAMs are AIM-9J1 Sidewinders.

Below: An F-16A of the 388th in low-visibility markings, seen in late 1979 at Nellis AFB with an AN/ASQ data-link probe on one wing and AIM-9L on the other.

379

►Northrop's simplified P.530 and evaluated two prototypes of each as the YF-16 and YF-17. GD's engineering team created a totally new aircraft with such advanced features as relaxed static stability (a basic distribution of shapes and masses to attain greater combat agility, overcoming a marginal longitudinal stability by the digital flight-control system), large wing/body flare to enhance lift at high angles of attack and house a gun and extra fuel, a straight wing with hinged leading and trailing flaps used to incrase manoeuvrability in combat (the trailing surfaces being rapid-action flaperons), fly-by-wire electrically signalled flight controls, a futuristic cockpit with reclining zero/zero seat for best resistance to g, with a sidestick controller instead of a control column and one-piece canopy/windscreen of blown polycarbonate, and a miniature multi-mode pulse-doppler radar. On 13 January 1975 the Air Force announced full development of the F-16 not just as a simple day air-combat fighter but also to meet a greatly expanded requirement calling for comprehensive all-weather navigation and weapon delivery in the air/surface role.

This vitally important programme growth was triggered largely by the recognition that there existed a near-term European market, and in June

Above: An F-16A of the 388th burdened by two AIM-9L, two AIM-9J, two Mk 84 (2,000-lb, 907-kg) bombs, two 370-US gal (1700-litre) drop tanks and a Westinghouse AN/ALQ-119 (V) ECM pod.

A pair of Fighting Falcons from Hill AFB. Later a suitable grey paint was discovered for the radome, reducing visibility.

1975 orders were announced by four European NATO countries (Belgium, Denmark, Netherlands and Norway). These organized with GD and P&WA a large multinational manufacturing programme which in the longer term has greatly expanded the production base. In July 1975 the Air Force ordered six pre-production F-16As and two F-16Bs with tandem dual controls and internal fuel reduced from 1,072.5 US gal (4,060lit) to 889.8 (3,368). Both introduced a flight-refuelling boom receptacle (into which a probe can be inserted) and provision for a 300 US gal (1,136lit) centreline drop tank and two 370gal (1,400lit) wing tanks. All eight aircraft were delivered by June 1978, by which time the Air Force had announced a programme for 1,184 F-16As and 204 F-16Bs, with the name Fighting Falcon.

Few aircraft have been as excitedly received as the F-16, which by sheer engineering excellence and painstaking development is as close to the optimum combat aircraft as it is possible to get in its timescale. Even so, it was naturally prey to occasional troubles, notably the prolonged stall-stagnation engine difficulty that had earlier hit the F-15 with an almost identical engine. Following intensive test programmes at Edwards, Nellis and by an MOT&E (multi-national operational test and evaluation) team the ▶

Above: In sharp contrast, this F-16A is flying in the minimum air-combat configuration, with no stores other than a pair of AIM-9J on the tip rails. Thrust/weight ratio can exceed unity.

▶ 388th TFW at Hill AFB, Utah, began to convert on 6 January 1979 and has subsequently not only achieved a string of 'firsts' with the F-16 but has set impressive records in the process. Next came the 56th TFW at MacDill, Florida, followed by the 474th at Nellis, Nevada, the 8th TFW at Kunsan, S Korea, the 50th TFW at Hahn, W. Germany (in USAFE) and the 363rd at Shaw, S. Carolina. Thanks to the large production base and wide international deployment (extending to Israel, S Korea, Egypt, Pakistan and other countries beyond those previously listed) global deployment of Air Force F-16 units is proving exceptionally simple, the aircraft having swiftly attained an exceptional level of reliabilty which is enhanced by outstanding maintenance and self-test features.

Enthusiasm by pilots and ground crew has been exceptional, but an event which dramatically highlighted how far the F-16 had come since 1974 was its first participation in a numerically scored inter-service competition. In the searching USAF/RAF contest held at RAF Lossiemouth on 16-19 June 1981 teams of F-16s (388th TFW), F-1111s, Jaguars and Buccaneers were required under realistic wartime scenarios to penetrate defended airspace, engage hostile fighters and bomb airfields and road convoys. The F-16s were the only aircraft to hit all assigned surface targets, while in air combat their score was 86 kills against no losses; rival teams suffered 42 losses and

Above: Low-visibility F-16A with instrumentation transmitter on right wing and ALQ-119 jammer pod on centreline.

Below: Shallow dive attack with two Mk 84 bombs by F-16A also carrying two tanks, two AIM-9L, two AIM-9J and jammer pod.

▶ collectively scored but a single kill. The F-16 also scored very much better against Rapier SAM threats, while in the ground-crew part of the contest the 388th achieved an average turnround time between sorties of 10½ minutes including refuelling, loading six Mk 82 bombs and 515 rounds of ammunition. Since its introduction to TAC the F-16 has had the highest Mission Capable Rate in the command, and has been the only multirole aircraft to achieve the command goal of 70%.

In 1982 production had passed 600 aircraft, with plenty of spare capacity at Fort Worth for up to 45 per month if necessary. Though this excellent output was attained by sticking to an agreed standard of build, improvements

Below: A F-16A of the 388th TFW, in the low-visibility markings now standard in Tactical Air Command. Tail designator letters for the next two wings to be completely equipped with the F-16 were: NA, 474th TFW, Nellis AFB; MC, 56th TFW, MacDill.

have been continual, and many more are in prospect. During production the nlet was strengthened to carry EO/FLIR and laser pods, a graphite/epoxy tailplane of larger size was introduced to match increased gross weight (see data), and the central computer and avionics were changed for a much expanded package'. Later the 30mm GEpod gun, Maverick missile, Lantirn and AMRAAM advanced missile will be introduced, the new AAM being inked with the programmable APG-66 radar for stand-off interception capability. Later still the striking bat-like SCAMP (supersonic-cruise aircraft modification program) may result in still higher performance with double bombloads.

Below: The F-16B being used to develop an F-16 with Wild Weasel anti-radar capability. The weapons installed here are AIM-9J (tips), AGM-45 Shrike (stations 2 and 8) and AGM-88 HARM (High-speed Anti-Radiation Missile) (stations 2 and 7).

General Dynamics F-106 Delta Dart

F-106A, B

Origin: General Dynamics Convair Division, San Diego, California.
Type: All-weather interceptor, (B) operational trainer.
Engine: One 24,500lb (11,130kg) thrust Pratt & Whitney J75-17 afterburning turbojet.
Dimensions: Span 38ft 3in (11.67m); length (both) 70ft 8¾in (21.55m) wing area 661.5 sq ft (61.52m²).
Weights: Empty (A) about 24,420lb (11,077kg); loaded (normal) 34,510lb (15,668kg).
Performance: Maximum speed (both) 1,525mph (2,455km/h) or Mach 2.3 at 36,000ft (11km); initial climb, about 29,000ft (8,839m)/min; service ceiling 57,000ft (17,374m); range with drop tanks 1,800 miles (2,897km).
Armament: One 20mm M61A-1 gun, two AIM-4F plus two AIM-4G Falcons, plus one AIR-2A or -2G Genie nuclear rocket.
History: First flight (aerodynamic prototype) 26 December 1956, (B) 9 April 1958; squadron delivery June 1959.

Development: Derived from the earlier F-102 Delta Dagger, the F-106 had a maximum speed approximately twice as high and completely met the requirements of Aerospace Defense Command (Adcom) for a manned interceptor to defend the continental United States. Linked via its complex and bulky MA-1 electronic fire-control system through a digital data link into the nationwide SAGE (semi-automatic ground environment), the 106 served much longer than intended and in fact never did see a successor, despite the continued threat of the manned bomber, though there were numerous engineering improvements and some substantial updates including the addition of the gun (in a neat installation in the missile bay, causing a

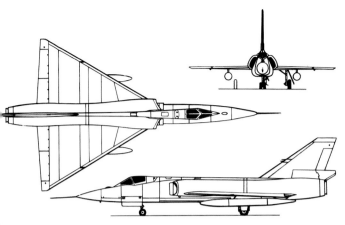

Above: Three-view of F-106A with IR seeker ahead of windscreen.

(light ventral bulge) as well as improved avionics, an infra-red sensor of great sensitivity facing ahead for detecting heat from hostile aircraft and assisting the lock-on of AAMs, and a flight-refuelling boom receptacle. Convair completed many other studies including improved electric power system, solid-state computer, the AIMS (aircraft identification monitoring system) and an enhanced-capability variant for Awacs control. The last of 277 F-106As and 63 tandem-seat F-106B armed trainers were delivered in 1961. Adcom was disbanded in 1980 and F-106s now fly only with fighter units in the ANG. One also flies with NASA on storm hazard research.

Below: Darts of one of the last TAC fighter interceptor squadrons. The Service type now flies only with the ANG.

General Dynamics F-111

F-111A, D, E and F, FB-111A and EF-111A

Origin: (except EF) General Dynamics Corporation, Fort Worth, Texas (EF) Grumman Aerospace Corporation, Bethpage, NY.

Type: A,D,E,F, all-weather attack; FB, strategic attack; EF, tactical ECM jammer.

Powerplant: Two Pratt & Whitney TF30 afterburning turbofans, as follow (A, C, EF) 18,500lb (8,390kg) TF30-3, (D,E) 19,600lb (8,891kg) TF30-9 (FB) 20,350lb (9,231kg) TF30-7, (F) 25,100lb (11,385kg) TF30-100.

Dimensions: Span (fully spread) (A,D,E,F,EF) 63ft 0in (19.2m), (FB) 70ft 0in (21.34m), (fully swept) (A,D,E,F,E,F) 31ft 11½in (9.74m), (FB) 33ft 11in (10.34m); length (except EF) 73ft 6in (22.4m), (EF) 77ft 1.6in (23.51m) wing area (A,D,E,F,EF, gross, 16°) 525 sq ft (48.77m²)

Weights: Empty (A) 46,172lb (20,943kg), (D) 49,090lb (22,267kg), (E about 47,000lb (21,319kg), (EF) 53,418lb) (24,230kg), (F) 47,481lb (21,537kg), (FB) close to 50,000lb (22,680kg); loaded (A) 91,500lb (41,500kg), (D,E) 92,500lb (41,954kg), (F) 100,000lb (45,360kg), (FB 114,300lb (51,846kg), (EF) 87,478lb (39,680kg).

Performance: Maximum speed at 36,000ft (11km), clean and with ma afterburner, (A,D,E) Mach 2.2, 1,450mph (2,335km/h), (FB) Mach 2 1,320mph (2,124km/h), (F) Mach 2.5, 1,653mph (2,660km/h), (EF) Mach 1.75, 1,160mph (1,865km/h); cruising speed, penetration, 571mph (919km/h); initial climb (EF) 3,592ft (1,95m)/min; service ceiling at comba weight, max afterburner, (A) 51,000ft (15,500m), (F) 60,000ft (18,290m) (EF) 54,700ft (16,670m); range with max internal fuel (A,D) 3,165 mile (5,093km), (F) 2,925 miles (4,707km), (EF) 2,484 miles (3,998km) takeoff run (A) 4,000ft (1,219m), (F) under 3,000ft (914m), (FB) 4,700f (1,433m), (EF) 3,250ft (991m).

Armament: Internal weapon bay for two B43 bombs or (D,F) one B43 and one M61 gun; three pylons under each wing (four inboard swivelling wit wing, outers being fixed and usable only at 16°, otherwise being jettisoned for max external load 31,500lb (14,288kg); (FB only) provision for up to si SRAM, two internal; (EF) no armament.

History: First flight 21 December 1964, service delivery (A) June 1967 (EF) July 1981.

Below: An F-111A of the 366th TFW (Mountain Home AFB, Idaho) lets go 24 bombs during a max-conventional load attack mission.

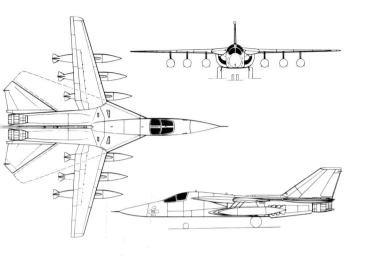

Above: Three-view of A,D,E or F model (gun not fitted).

Above: An early F-111E on test with a white radome; this model has since 1970 been deployed in England (20th TFW).

Below: View of an F-111 of TAC as it edges in under a KC-135 with its boom receptacle door open above the fuselage.

389

▶**Development:** In 1960 the Department of Defense masterminded the TFX (tactical fighter experimental) as a gigantic programme to meet all the fighter and attack needs of the Air Force, Navy and Marine Corps, despite the disparate requirements of these services, and expected the resultant aircraft to be bought throughout the non-Communist world. In fact, so severe were the demands for weapon load and, in particular, mission range that on the low power available the aircraft had inadequate air-combat capability and in fact it was destined never to serve in this role, though it is still loosely described as a 'tactical fighter'. After prolonged technical problems involving escalation in weight, severe aerodynamic drag, engine/inlet mismatch and, extending into the early 1970s, structural failures, the F-111 eventually matured as the world's best long-range interdiction attack aircraft which in the hands of dedicated and courageous Air Force crews pioneered the new art of 'skiing'--riding the ski-toe locus of a TFR (terrain-following radar) over hills, mountains and steep-sided valleys in blind conditions, in blizzards or by night, holding a steady 200ft (91m) distance from the ground at high-subsonic speed, finally to plant a bomb automatically within a few metres of a previously computed target.

Basic features of the F-111 include a variable-sweep 'swing wing' (the first in production in the world) with limits of 16° and 72.5°, with exceptional high-lift devices, side-by-side seating for the pilot and right-seat navigator (usually also a pilot) or (EF) electronic-warfare officer, large main gears with low-pressure tyres for no-flare landings on soft strips (these prevent the carriage of ordnance on fuselage pylons), a small internal weapon bay, very great internal fuel capacity (typically 5,022 US gal, 19,010 litres), and emergency escape by jettisoning the entire crew compartment, which has its own parachutes and can serve as a survival shelter or boat.

General Dynamics cleared the original aircraft for service in 2½ years, and

Above: By far the best of the tactical attack models, the F-111F
equips the 48th TFW at RAF Lakenheath, England. The avionics
represent an attempt to combine some of the advanced features of
the Mk II system (F-111D) without the latter's frustrating costs and
problems, while the engine is much more powerful than that of any
other F-111 (and much more powerful than any TF30 fitted to the
Navy's Grumman F-14 Tomcat for that matter!).

Below: A pair of FB-111A bombers from Strategic Air Command
are seen here in long-range cruise with no external load except a
pair of 500-US gal (2271-litre) tanks. Two Mk 43, Mk 57 or TX-61
bombs may be aboard.

▶built 141 of this F-111A version, which equips 366TFW at Mountain Home AFB, Idaho (others have been reserved for conversion into the EF-111A). It is planned to update the A by fitting a digital computer to the original analog-type AJQ-20A nav/bomb system, together with the Air Force standard INS and a new control/display set. The F-111E was similar but had larger inlet ducts and engines of slightly greater power; 94 were delivered and survivors equip the 20th TFW at Upper Heyford, England. These are to receive the same updates as the A. Next came the F-111D, which at great cost was fitted with an almost completely different avionic system of a basically digital nature including the APQ-30 attack radar, APN-189 doppler and HUDs for both crew-members. This aircraft had great potential but caused severe technical and manpower problems in service and never fully realized its capabilities, though it remains a major advance on the A and E. The 96 built have always equipped the 27th TFW at Cannon AFB, New Mexico. The F-111F is by far the best of all tactical F-111 versions, almost entirely because Pratt & Whitney at last produced a really powerful TF30 which incorporated many other advanced features giving enhanced life with fewer problems. With much greater performance than any other model the F could if necessary double in an air-combat role though it has no weapons for this role except the gun and if necessary AIM-9. The 106 of this model served at Mountain Home until transfer to the 48th TFW in England, at Lakenheath. The most important of all F-111 post-delivery modifications has been the conversion of the F force to use the Pave Tack pod, normally stowed in the weapon bay but rotated out on a cradle for use. This complex package provides a day/night all-weather capability to acquire, track, designate and hit surface targets using EO, IR or laser guided weapons. The first squadron to convert was the 48th TFW's 494th TFS, in September 1981. Their operations officer, Maj Bob Rudiger, has said: 'Important targets that once required several aircraft can now be disabled with a single Pave Tack aircraft, the radar tells the pod where to look, and the laser allows us to put the weapon precisely on target.'

The long-span FB-111A was bought to replace the B-58 and early models of B-52 in SAC, though the raising price resulted in a cut in procurement from 210 to 76, lentering service in October 1969. It has so-called Mk IIB avionics, derived from those of the D but configured for SAC missions using nuclear bombs or SRAMs. With strengthened structure and landing gear the FB has a capability of carrying 41,250lb (18,711kg) of bombs, made up of 50 bombs of 825lb (nominal 750lb size) each. This is not normally used, and the outer pylons associated with this load are not normally installed. The FB equips SAC's 380th BW at Plattsburgh AFB, NY, and the 509th at Pease, New Hampshire. No go-ahead has been received for numerous extremely capable stretched FB versions.

Left: F-111F No 70-369 cruises above fine-weather cumulus clouds as it heads across England for practice TFR (terrain-following radar) flight and a simulated bomb drop on an instrumented range in the Isle of Man.

Below: This EF-111A still bears its original tail number 66-051, showing it was one of the fourth block of the F-111A version before its total reconstruction. The Air Force has a desperate need for considerably more advanced EW (electronic-warfare) platforms than the 42 of this type which it hopes to be able to afford.

Above: The first production EF-111A was former F-111A No 66-049, seen here on flight test at Grumman's facility at Calverton, NY.

Last of the F-111 variants, the EF-111A is the USAF's dedicated EW platform, managed by Grumman (partner on the original Navy F-111B version) and produced by rebuilding F-111As. The USA acknowledges the Soviet Union to have a lead in both ground and air EW, and thousands of radars and other defence emitters in Eastern Europe would make penetration by NATO aircraft extremely dangerous. The vast masking power of the EF-110A, which equals that of the Navy EA-6B and in fact uses almost the same ALQ-99E tac-jam system (but with a crew of only two instead of four), is expected to be able to suppress these 'eyes' and enable NATO aircraft to survive. An aerodynamic prototype flew in March 1977, the ALQ-99 was flying in an F-111 in May 1977, and production deliveries began in mid-1981 to the 366th TFW. The Air Force plans to have 42 aircraft rebuilt as EFs, for service with all USAFE penetrating attack units and others in TAC and possibly other commands.

Lockheed C-5A Galaxy

C-5A

Origin: Lockheed-Georgia Company, Marietta, Ga.

Type: Heavy strategic airlift transport.

Powerplant: Four 41,000lb (18,597kg) thrust General Electric TF39-1 turbofans.

Dimensions: Span 222ft 8½in (67.88m); length 247ft 10in (75.54m), height 65ft 1½in (19.85m); wing area 6,200sq ft (576.0m²).

Weights: Empty (basic operating) 337,937lb (153,285kg), loaded (2,25g 769,000lb (348,810kg).

Performance: Maximum speed (max weight, 25,000ft/7,620m) 571mph (760km/h); normal long-range cruising speed, 518mph (834km/h); initial climb at max wt., rated thrust, 1,800ft (549m)/min; service ceiling (615,000lb/278,950kg) 34,000ft (10.36km); range with design payload of 220, 967lb (100,228kg), 3,749 miles (6,033km); range with 112,600lb (51,074kg) payload, 6,529 miles 7,991 miles (12,860km); takeoff distance at max wt. over 50ft (15m), 8,400ft (2,560m); landing from 50ft (15m), 3,600ft (1,097m).

Armament: None.

History: First flight 30 June 1968; service delivery, 17 December 1969; final delivery from new, May 1973.

Development: Growing appreciation of the need for an extremely large logistics transport to permit deployment of the heaviest hardware items on a global basis led in 1963 to the CX-HLS (Heavy Logistics System) specification calling for a payload of 250,000lb (113,400kg) over a coast-to-coast range and half this load over the extremely challenging unrefuelled range of 8,000 miles (12,875km); it also demanded the ability to fly such loads into a 4,000ft (1,220m) rough forward airstrip. Such performance was theoretically possible using a new species of turbofan, of high bypass ratio, much more powerful than existing engines. In August 1965 GE won the engine contract, and two months later Lockheed won the C-5A aircraft. Design was undertaken under extreme pressure, the wing being assigned to CDI, a group of British engineers from the cancelled HS.115 and TSR.2 programmes. About half the value of each airframe was subcontracted to

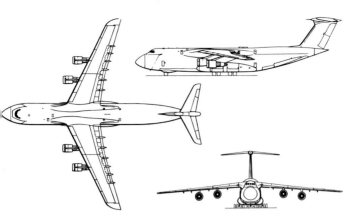

Above: Three-view of C-5A Galaxy as delivered to MAC.

Above: First takeoff by the prototype on 30 June 1968; subsequently the TF39 engine was made almost free from visible smoke.

Above: An almost grotesque appearance results from a camera resting on the ground and the nose door partly open.

Left: Production took place in batches of 53 and 23 (plus five prototypes). This is 68-0216 from the main block of 53.

▶suppliers in the US and Canada, and construction of the first aircraft (66 8303) began as early as August 1966.

Meeting the requirements proved impossible, and cost-inflation reduced the total buy from 115 (six squadrons) to 81 (four squadrons), of which 30 were delivered by the end of 1970. As a cargo airlifter the C-5A proved in a class of its own, with main-deck width of 19ft (5.79m) and full-section access at front and rear. The upper deck houses the flight crew of five, a rest area for a further 15 and a rear (aft of the wing) area with 75 seats. Features include high-lift slats and flaps, an air-refuelling receptacle, advanced forward-looking radars and a unique landing gear with 28 wheels offering the required 'high flotation' for unpaved surfaces, as weel as free castoring to facilitate ground manoeuvring, an offset (20° to left or right) swivelling capability for use in crosswinds, fully modulating anti-skid brakes and the ability to kneel to bring the main deck close to the ground. Despite highly publicized faults, most of which were quickly rectified, the C-5A was soon

Above: C-5A No 67-0171 in a remarkably tight turn at low level.

Below: The C-5A (this is 69-0013) dwarfs even the KC-10A.

iving invaluable service; but a deep-rooted difficulty was that the wing ccrued fatigue damage much more rapidly than had been predicted. everal costly modification programmes proved incomplete solutions, and 1978 Lockheed's proposal for the introduction of a new wing was ccepted. This wing uses a totally different detailed design in different naterials, and though the moving surfaces are largely unchanged even these re to be manufactured again, the slats, ailerons and flap tracks for the econd time being assigned to Canadair. Between 1982-87 all 77 surviving rcraft are to be re-winged. This is being done with minimal reduction in rlift capability by MAC's 60th MAW at Travis, 436th at Dover, Delaware, nd 443rd at Altus AFB, Oklahoma.

In 1982 the US Congress authorized a programme to procure an additional 50 aircraft to a new C-5B standard, with a long crack-free airframe 'e, improved avionics and four General Electric TF39-GE-1C turbofan ngines. The first flew on 10 September 1985.

bove: Taken during manoeuvres with the USA in the United States his landing picture shows both the multi-segment flaps and the 28 nding wheels needed to confer 'flotation' for soft fields.

Lockheed C-130 Hercules

C-130A to P, DC-130, EC-130, HC-130, JHC-130, JC-130, MC-130, RC-130, WC-130.

Origin: Lockheed-Georgia Company, Marietta, Ga.

Type: Originally, multirole airlift transport; special variants, see text.

Powerplant: Four Allison T56 turboprops, (B and E families) 4,050ehp, T56-7, (H family) 4,910ehp T56-15 flat-rated at 4,508ehp.

Dimensions: Span 132ft 7in (40.41m); length (basic) 97ft 9in (29.79m) (HC-130H, arms spread) 106ft 4in (32.41m); wing area 1,745sq f (162.12m²).

Weights: Empty (basic E, H) 72,892lb (33 063kg); operating weight (H 75,832lb (34,397kg); loaded (E,H) 155,000lb (70,310kg), max overloa 175,000lb (79,380kg).

Performance: Maximum speed at 175,000lb (E, H), also max cruisin speed, 386mph (621km/h); economical cruise, 345mph (556km/h); initia SL climb (E) 1,830ft (558m)/min, (H) 1,900ft (579m)/min; service ceilin at 155,000lb, (E) 23,000ft (7,010m), (H) 26,500ft (8,075m); range (H with max payload of 2,487 miles (4,002km; ferry range with reserves (H) 4,606 miles (7,412km); takeoff to 50ft (15m) (H at 175,000lb), 5,160f (1,573m); landing from 50ft (15m) (H at 100,000lb/45,360kg), 2,700f (823m).

Armament: Normally none.

History: First flight (YC-130A) 23 August 1954, (production C-130A) 7 April 1955; service delivery December 1956.

Development: When the Berlin Airlift and Korean war highlighted the nee for more capable military transport aircraft, several obvious features wer waiting to be combined in one design. Among these were a high wing an unobstructed cargo compartment, a flat level floor at truck-bed height abov

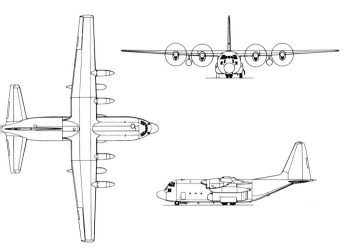

Above: Three-view of standard C-130E or C-130H.

Below: One of seven sub-variants equipped for the aerial recovery of spacecraft or other items or the pick-up of passengers from the ground. Main user is ARRS (Aerospace Rescue and Recovery Service) whose models included the HC-130H, JHC-130H, DC-130H, HC-130N and HC-130P.

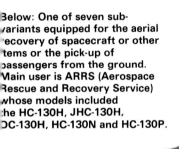

Below: All models of C-130 (this is a standard C-130H) are cleared for unrestricted weight operation from unpaved airstrips.

Above: Fine picture of C-130H No 63-7798, in regular camouflage with one of the MAC airlift squadrons on inter-theatre duties.

▶the ground, pressurization and air-conditioning, full-section rear door and vehicle ramp, turboprop propulsion for high performance, a modern flight deck with all-round vision, and retractable landing gear with 'high flotation tyres for use from unprepared airstrips. All were incorporated in th Lockheed Model 82 which in June 1951 won an Air Force requirement for new and versatile transport for TAC. By sheer good fortune the Alliso single-shaft T56 turboprop matured at precisely the right time, along with new species of advanced Aeroproducts or HamStan propeller and severa other new-technology items including high-strength 2024 aluminium allo machined skin planks for the wings and cargo floor, metal/metal bondin and titanium alloys for the nacelles and flap skins. Another new feature was miniature APU (auxiliary power unit) in one of the landing-gear blisters t provide ground power for air-conditioning and main-engine pneumati starting.

Two YC-130 prototypes were built at Burbank, with 3,250hp T56-1 engines, but long before these were completed the programme was move to the vast Government Plant 6 in Georgia which had been built to produc the B-29 under Bell management and restored to active use by Lockheed i January 1951. The new transport was ordered as the C-130A in Septembe 1952 and the work phased in well with the tapering off of the B-47. Whe the 130, soon dubbed the Herky-bird, joined the 463rd Troop Carrier Win at Ardmore in 1956 it caused a stir of a kind never before associated with mere cargo transport. Pilots began to fly their big airlifters like fighters, an to explore the limits of what appeared to be an aircraft so willing it would d impossible demands. This was despite increases in permitted gross weigh from 102,000lb to 116,000 and then to 124,200lb (56,335kg). At an earl stage the nose grew a characteristic pimple from switching to the APN-5 radar, and provision was made for eight 1,000lb (454kg) Aerojet assistec takeoff rockets to be clipped to the sides of the fuselage, to augment th thrust of full-rated 3,750hp engines.

In December 1958 Lockheed flew the first extended-range C-130B with more powerful engines driving four-blade propellers. The Air Force bough 132 to supplement the 204 A-models, the latter progressively being rebui as AC-130 gunships, DC-130 drone (RPV) controllers, JC-130 spacecraft tracking and retrieval aircraft and C-130D wheel/ski aircraft with Arctic/Antarctic equipment. The next basic model, and bought in larges numbers (389), was the E, first flown on 25 August 1961. With this a mino

Above: Delivery from high level of an armoured car by parachuted pallet; the aircraft is a MAC C-130H.

Below: Delivery of an M551 Sheridan light tank by the alternative method of ground-proximity extraction without parachutes.

Above: Exceptional C-130 force on manoeuvres at Dyess AFB, Texas.

▶ structural rework enabled wing pylons to carry large drop tanks of 1,360 US gal (5,145lit), meeting the strategic range requirements of MATS (now MAC) and thus opening up a new market for the 130 beyond the tactical sphere. MATS (MAC) received 130 of the E model, and TAC re-equipped with 245 and transferred the A and B models to the ANG and Reserve, giving these reserve forces undreamed-of airlift capability. Some B-models were converted for other roles, new duties including weather reconnaissance (WC-130) and a single STOL aircraft with extra pod-mounted T56 engines supplying a boundary-layer control system, designated NC-130. Among currently serving rebuilds of the E are the EC-130E tactical command and control platform, with several unique avionic systems, and the MC-130E used with special avionics and low-level flight techniques for clandestine exfiltration and airdrop missions.

Latest basic type is the C-130H, first delivered in April 1975, with more powerful engines flat-rated at the previous level to give improved takeoff from hot/high airstrips. Variations include the HC-130H extended-range model for the Aerospace Rescue and Recovery Service with a fold-out nose installation for the snatching of people or payloads from the ground. The JHC-130H model has further gear for aerial recovery of space capsules. A more advanced model, with special direction-finding receivers but without long-range tanks, is the HC-130N. The HC-130P model combines the mid-air retrieval capability with a tanking and air-refuelling function for helicopters.

This evergreen aircraft is by far the most important Air Force tactical airlifter and fulfils a host of secondary functions. Though civil and RAF versions have been stretched to match capacity to payload, this has not been done by the USAF. Production continues, and six H models were ordered for the AFRes and ANG in July 1981. New roles being studied by the Air Force include the C-130H-MP maritime patroller with offshore surveillance equipment, and the CAML (cargo aircraft minelayer) system using hydraulically powered pallets for rapid-sequence deployment of large sea mines. Should CAML be adopted, Air Force C-130s could fly minelaying missions for the Navy.

Below: No longer in use, the AC-130A was the first AC-130 armed gunship version for truck-killing at night. Two 20-mm M61s are firing.

Top: A C-130—apparently an HC-130 of the ARRS—moving off during a 1979 exercise. Some models have heated ski landing gears.

Above: Gunship models, developed during the Vietnam War, are still active in Special Forces operations; this is an AC-130H seen in 1980.

Lockheed C-141 StarLifter

C-141A and B

Origin: Lockheed-Georgia Company, Marietta, Ga.
Type: Strategic airlift and aeromedical transport.
Powerplant: Four 21,000lb (9,525kg) thrust Pratt & Whitney TF33-turbofans.
Dimensions: Span 159ft 11in (48.74m); length (A) 145ft. 0in (44.2m), (B) 168ft 3½in (51.29m); wing area 3,228sq. ft (299.9m²).
Weights: Empty (A) 133,733lb (60,678kg), (B) 148,120lb (67,186kg) loaded (A) 316,600lb (143,600kg), (B) 343,000lb (155,585kg).
Performance: Maximum speed (A) 571mph (919km/h), (B, also ma cruising speed) 566mph (910km/h); long-range cruising speed (both 495mph (796km/h); initial climb (A) 3,100ft (945m)/min, (B) 2,920 (890m)/min; service ceiling, 41,600ft (12,68km); range with maximur payload of (A, 70,847lb/32,136kg) 4,080 miles (6,565km), (E 90,880lb/41,222kg) 2,935 miles (4,725km); takeoff to 50ft (15m) (E 5,800ft (1,768m).
Armament: None.
History: First flight 17 December 1953; service delivery 19 October 1964 first flight of C-141B, 24 March 1977.

Development: In the late 1950s MATS (now MAC) anticipated a sever future shortage of long-range airlift capacity, the C-133 being an interin propeller aircraft and the much larger C-132 being cancelled. As interin solutions orders were placed for the C-135 jet and for a long-range version of the C-130, but on 4 May 1960 a requirement was issued for a purpose designed transport which was won by Lockheed's Model 300 submission i March 1961. Ordered at once as the C-141, it followed the lines of the C 130, and even had the same 10ft x 9ft (3.1 x 2.77m) body cross-section (a choice which perhaps proved erroneous, as from the start the internal cub volume was totally inadequate for the available weightlifting ability). Th C-141 was, in other respects, much larger, with a wing of almost twice th area, swept at only 23° (¼-chord) for good field length but resulting in lowe speeds than equivalent civil transports. Features included a full-sectio ramp/door, side paratroop doors, upper-surface roll/airbrake spoilers, fou reversers, tape instruments, an all-weather landing system and advance loading and positioning systems for pallets and other loads.

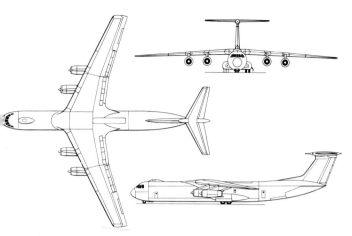

Above: Three-view of the new model, the stretched C-141B.

Above: Takeoff by a C-141A of the 438th MAW, based at McGuire AFB, New Jersey, in the 21st AF. Outstanding in most respects, the C-141 design erred in adhering to the same fuselage cross-section as the C-130, resulting in a basic inability to accommodate the loads it could otherwise lift. This has been rectified in the lengthened C-141B, though the width/height problems still remain.

Left: Arrival in Japan of a C-141A then serving with the 60th MAW.

▶ The first five C-141As were ordered in August 1961, at which time the requirement was for 132 aircraft, but following extremely rapid development and service introduction further orders were placed for a total of 285. Several of the first block were structurally modified to improve the ability of the floor to support the skids of a containerized Minuteman ICBM, a weight of 86,207lb (30,103kg). One of these aircraft set a world record in parachuting a single mass of 70,195lb (31,840kg). Standard loads included 10 regular 463L cargo pallets, 154 troops, 123 paratroops or 80 litter (stretcher) patients plus 16 medical attendants. Usable volume was 5,290 cu ft (150m³), not including the ramp. Service experience proved exemplary and in the Vietnam war C-141s, many of them specially equipped for medical missions and flown with extraordinary skill to ensure a smooth ride even through severe weather, maintained essentially a daily schedule on a 10,000-mile (16,000km) trip with full loads both ways.

It was this full-load experience which finally drove home the lesson that the C-141 could use more cubic capacity. Lockheed devised a cost/effective

Below: The first of three M-113 amphibious armoured carriers of the US Army emerges from an unmodified C-141A in the 1970s.

This StarLifter, at the time designated as the YC-141B, was the first of MAC's 271 aircraft of this type to be 'stretched'. The bulge aft of the cockpit is the UARRSI (Universal Aerial Refuelling Receptacle Slipway Installation).

U.S. AIR FORCE

stretch which adds 'plugs' ahead of and behind the wing which extend the usable length by 23ft 4in (7.11m), increasing the usable volume (including the ramp) to 11,399cu ft (322.71m³). The extended aircraft, designated C-141B, carriers 13 pallets or much larger numbers of personnel. It also incorporates an improved wing/body fairing which reduces drag and fuel burn per unit distance flown, while among other modifications the most prominent is a dorsal bulge aft of the flight deck housing a universal (boom or drogue) flight-refuelling receptacle. The first conversion, the YC-141B, was so successful that the Air Force decided to have Lockheed rework all the surviving aircraft (277), to give in effect the airlift ability of 90 additional aircraft with no extra fuel consumption.

Two hundred and seventy C-141As were converted to B standard in the early 1980s and equip 14 squadrons assigned to the following MAWs: 60th at Travis, California; 63rd at Norton, California; 437th at Charleston, S Carolina; 438th at McGuire, NJ; 443rd at Altus, Oklahoma; and to part of the 314th TAW at Little Rock, Arkansas.

Below: As noted in the text, a C-141 once held the world record for a heavy-dropped load. Here pallets leave a C-141B in late 1980.

Lockheed SR-71

SR-71A, B and C

Origin: Lockheed-California Company, Burbank, California.
Type: A, strategic reconnaissance; B, C, trainer.
Powerplant: Two 32,500lb (14,742kg) thrust Pratt & Whitney J58-1 (JT11D-20B) continuous-bleed afterburning turbojets.
Dimensions: Span 55ft 7in (16.94m); length 107ft 5in (32.74m); wing area 1,800sq ft (167.2m²).
Weights: Empty, not disclosed, but about 65,000lb (29.5t); loaded 170,000lb (77,112kg).
Performance: Maximum speed (also maximum cruising speed), about 2,100mph (3,380km/h) at over 60,000ft (18,29m); world record speed over 15/25km course, 2,193mph (3,530km/h), Mach 3.31); maximum sustained height (also world record), 85,069ft (25,929m); range at 78,740ft (24km) at 1,983mph (3191km/h, Mach 3) on internal fuel, 2,982 miles (4,800km); corresponding endurance, 1h 30min; endurance at loiter speed, up to 7h.
Armament: None.
History: First flight (A-11) 26 April 1962; (SR-71A) 22 December 1964; service delivery, January 1966.

Development: Unbelievably, Lockheed and the Air Force succeeded in designing, building and completing the flight-test programme of these extremely large and noisy aircraft in total secrecy. President Johnson disclosed the existence of the basic A-11 design in February 1964. It was created by Lockheed's Advanced Development Projects team--the so-called Skunk Works--under vice-president C.L. 'Kelly' Johnson in 1959-61 The requirement was for a platform able to succeed the U-2 for clandestine reconnaissance, and as height was no longer sufficient protection, speed ▶

Below: SR-71As used on combat missions over Southeast Asia in 1967-73 still wear a snake emblem on their vertical tails.

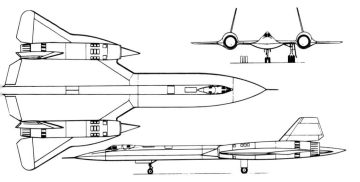

Above: Standard SR-71A with spikes out and nozzles closed.

Above: A Blackbird of the 9th SRW taxis in at Beale after a
mission, its braking-parachute doors still open above the body.

U.S. AIR FORCE

▶ had to be added (which in turn translated into still greater height). The engineering problems with the titanium-alloy airframe, the unprecedented propulsion system (which at cruising speed glows orange-white at the rear yeat gets most of its thrust from the inlet) and even the hydraulic system which had to use totally new materials and techniques. Basic features included a modified delta wing with pronounced camber on the outer leading edges, extremely large lifting strakes extended forwards along the body and nacelles, twin inwards-canted pivoted fins above the nacelles, outboard ailerons, inboard elevators and main gears with three wheels side-by-side. The original A-11 shape also featured fixed ventral fins under the rear of the nacelles and a larger hinged central ventral fin.

The first three aircraft (60-6934/6) were built as YF-12A research interceptors, with a pressurized cockpit for a pilot and air interception officer, Hughes ASG-18 pulse-doppler radar, side chines cut back to avoid the radome and provide lateral locations for two IR seekers, and tandem missile bays for (usually) eight AIM-47 AAMs. In 1969-72 two participated in a joint programme with NASA to investigate many aspects of flight at around Mach 3. These aircraft investigated surface finishes other than the normal bluish-black which resulted in the popular name of 'Blackbird' for all aircraft of this family.

It is believed that about 15 aircraft were delivered to the Air Force with a generally similar standard of build, though configured for the reconnaissance/strike role. Designated A-11, they could carry a centreline pod which could be a 1-megaton bomb but was usually a GTD-21 reconnaissance drone looking like a scaled-down single-engined A-11 and with cameras, IR and (variously, according to mission) other sensors in a bay behind the multi-shock centrebody nose inlet. Some dozens of these RPVs were delivered, painted the same heat-reflective black and with similar flight performance (engine has not been disclosed) but with rather shorter endurance. Those not consumed in missions (about 17) were stored at Davis-Monthan.

The A-11/GTD-21 held the fort until, in 1964, the definitive long-range recon/strike RS-71A came into service. (It was announced by President Johnson as the SR-71A and as he was never corrected the 'SR' designation became accepted.) This also can carry a 1-MT bomb pod or GTD-21 or derived RPV, but details of missions and payloads have not been disclosed. With an airframe and increased-capacity fuel system first flown on the fourth

Left: The crew disembark from their incredible vehicle as a ground-crewman begins to open one of the inlet-duct doors (still too hot to touch). The SR-71 needs very special ground-support equipment.

Below: The setting sun is reflected off this SR-71A caught by the camera in a rare slow-speed let-down above a thick cloud layer. The aircraft is No 71-7964. The number of SR-71s built has not been disclosed.

Above: The Air Force no longer uses the Lockheed YF-12A, shorter and much lighter (because of smaller fuel capacity) than an SR-71.

▶ A-11 (designated YF-12C) it is longer, has no rear ventrals, optimized forward chines extending to the tip of the nose, and no missile bay but extremely comprehensive and in some cases unique reconnaissance systems for the surveillance of from 60,000 to 80,000 square miles (155,000 to 207,000km²) per hour. The backseater, with a separate clamshell canopy with inserted panes of heat-resistant glass, is the RSO, reconnaissance systems officer. Both crew wear Astronaut suits and follow pre-flight procedures based on those of space missions. The first SR-71A was assigned to a new unit, the 4,200th SRW, at Beale AFB, California, in 1966, which worked up the optimum operating procedures and techniques for best coverage, optimum fuel consumption, minimal signatures and precision navigation, burning special JP-7 fuel topped up in flight by KC-135Q tankers also based at Beale. To facilitate the demanding process of crew conversion to this extremely costly aircraft an operational trainer, the SR-71B, was purchased, at least two being slotted into the main batch of 29

Below: A loose formation with a T-38A emphasizes the impressive size of the SR-71A; this example carries the Vietnam snake badge.

Above: This view of an SR-71 on the landing approach shows the remarkable breadth of the sharp-edged forward fuselage.

Right: Special JP-7 fuel streams from the receptacle of SR-71A No 71-7974 as the boomer in the KC-135Q breaks contact.

(or more) which began at 61-7950. This has a raised instructor cockpit and dual pilot controls, and also includes the reconnaissance systems for RSO training.

After the first crews had qualified as fully operational, in 1971, the parent wing was restyled the 9th SRW, with two squadrons. This has ever since operated in a clandestine manner, rarely more than two aircraft being despatched to any overseas theatre and missions normally being flown by single aircraft. It is not known to what extent subsonic cruise is used; in the normal high-speed regime the skin temperature rises from -49°C to 550/595°C, and the fuel serves as the heat sink and rises to a temperature of about 320°C before reaching the engines, at least one SR-71C was produced as an SR-71A rebuild, following loss of an SR-71B. It has been estimated that the SR-71As seldom fly more than 200 hours per year, mainly on training exercises. No recent estimate has been published of their vulnerability.

Below: Touchdown by an SR-71B trainer, showing both the all-moving canted vertical tails and the 40ft (12.2m) braking parachute.

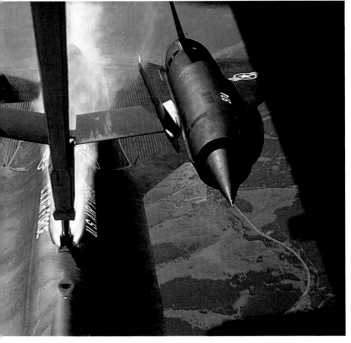

Lockheed TR-1

U-2A, B, C, CT, D, R, WU-2 family and TR-1A & B.

Origin: Lockheed California Company, Burbank, California.
Powerplant: One Pratt & Whitney unaugmented turbojet, (A and some derivatives) 11,200lb (5,080kg) thurst J57-13A or -37A, (most other U-2) versions) one 17,000lb (7,711kg) thrust J75-13, (TR-1) 17,000lb (7,711kg) J75-13B.
Dimensions: Span (A,B,C,D,CT) 80ft 0in (24,38m), R, WU-2C, TR-1) 103ft 0in (31.39m); length (typical of early versions) 49ft 7in (15.1m), (R, TR) 63ft 0in (19.2m); wing area (early) 565sq ft (52.49m²), (R, TR) 1,000sq ft (92.9m²).
Weights: Empty (A) 9,920lb (4,500kg), (B,C,CT,D) typically 11,700lb (5,305kg), (R) 14,990lb (6,800kg), (TR) about 16,000lb (7,258kg); loaded (A) 14,800lb (6,713kg), (B,C,CT,D, clean) typically 16,000lb (7,258kg), (with 89 US gal wing tanks) 17,270lb (7,833kg), (R) 29,000lb (13,154kg), (TR) 40,000lb (18,144kg).
Performance: Maximum speed (A) 494mph (795km/h), (B,C,CT,D) 528mph (850km/h), (R) about 510mph (8211km/h), (TR) probably about 495mph (797km/h); maximum cruising speed (most) 460mph (740km/h), (TR) 430mph (692km/h); operational ceiling (A) 70,000ft (21.34km), (B,C, CT, D) 85,000ft (25.9km), (R,TR) about 90,000ft (27.43km); maximum range (A) 2,200 miles (3,540km), (B,C,CT,D) 3,000 miles (4,830km), (R) about 3,500 miles (5,833km), (TR) about 4,000 miles (6,437km); endurance on internal fuel (A) 5½ h, (B,C,CT,D) 6½ h, (R) 7½ h, (TR) 12 h.
Armament: None.

Above: Two-seat U-2D at Air Force Flight Test Center, Edwards AFB.

Below: Landing by U-2R No 68-10333, without mission pods.

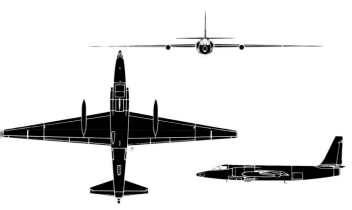

Above: Three-view of original (small) U-2B with slipper tanks.

History: First flight (A) 1 August 1955; service delivery February 1956; operational service, June 1957.

Development: First of the two families of clandestine surveillance aircraft produced by Lockheed's 'Skunk Works' under the brilliant engineering leadership of C.L. 'Kelly' Johnson, the U-2 was conceived in spring 1954 to meet an unannounced joint USAF/CIA requirement for a reconnaissance and research aircraft to cruise at the highest attainable altitudes. The entire programme was cloaked in secrecy, test flying (under Tony LeVier) took ▶

Above: Another of the many rebuilds was this black-painted example, believed to be a U-2L, originally the penultimate U-2B but converted for upper-atmosphere radiation measurements.

▶ place at remote Watertown Strip, Nevada, and no announcement was made of delivery to the Air Force of 56-675 and -676, the two prototypes. The original order comprised 48 single-seaters and five tandem-seat aircraft, initially the back-seater being an observer or systems operator. The operating unit was styled Weather Reconnaissance Squadron, Provisional (1st) and soon moved to Atsugi AB, Japan, while the WRS,P (2nd) moved to Wiesbaden, Germany, with basing also at Lakenheath, England. The WRS,P(3rd) remained at Edwards to develop techniques and handle research.

Intense interest in the aircraft, grey and without markings, prompted an announcement that they were NASA research aircraft, with Utility designation U-2, but after numerous unmolested missions over the Soviet Union, China and other territories, one of the CIA aircraft was shot down near Sverdlovsk on 1 May 1960. Future missions were flown by USAF pilots in uniform, with USAF markings on the aircraft. Several more J75-powered aircraft were shot down over China and Cuba, and attrition was also fairly high from accidents, because the U-2 is possibly the most difficult of all modern aircraft to fly. Features include an all-metal airframe of sailplane-like qualities, with a lightly loaded and extremely flexible wing, tandem bicycle landing gears, outrigger twin-wheel units jettisoned on takeoff (the landing tipping on to a downturned wingtip), an unpressurized cockpit with UV-protected sliding canopy of F-104 type, special low-volatility fuel, and large flaps, airbrakes and braking parachute.

From 1959 the J75 engine was installed, and with the U-2C the inlets

Below: Landing a TR-1 is almost as difficult as landing early U-2s.

Above: U-2R No 68-10336 flying with mission containers in place.

Above: One of the original black-painted U-2Bs photographed without pinion tanks over Edwards AFB in 1968. The non-reflective paint then used was to a different specification from that on today's Lockheed TR-1.

Left: The U-2CT is still the type-conversion pilot trainer, used by the 100th SRW at Davis-Monthan AFB.

▶ were splayed out at the front, the U-2D being the original two-seat versi◌
and the U-2CT (conversion trainer) being one of at least six rebuilds, in th◌
example as a dual-control pilot trainer with the instructor seated at an upp◌
level. Most CTs have been stationed at the Air Force Flight Test Center ar◌
Test Pilot School, both at Edwards. The AFFTC also uses several oth◌
versions, including D variants with special instrumentation, dorsal or vent◌
inlets for sampling, and various external payloads, with a variety of blac◌
white and other paint schemes. Both C and D models have large dors◌
'doghouse' fairings for sampling, sensing or avionic equipment.

Because of high attrition the line was reopened in 1968 with ◌
considerably larger aircraft styled U-2R (68-10329 to 10340). While mo◌
earlier models could carry 80 US gal (336lit) tanks on the leading edge, the◌
was supplied with large wing pods permanently installed and accommodatir◌
various payloads as well as 105 US gal (398lit) fuel. Wet wings increase◌
internal capacity, and the R also introduced a stretched airframe able◌
accommodate all necessary fuel and equipment internally. Front and re◌
main gears were moved closer together and the rear fuselage was form◌

Below: A U-2R, No 68-10331, flying almost silently without the mission pods. This, the first of the greatly enlarged variants, introduced a fin platform instead of a dorsal spine.

The first TR-1A single-seater, No 80-1066, seen outside its hangar at Palmdale in July 1981. The TR-1s will be operated by special SAC units on behalf of TAC, the bases being in Euro◌

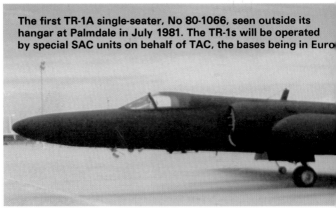

into a bulged upper platform carrying the tailplane. All known U-2R aircraft have been matt black, serving with various overseas commands.

The latest variant, the TR-1, is basically a further updated U-2R with ASARS (advanced Synthetic-Aperture Radar System), in the form of the UPD-X side-looking airborne radar, and with dramatically increased integral-tank fuel capacity, which results in very much higher gross weight. A single-seater, like the R, the TR-1A carries extensive new avionics in its pods, as well as much more comprehensive ECM. Mission equipment is also carried in the nose, in the Q-bay behind the cockpit and between the inlet ducts. Because of the long endurance the Astronaut-suited pilot has special facilities for his personal comfort and for taking warm food. The first batch comprised two TR-1As (80-1061 and 1062) and a third aircraft (1063) which was actually first to be delivered, on 10 June 1981, via the Air Force to NASA with designation ER-2 for earth-rescource missions. Next followed three more TR-1As and a two-seat TR-1B, the eventual fleet expected to number 33 As and two Bs. The main base is at Alconbury, England and the mission is to look 35 miles (55km) into Communist territory.

Below: Only the expert could tell that this is a U-2R (actually ship 10329) instead of a TR-1. The latter (foot of page) has totally different sensors and more advanced ECM installations.

McDonnell Douglas C-9

C-9A, VC-9A

Origin: Douglas Aircraft Company, Long Beach, California.
Type: Aeromedical airlift transport.
Powerplant: Two 14,500lb (6,577kg) thrust Pratt & Whitney JT8D-9 turbofans.
Dimensions: Span 93ft 5in (28.47m), length 119ft 3½in (36,37m), wing area 1,000.7sq ft (92.97m²).
Weights: Empty about 60,500lb (27,443kg); loaded 108,000 or 121,000lb (48,989 or 54,884kg).
Performance: Maximum speed 583mph (938km/h); maximum cruising speed 564mph (907km/h); initial climb 2,900ft (885m)/min; takeoff field length, 5,530ft (1,685m); range with maximum payload of 22,000lb (9,979kg), about 1,990 miles (3,203km).
Armament: None.
History: First flight (DC-9) 25 February 1955; service delivery 10 August 1968.

Development: While the Navy requested a completely re engineered DC-9 (as the C-9B Skytrain II) the Air Force bought the DC-9-30 off the shelf, with few modifications as its standard aeromedical transport over tactical ranges. It has three entrances, two with special hydraulic stairways and the third a large door forward on the left side with a hydraulic elevator for loading litters (stretcher patients). Normal loads can be up to 40 litter patients and/or 40 seated, plus two nurses and three aeromedical technicians. There are galleys

Above: Interior of a C-9A Nightingale showing litters and seats.

Above: Unlike the Navy C-9B the C-9A has no windows left forward.

and toilets front and rear, as well as a special care compartment with its own environmental controls. A total of 21 C-9As was delivered in 1968-73, equipping the 375th AAW at MAC's headquarters at Scott AFB, Illinois, and the 435th TAW at Rhein Main airport, Germany. The VIP VC-9A (originally VC-9C) force comprises three aircraft assigned to the 89th MAG SAMW at Andrews, near Washington DC.

Above: The first C-9A to be delivered was 67-22583, entering MAC service in August 1968. Curiously, even though it is used in all DC-9 USAF and Navy/Marines versions, and the T-43A, the JT8B engine has never received a military designation.

Left: This Nightingale, No 68-8932, was the first of the second batch. Predictably, this off-the-shelf civil transport (apart from the special interior) has an exemplary record of high-utilization service.

McDonnell Douglas C-17

C-17A

Origin: Douglas Aircraft Company, Long Beach, California.
Type: Long-range heavy airlift transport.
Powerplant: Four 37,600lb (17,055kg) thrust Pratt & Whitney PW2037 turbofans.
Dimensions: Span 165ft 0in (50.29m); length 170ft 8in (52.02m); height 53ft 6in (16.31m); wing area 3,800sq ft (353m²).
Weights: Empty 259,000lb (117,480kg); loaded 572,000lb (259,455kg).
Performance: Normal cruising speed about 495mph (797km/h); takeoff field length with maximum payload, 7,600ft (2,320m); landing field length with max payload, 3,000ft (914m); range with maximum payload, 2,765 miles (4,445km); ferry range 5,755 miles (9,265km).
Armament: None.
History: First flight, possibly 1986; delivery about 1989; full operational capability, 'early 1990s'.

Development: After years of study, which originally centred on tactical aircraft to replace the C-130 (YC-14 and YC-15) but moved to global ranges with the announcement of the Rapid Deployment Force, the USAF was able to issue an RFP for the new C-X long-range heavy airlift transport in October 1980. Douglas's selection was announced in August 1981, but it took until 1985 before the USAF firmly committed itself to the programme.

In early 1982 the Reagan administration stated that it did not plan further velopment of the C-17, but in mid-year let a "modestly paced" R&D ogramme to McDonnell Douglas for further work on the project. The scal Year 1985 programme, however, announced full-scale engineering velopment; the first prototype will fly in 1989 and IOC is expected for late 991, in a programme which may eventually rival that of the C-130.

The C-17 will be an extremely modern aircraft in all respects, with a 25° percritical wing carrying four of the newest engines, each with a reverser, owing back close under the wing to give powered lift when the titanium ps are lowered. Ground mobility will be exceptional, with four main gears ch with a row of three low-pressure tyres, allowing the fully loaded air- aft to turn in an 80ft (24.5m) strip and reverse back up a 2.5% (1 in 40) adient. The cargo floor will be 87ft (26.5m) long, 216in (5.49m) wide and ve headroom of 142in (3.6m) under the wing and 162in (4.1m) else- here. Maximum payload will be 17,200lb (78.1t), and apart from an M1 nk (plus other loads) the C-17 could carry wheeled vehicles two-abreast d Jeeps three-abreast. Three electronic displays on the flight deck enable e flight crew to be reduced to two pilots and a loadmaster. The C-17 will mbine ground mobility at least as good as a C-130 with cargo capability a C-5A.

elow: Though the four PW2037 turbofan engines would blow to the large flaps, the C-17A would not be such a dedicated STOL hort-takeoff and landing) aircraft as its smaller predecessor the C-15. This is an early McDonnell Douglas artist's impression.

McDonnell Douglas F-4 Phantom II

F-4C, D, E, G and RF-4C

Origin: McDonnell Aircraft Company, St Louis, Missouri.

Type: (C,D,E) all-weather interceptor and attack, (G) EW platform, (RF reconnaissance.

Powerplant: (C,D,RF) to 17,000lb (7,711kg) thrust General Electric J79-15 afterburning turbojets, (E,G) two 17,900lb (8,120kg) J79-17.

Dimensions: Span 38ft 5in (11.7m); length (C,D) 58ft 3in (17.76m), (E,RF 63ft 0in (19.2m); wing area 530sq ft (49.2m²).

Weights: Empty (C) about 28,000lb (12.7t), (D) 28,190lb (12,787kg), (E 30,328lb (13,757kg), (G) about 31,000lb (14.06t), (RF) 29,300lb (13.29t) maximum loaded (C,D,RF) 58,000lb (26.3t), (E,G) 60,360lb (27.5t).

Performance: Maximum speed (C,D,E, Sparrow AAMs only external load 910mph (1,464km/h, Mach 1.19) at low level, 1,500mph (241km/h, Mach 2.27) over 35,000ft (10.67km); initial climb, low level (AAMs only external load) 28,000ft (8,534m)/min; service ceiling 60,000ft (18.29km) withou external stores; range on internal fuel (no external weapons) typically 1,750 miles (2,817km), ferry range (clean except three tanks), (C,D,RF) 2,300 miles (3,700km), (E,G) 2,660 miles (4,281km); takeoff run (clean) 5,000f (1,525m); landing run 3,000ft (914m).

Armament: (C,D) Up to 16,000lb (7,257kg) assorted stores on externa pylons including four AIM-7 Sparrow AAMs recessed into underside o fuselage/wing junction and two more AIM-7, or four AIM-9 Sidewinder, or inboard pylons: (E) same plus 20mm M61A-1 gun under nose; (G) typically three AIM-7 Sparrow recessed, three Mavericks or one Standard ARM plus two AIM-9 on each inboard pylon, and one Shrike on each outboard pylon plus any other ordnance carried by other versions; (RF) none.

History: First flight (Navy F4H-1) 27 May 1958, (Air Force F-4C) 27 May 1963. ▶

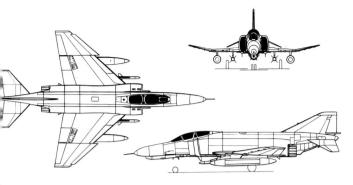

Above: Three-view of an F-4E.

Above: A TAC F-4E in one of the several experimental colour schemes, in this case green, tan and buff (café au lait). This aircraft has its slats open and a Tiseo electro-optical sensor pod on the inboard end of the left-wing leading edge.

Above left: F-4G Advanced Wild Weasels are F-4E rebuilds dedicated to electronic warfare; this one is based at Spangdahlem.

Left: The RF-4C was developed by the Air Force as an unarmed multi-sensor recon platform; this one is from the 1st Tac Recon Sqn at RAF Alconbury.

▶**Development:** Though it was the result of the manufacturer's initiative rather than an order by a customer, the F4H-11 Phantom II was by a wide margin the most potent fighter of the late 1950s, with outstanding all-round flight performance (resulting in 21 world records), the best radar performance of any Western fighter, the greatest load-carrying capability, and exceptional range and slow-flying qualities to fit it for oceanic operations from carriers. By the early 1960s the Air Force had recognised that it beat even the specialist land-based types at their own missions, and after prolonged study decided to buy the basic F-4B version with minimal changes. The original Air Force designation of F-110 Spectre was changed to F-4C Phantom II under the unified 1962 system, the F-4C being a minumum-change version of the Navy B and preceded (from 24 January 1962) by the loan to TAC of 30 B models ex-Navy.

Right: Takeoff of an F-4E of the 51st Composite Wing, Osan AB, South Korea, with ALQ-101 ECM pod and Sidewinders. Parked are F-4Ds.

Above: An immaculate F-4E from Langley AFB, with TAC badge on the fin and unit badge on the inlet duct. Four AIM-9J are loaded.

Left: One of the older
species is this F-4C, the
original Air Force version
intended as a minimum-
change derivative of the
Navy F-4B. Without an
internal gun, but with an
infra-red sensor in a nose
fairing, it is shown in
overall air-superiority pale
grey in the Air National
Guard's 171st FIS,
Selfridge AFB, Michigan.

▶ After buying 583 F-4Cs with dual controls, a boom receptacle, Dash-1
engines with cartridge starters, larger tyres and increased-capacity brake
inertial navigation and improved weapon aiming, the Air Force procure
793 of the F-4D model which was tailored to its own land-based mission
with APQ-109 radar, ASG-22 servoed sight, ASQ-91 weapon-releas
computer for nuclear LABS manoeuvres, improved inertial system and 30
kVA alternators. Visually, many Ds could be distinguished by removal of th
AAA-4 IR detector in a pod under the radar, always present on the C. Ne
came the extremely sophisticated RF-4C multi-sensor reconnaissanc
aircraft, a major rebuild in a programme which preceded the D by two year
and was the first Air Force variant to be authorised. Designed to suppleme
and then replace the RF-101 family the RF-4C was unarmed but wa
modified to carry a battery of forward-looking and oblique cameras, l
linescan, SLAR (side-looking airborne radar) and a small forward obliqu
mapping radar, as well as more than 20 auxiliary fits including pho
flash/flare cartridges in the top of the rear fuselage, special ECM and H
shunt aerials built into the fin behind the leading edge on each side. TA
purchased 505 of this model in 1964-73.

All these variants were very heavily engaged in the war in SE Asia
1966-73, where political rules combined with other problems to reduc
their air-combat performance. Prolonged call for an internal gun resulted
the F-4E, which had the most powerful J79 engine to permit the flig
performance to be maintained despite adding weight at both ends. In th
nose was the new solid-state APQ-120 radar and the M61 gun, slantin
down on the ventral centreline with the 6 o'clock firing barrel nea
horizontal, and at the rear was a new (No 7) fuel cell giving enhanced rang
The first E was delivered to TAC on 3 October 1967, about three month
after first flight, and a total of 949 in all were supplied to maintain the F-4 a
leading TAC aircraft with an average of 16 wings equipped throughout th
period 1967/77. From 1972 all Es were rebuilt with a slatted leading edg
replacing the previous blown droop which permitted much tighte
accelerative manoeuvres to be made, especially at high weights, withou
stall/spin accidents of the kind which had caused many losses in Vietnam

Above: This F-4E carries various advanced electronic systems for night ground attack, including the Pave Tack pod on the ventral centreline. The stablized head of this pod contains a laser and FLIR (forward-looking infra-red) boresighted together and interfaced with the ARN-101 digital electronics on board the aircraft.

Left: F-4G Advanced Wild Weasel of the 35th TFW, George AFB, California. The camouflage is standard tan/dark green/medium green, with the unit badge on the inlet duct and TAC badge on the fin.

The final Air Force variant is the F-4G, the standard Advanced Wild Weasel platform replacing the F-105F and G which pioneered Wild Weasel missions in the late 1960s. The name covers all dedicated EW and anti-SAM missions in which specially equipped electronic aircraft hunt down hostile SAM installations (using radar for lock-on, tracking or missile guidance) and destroy them before or during an attack by other friendly aircraft on nearby targets. The F-4G (the same designation was used previously for modified F-4Bs of the Navy) is a rebuild of late-model F-4E (F-4E-42 through -45) fighters, and has almost the same airframe. It is the successor to the EF-4C, two squadrons of which were fielded by TAC from 1968 and which demonstrated excellent performance with a simpler system. In the F-4G the main EW system is the AN/APR-38, which provides very comprehensive radar homing and warning and uses no fewer than 52 special aerials, of which the most obvious are pods facing forward under the nose (replacing the gun) and facing to the rear at the top of the vertical tail. The system is governed by a Texas Instruments reprogrammable software routine which thus keeps up the date on all known hostile emitters. Offensive weapons normally comprise triple AGM-65 EO-guided Mavericks on each inboard pylon plus a Shrike on each outer pylon; alternatively weapons can include the big Standard ARM (Anti-Radiation Missile), AGM-88 HARM (High-speed ARM) or various other precision air/ground weapons. A Westinghouse ALQ-119 jammer pod is fitted in the left front missile recess, the other three recesses carrying Sparrow AAMs for self-protection. Another change is to fit the F-15 type centreline tank which can take 5g when full with 600 US gal (2,271lit). The G total is 116 aircraft.

Today the F-4 is still the most numerous combat aircraft in the Air Force. User units include: TAC, 4th TFW (E) at Seymour-Johnson, N Carolina; 31st TFW (E), Homestead, Florida; 33rd TFW (E), Eglin, Florida; 35th TFW (C,E,G), George, California; 56th TFW (D,E), MacDill, Florida; 57th FIS (E), Keflavik, Iceland; 57th TTW (E), Nellis, Nevada; 58th TTW (C), Luke, Arizona; 67th TRW (RF), Bergstrom, Texas; 347th TFW (E), Moody, Georgia, 363rd TRW (RF), Shaw, S Carolina; and 474th TFW (D), Nellis. USAFE, 10th TRW (RF), Alconbury, England; 26th TRW (RF), Zweibrücken, ▶

► Germany; 50th TFW (E), Hahn, Germany; 52nd TFW (E,G), Spangdahlem
Germany; 86th TFW (E), Ramstein, Germany; 401st TFW (C), Torrejo
Spain; and 406th TFT (various), Zaragoza, Spain. Pacaf, 3rd TFW (D), Clar
Philippines; 8th TFW (E), Kunsan, Korea; 18th TFW (C, RF), Kader
Okinawa; and 51st CW (E), Osan, Korea. Alaska, 21st CW (E), Elmendo
Afres, 915th TFG (C), Homestead. ANG, 117th TRW (RF), Birmingha
Alabama, 119th FIG (C), Fargo, N Dakota, 122nd TFW (C), Ft Wayn

Indiana; 123rd TRW (RF), Louisville, Kentucky; 124th TRG (RF), Boise, Idaho; 131st TFW (C), St Louis, Mo; 148th TRG (RF), Duluth, Minnesota; 149th TFG (C), Kelly, Texas; 152nd TRG (RF), Reno, Nevada; 154th CG (C), Hickam, Hawaii; 155th TRG (RF), Meridian, Mississippi; 159th TFG (C), New Orleans, Louisiana; 183rd TFG (C), Springfield, Illinois; 186th TRG (RF), Meridian; 187th TRG (RF), Montgomery, Alabama; and the 191st FIG (D), Selfridge, Michigan.

Left: Recovery of two F-4Es of the 35th TFW at George AFB, with drag chutes deployed. Note that the same wing's F-4Gs (previous page) have the different tail code WW (Wild Weasel ?).

Below: This F-4G is carrying an AGM-45 Shrike, AGM-78 Standard ARM, ALQ-119 ECM pod and the 600-gal F-15 type tank used by this model.

McDonnell Douglas F-15 Eagle

F-15A,B,C,D and E

Origin: McDonnell Aircraft Company, St Louis, Missouri.

Type: Air-superiority fighter with secondary attack role.

Powerplant: Two 23,930lb (10,855kg) thrust Pratt & Whitney F100-100 afterburning turbofans.

Dimensions: Span 42ft 9¾in (13.05m); length (all) 63ft 9in (19.43m); wing area 608sq ft (56.5m²).

Weights: Empty (basic equipped) 28,000lb (12.7t); loaded (interception mission, max internal fuel plus four AIM-7, F-15A) 41,500lb (18,824kg), (C) 44,500lb (20,185kg); maximum with max external load (A) 56,500lb (25,628kg), (C) 68,000lb (30,845kg).

Performance: Maximum speed (over 36,000ft/10 973m with no external load except four AIM-7), 1,653mph (2,660km/h, Mach 2.5); with max external load or at low level, not published; initial climb (clean) over 50,000ft (15.24km)/min, (max wt) 29,000ft (8.8km)/min; service ceiling 65,000ft (19.8km); takeoff run (clean) 900ft (274m); landing run (clean, without brake chute) 2,500ft (762m); ferry range with three external tanks, over 2,878 miles (4,631km), (with Fast packs also) over 3,450 miles (5,560km).

Armament: One 20mm M61A-1 gun with 940 rounds, four AIM-7F (later AMRAAM) fitting against fuselage, four AIM-9L (later Asraam) on flanks of wing pylons, total additional ordnance load 16,000lb (7,257kg) on five stations (two each wing, one centreline).

History: First flight (A) 27 July 1972, (B) 7 July 1973; service delivery (Cat II test) March 1974, (inventory) November 1974.

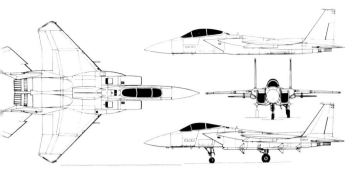

Above: Three-view of F-15A or C with side view (top) of F-15B or D.

Development: Recognizing its urgent need for a superior long-range air-combat fighter the Air Force requested development funds in 1965 and issued an RFP in September 1968 for the FX, the McDonnell proposal being selected in late 1969, with the F100 engine and Hughes APG-63 radar following in 1970. Inevitably the demand for long range resulted in a large aircraft, the wing having to be so large to meet the manoeuvre requirement that it has a fixed leading edge and plain unblown trailing-edge flaps. Two of ▶

Below: There are actually three F-15As in this photograph, which was taken from the back seat of an F-15B. Carrying no missiles except single AIM-9Js, they come from the 58th Tactical Training Wing at Luke AFB, Arizona, which rivals Nellis as a piloting centre.

▶ the extremely powerful engines were needed to achieve the desired ratio of thrust/weight, which near sea level in the clean condition exceeds unity. The inlet ducts form the walls of the broad fuselage, with plain vertical rectangular inlets giving external compression from the forward-raked upper lip and with the entire inlet pivoted at the top and positioned at the optimum angle for each flight regime. The upper wall of the inlet forms a variable ramp, and the lower edge of the fuselage is tailored to snug fitting of the four medium-range AAMs. The gun is in the bulged strake at the root of the right wing, drawing ammunition from a tank inboard of the duct. There is no fuel between the engines but abundant room in the integral-tank inner wing and between the ducts for 11,600lb (5,260kg, 1,739 US gal, 6,592lit), and three 600 US gal (2,270lit) drop tanks can be carried each, stressed to 5g manoeuvres when full. Roll is by ailerons, only at low speeds, the dogtoothed slab tailplanes taking over entirely at over Mach 1, together with the twin rudders, which are vertical.

Avionics and flight/weapon control systems are typical of the 1970 period, with a flat-plate scanner pulse-doppler radar, vertical situation display presenting ADI (attitude/director indicator), radar and EO information on one picture, a HUD, INS and central digital computer. In its integral ECM/IFF subsystems the F-15 was far better than most Western fighters, with Loral radar warning (with front/rear aerials on the left fin tip), Northrop ALQ-135 internal counter-measures system, Magnavox EW warning set and Hazeltine APX-76 IFF with Litton reply-evaluator. High-power jammers, however, must still be hung externally, any of various Westinghouse pods normally occupying an outer wing pylon. While the APG-63 offered a fantastic improvement (over any previous Air Force radar) in its ability to track low-level targets, fairly straightforward location of cockpit switches giving a Hotas (Hands on throttle and stick) capability which dramatically improved dogfight performance. Though it was, and remains, concerned at the price, the Air Force got in the F-15A everything it was looking for, and in

Below: 32nd TFW F-15s display their full armament.

Top: Scramble by 32nd TFW F-15 from Camp New Amsterdam.

Above: Dive bombing by F-15B flown solo; heavy loads are possible.

435

▶1973 announced a force of 729 aircraft including a proportion of tandem dual-control F-15B operational trainers.

Production at St Louis has been running at 90 to 144 aircraft per year, with some 1,000 F-15s delivered by late 1986. Recipient units began with TAC's 57th TTW at Nellis, 58th TTW at Luke, 1st TFW at Langley, 36th TFW at Bitburg (Germany), 49th TFW at Holloman, 33rd TFW at Eglin, 32nd TFS at Camp New Amsterdam (Netherlands) and 18th TFW at Kadena (Okinawa). Some of these units have received the current production variants, the F-15C and two-seat F-15D. These have a vital electronic modification in a reprogrammable signal processor, giving instant ability to switch from one locked-on target to another, to keep looking whilst already locked to one target, to switch between air and ground targets and, by virtue of an increase in memory from 24K to 96K (96,000 'words'), to go into a high-resolution mode giving the ability to pick one target from a tight formation even at near the limit of radar range. To some extent the latter capability will remain not fully realized until a later medium-range AAM is used (the Air Force has studied the Navy AIM-54 Phoenix but not adopted it). The British Sky Flash would give a major improvement now, especially in severe jamming, but again has not been adopted. The C and D also have 2,000lb (907kg) of additional internal fuel and can carry the Fast (Fuel and sensor, tactical) packs cunningly devised by McDonnell to fit flush along the sides of the fuselage. These actually reduce subsonic drag and offer far less supersonic drag than the drop tanks whilst adding a further 9,750lb

4,422kg) fuel, or an assortment of sensors (cameras, FLIR, EO, LLTV or laser designator) or a mix of fuel and sensors.

In the second half of 1981 the F-15C re-equipped the 48th FIS at Langley, previously an F-106A unit in now-defunct Adcom, and the Air Force is now procuring aircraft to an eventual level of 1,266, partly in order to replace the aged F-106 in CONUS defence. For the future, while one variant of F-1 has been subjected to prolonged study as the USAF's Asat (Anti-satellite) aircraft, firing a large air/space missile based on a SRAM motor followed by an Altair II carrying a nuclear warhead, prolonged testing and demonstration of a company-funded Strike Eagle has now led to the F-15E of which 392 are to be procured, with IOC in 1988. This will serve as the Enhanced Tactical Fighter to replace the F-111 (the alternative being the Panavia Tornado) and also as the Advanced Wild Weasel (with far greater capability than the F-4G). The key is the SAR (synthetic-aperture radar) built into the APG-63, which very greatly improves resolution of fine detail against even distant ground targets. With a Pave Tack (FLIR/laser) pod the backseater in the two-seat F-15E can handle what are considered to be the best tactical navigation/target/weapon avionics in the world (apart from the strictly comparable Tornado). External weapon carriage is increased to 24,000lb (10,885kg), including laser-guided and anti-radiation weapons, Harpoon anti-ship missiles, dispensers and other stores. Whether the large existing F-15 force can eventually be brought up to this impressive standard has not been disclosed.

Left: F-15C in current low-visibility two-tone grey. The F-15 has large surface area in relation to its mass.

Below: An F-15A of the 49th TFW, from Holloman AFB, New Mexico, pulls round in a loop.

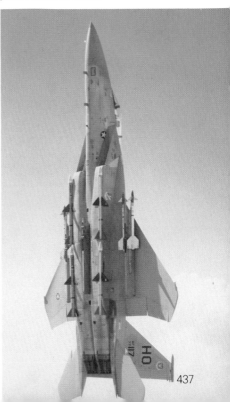

437

McDonnell Douglas F-101

F-101B

Origin: McDonnell Aircraft Company, St Louis, Missouri.
Type: All-weather interceptor.
Powerplant: Two 14,990lb (6,800kg) thrust Pratt & Whitney J57-55 afterburning turbojets.
Dimensions: Span 39ft 8in (12.09m); length 67ft 4¾in (20.55m); wing area 368sq ft (34.22m²).
Weights: Empty (equipped) 28,000lb (12.7t); loaded (intercept) 39,900lb (19.1t), maximum 46,673lb (21,171kg).
Performance: Maximum speed (40,000ft/18.1km, clean), 1,220mph (1963km/h, Mach 1.85); initial climb, 17,000ft (5,180m)/min; service ceiling, 52,000ft (15.85km); range on internal fuel, 1,550 miles (2,495km).
Armament: Three AIM-4D or AIM-26 Falcon AAMs in internal bay and/or two AIR-2A Genie nuclear rockets externally.
History: First flight (F-101A) 29 September 1954, (B) 27 March 1957, service delivery (B) 18 March 1959.

Development: The original F-101A was intended as a 'penetration fighter' for SAC, but actually went to TAC as an attack aircraft. The F-101B interceptor, one of a series of later variants, differed from all others in having engines with large high-augmentation afterburners, and a second crew member, accommodated at the expense of reduced fuselage fuel, to manage the MG-13 radar fire-control system tied in with the missile armament. By 1961 the Air Force had received 480 of this version together with the closely related TF-101B dual trainer which retained full armament. At one time 16 Adcom squadrons flew this reliable and well-liked aircraft, and it was also in wide-scale service with the CAF. Its final days of front-line service were seen with various units of the Air National Guard, before being replaced by the F-4 and F-15 in US service and by the CF-18 in the CAF. A number of examples are still flying, however, particularly on EW tasks.

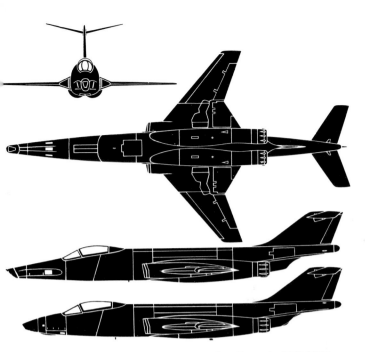

Above: Three-view of RF-101C with side view (lower) of RF-101G.

Above left: Externally similar to the RF-101G the RF-101H was a rebuild for the Air National Guard of the original unarmed RF-101C reconnaissance version.

Left: The last F-101 model in front-line service was the F-101B all-weather interceptor, which was flown with great success by the Air National Guard. This version was distinguished by its large afterburner nozzles.

McDonnell Douglas KC-10

KC-10A

Origin: Douglas Aircraft Company, Long Beach, California.
Type: Air-refuelling tanker and heavy cargo transport.
Powerplant: Three 52,500lb (23,814kg) thrust General Electric F103 (CF6-50C2) turbofans.
Dimensions: Span 165ft 4.4in (50.41m); length 181ft 7in (55.35m); height 58ft 1in (17.7m); wing area 3,958sq ft (367.7m²).
Weights: Empty (tanker role) 240,026lb (108,874kg); maximum loaded 590,000lb (267,620kg).
Performance: Maximum speed (max weight, tanker) about 600mph (9,66km/h) at 25,000ft (7,620m); maximum cruising speed, 555mph (8,93km/h) at 30,000ft (,144m); takeoff field length, 10,400ft (3,170m);

maximum range with maximum cargo load, 4,370 miles (7,032km); maximum range with max internal fuel, 11,500 miles (18,507km); landing speed at max landing weight, 171mph (275km/h).
Armament: None.
History: First flight (DC-10) 29 August 1970, (KC-10A) 12 July 1980.

Development: During the early 1970s the Air Force studied available commercial wide-body transports as a possible ATCA (Advanced Tanker/ Cargo Aircraft), and on 19 December 1977 announced the choice of a special version of the DC-10-30CF. The need had been highlighted by the difficulty of airlifting and air-fuelling USAF air units to the Middle East during the 1973 war, when some countries refused the USAF refuelling rights and the KC-135 and supporting cargo force found mission planning extremely ▶

Above and left: The KC-10A Extender is important to the USAF and to McDonnell Douglas. Commercial DC-10 production has reduced to a trickle, but the KC-10A will keep the line open through to the early 1990s. 16 were funded up to 1982 and since then a further 44 have been authorised. The KC-10A provides a major enhancement to the USA's global capability, especially as it can carry a substantial load of troops or cargo at the same time that it is serving as an airborne refueller. The KC-10A can use the extra fuel itself and in 1985 one of these aircraft flew from Saudi Arabia to the USA in 17.8 hours.

441

▶difficult. The ATCA was bought to fly global missions not only with several times the overall payload of the KC-135, to a maximum of 169,409lb (76,842kg), but with the ability to provide tanker support to combat units whilst simultaneously carrying spares and support personnel. Compared with the DC-10-30 the KC-10A has a windowless main cabin, with large freight door and five passenger doors, a McDD high-speed boom with fly-by-wire control and able to transfer fuel at 1,500 US gal (5,678lit)/min, and a completely redesigned lower lobe to the fuselage housing seven Goodyear rubberized fabric fuel cells with capacity of about 18,125 US gal (68,610lit). Together with its own fuel the KC-10A has the ability to transfer 200,000lb (90,718kg) to receiver aircraft at a distance of 2,200 miles (3,540km) from home base, and accompany the refuelled aircraft to destination. The cargo floor has improved power rollers and portable winch handling systems, and can accommodate 27 standard USAF Type 463L pallets.

The Air Force initially planned to fund 36 KC-10A Extenders, and in FY79 two aircraft were bought ($148 million, including some engineering costs), in FY80 a total of four, and in FY81 six. The second aircraft was the first to be delivered to SAC at Barkdale AFB, Louisiana, on March 17 1981. Orders for a further 44 will result in a force of 60 by the end of the decade; more orders may follow as the full extent of the force multiplication provided by this remarkable aircraft become apparent.

Above: The centreline gear is prominent in this takeoff picture.

Below: Refuelling trials with a TAC A-10A. The NKC-135A is used for radiation measures by the Aeronautical Systems Division.

Northrop F-5

F-5A Freedom Fighter, F-5B, F-5E Tiger II, F-5F

Origin: Northrop Corporation, Hawthorne, California.

Type: Light tactical fighter.

Powerplant: Two General Electric J85 afterburning turbojets, (A/B) 4,080lb (1,850kg) thrust J85-13 or -13A, (E/F) 5,000lb (2,270kg) thrust -21A.

Dimensions: Span (A/B) 25ft 3in (7.7m) (A/B over tip tanks) 25ft 10in (7.87m), (E/F) 26ft 8in (8.13m), (E/F over AAMs) 27ft 11^{7}in (8.53m) length (A) 47ft 2in (14.38m), (B) 46ft 4in (14.12m), (E) 48ft 2in (14.68m), (F) 51ft 7in (15.72m); wing area (A/B) 170sq ft (15.79m^2), (E/F) 186sq ft (17.3m^2).

Weights: Empty (A) 8,085lb (3,667kg), (B) 8,361lb (73,792kg), (E) 9,683lb (4,392kg), (F) 10,567lb (4,793kg); max loaded (A) 20,576lb (9,333kg), (B) 20,116lb (9,124kg), (E) 24,676lb) (11,193kg), (F) 25,225lb (11,442kg).

Performance: Maximum speed at 36,000ft (11km), (A) 925mph (1,489km/h, Mach 1.4), (B) 886mph (1,425km/h, Mach 1.34), (E) 1,077mph (1,734km/h, Mach 1.63), (F) 1,011mph (1,628km/h, Mach 1.53); typical cruising speed 562mph (904km/h, Mach 0.85); initial climb (A/B) 28,700ft (8,750m)/min, (E) 34,500ft (100,516m)/min, (F) 32,890ft (1,025m)/min; service ceiling (all) about 51,000ft (15.54km); combat radius with max weapon load and allowances, (A, hi-lo-hi) 215 miles (346km), (E, lo-lo-lo) 138 miles (222km); range with max fuel (all hi, tanks dropped, with reserves) (A) 1,565 miles (2,518km), (E) 1,779 miles (2,863km).

Armament: (A/B) total military load 6,200lb (2,812kg) including two 20mm M-39 guns and wide variety of underwing stores, plus AIM-9 AAMs for air combat; (E/F) Very wide range of ordnance to total of 7,000lb (3,175kg) not including two (F-5F, one) M-39A2 guns each with 280 rounds and two AIM-9 missiles on tip rails.

History: First flight (N-1,56C) 30 July 1959, (production F-5A) October 1963, (F-5E) 11 August 1972.

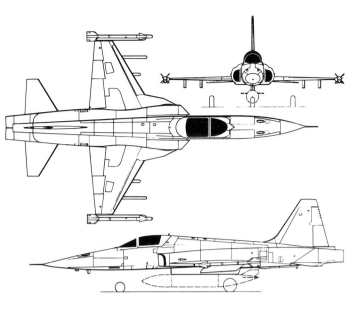

Above: Three-view of F-5E Tiger II; two-seat F-5F is 42in longer.

Development: The Air Force showed almost no interest in Northrop's N-156C Freedom Fighter, which was built with company funds and rolled out in 1959 without US markings. Eventually Northrop secured orders for over 1,000 F-5A and B fighters for foreign customers, and 12 of the MAP ▶

Left: This F-5E is used in the Aggressor role for Dissimilar Air Combat Training at the USAF Fighter Weapons School at Nellis AFB (badge painted on inlet duct).

Above: Another F-5E painted in a Warsaw Pact type colouring, with nose number, this example is from the 527th Tac Ftr Training Sqn at RAF Alconbury, England.

Left: The F-5E Aggressors flight line at Alconbury is constantly busy honing the edge of the sharpest USAF air-combat pilots. Costs are extremely modest.

445

▶ (Mutual Assistance Program) F-5As were evaluated by the Air Force in Vietnam in a project called Skoshi Tiger, which demonstrated the rather limited capability of this light tactical machine, as well as its economy and strong pilot appeal. When the USAF withdrew from SE Asia it left behind many F-5As and Bs, most having been formally transferred to South Vietnam, and few of these remain in the inventory. In contrast the slightly more powerful and generally updated F-5E Tiger II succeeded in winning Air Force support from the start, and the training of foreign recipients was handled mainly by TAC, with ATC assistance. The first service delivery of this version was to TAC's 425th TFS in April 1973. This unit at Williams AFB, Arizona (a detached part of the 58th TTW at Luke), proved the training and combat procedures and also later introduced the longer F which retains both the fire-control system and most fuselage fuel despite the second seat.

Below: An older F-5A making a steep dive-bombing attack, with aiming by the optical gunsight using a manually depressed reticle.

Ultimately the Air Force bought 112 F-5Es, both as tactical fighters and (over half the total) as Aggressor aircraft simulating potential enemy aircraft in DACT (Dissimilar Air Combat Training). About 60 F-5Es and a small number of Fs continue in Air Force service in the development of air-combat techniques, in Aggressor roles, in the monitoring of fighter weapons meets and various hack duties. The F-5Es are painted in at least eight different colour schemes, three of which reproduce Warsaw Pact comouflage schemes while others are low-visibility schemes. The F-5Fs at Williams are silver, with broad yellow bands and vertical tails. User units include the 58th TTW (425th TFS, as described), 57th TTW at Nellis (a major tactical and air combat centre for the entire Air Force), 3rd TFW, Clark AFB, Philippines (Pacaf), 527th Aggressor TFS, attached to the 10th TRW at RAF Alconbury, England; and various research establishments in Systems Command.

Below: Unusual photograph taken by the pilot of one of a pair of Aggressors F-5Es of the 527th; his partner has AIM-9J missiles.

Above: All four Aggressors colour schemes are seen in this formation of Alconbury F-5Es (no AIM-9s).

Left: This colourful F-5E serves with the 425th Tac Ftr Training Sqn at Luke AFB; it has old AIM-9Bs.

Northrop T-38 Talon

T-38A

Origin: Northrop Corporation, Hawthorne, California.
Type: Advanced trainer.
Powerplant: Two 3,850lb (1,746kg) thrust General Electric J85-5A afterburning turbojets.
Dimensions: Span 25ft 3in (7.7m); length 46ft 4½in (14.1m); wing area 170sq ft (15.79m²).
Weights: Empty 7,200lb (3,266kg); loaded 11,820lb (5,361kg).
Performance: Maximum speed, 858mph (1,381km/h, Mach 1.3) at 36,000ft (11km); maximum cruising speed, 627mph (1,009km/h) at same height; initial climb 33,600ft (10.24km)/min; service ceiling 53,600ft (16.34km); range (max fuel, 20min loiter at 10,000ft/3km) 1,140 miles (1,835km).
Armament: None.
History: First flight (YT-38) 10 April 1959, (T-38A) May 1960; service delivery 17 March 1961.

Development: Throughout the second half of the 1950s Northrop's project team under Welko Gasich studied advanced lightweight fighters of novel design for land and carrier operation, but the first genuine service interest was in the N-156T trainer, a contract for Air Force prototypes being signed in December 1956. Unique in the world, except for the Japanese FST-2, in being designed from the outset as a jet basic trainer with supersonic speed on the level, the T-38 was an attractive lightweight version of contemporary fighters, with twin afterburning engines, extremely small sharp-edged wings, area ruling for reduced transonic drag, inboard powered ailerons and slab tailplanes with slight anhedral. The instructor is seated behind and 10in (0.25m) higher than his pupil, both having rocket-assisted seats. To assist the pilot, yaw and pitch flight-control channels incorporate stability augmenters, and great care was taken in 1959-61 to produce an aircraft that pupils could handle. Strictly classed as a basic pilot trainer, the T-38A nevertheless is an advanced machine to which undergraduate pilots come only after completing their weed-out on the T-41A and their complete piloting course on the T-37A jet. The Air Force procured about 1,114 Talons, of which some 800 remain in inventory service with ATC. Their accident rate of some 0.9/11,2 per 100,000 flight

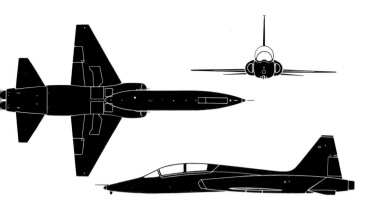

Above: Three-view of T-38A without centreline pod.

hours is half that for the USAF as a whole. An Advanced Squadron of T-38As is based at each ATC school (see Cessna T-37 for list). Many Talons are used as hacks by senior officers, for command liaison and for research, while others are assigned to TAC's 479th TTW at Holloman.

Above: Popularly called the White Rocket, the T-38A has helped 50,000 pilots get their wings. This picture was taken during routine formation training. According to Northrop the T-38 saved taxpayers more than $1 billion because of better-than-predicted safety and maintenance.

Left: Talons equip the USAF Thunderbirds display team, which has found the T-38 easy and economical. Loss of four team-members in January 1982 was tragic, but in no way connected with the aircraft.

Republic F-105 Thunderchief

F105B, D, F and G

Origin: Republic Aviation Corporation (now Fairchild Republic Co) Farmingdale, NY.

Type: (B,D) single-seat fighter/bomber, (F) two-seat operational trainer, (G EW/ECM platform.

Engine: One Pratt & Whitney J75 two-shaft afterburning turbojet; (B 23,500lb (10,660kg) J75-5; (D, F, G) 24,500lb (11,113kg) J75-19W.

Dimensions: Span 34ft 11¼in (10.65m); length (B, D) 64ft 3in (19.58m) (F, G) 69ft 7½in (21.21m); height (B, D) 19ft 8in (5.99m), (F, G) 20ft 2ir (6.15m).

Weights: Empty (D) 27,500lb (12,474kg); (F, G) 28,393lb (12,879kg) maximum loaded (B) 40,000lb (18,144kg); (D) 52,546lb (23,834kg) (F, G) 54,000lb (24,495kg).

Performance: Maximum speed (B) 1,254mph; (D, F, G) 1,480mph (2,382km/h, Mach 2.25); initial climb (B, D, typical) 34,500ft (10,500m)/min (F, G) 32,000ft (9,750m)/min; service ceiling (typical) 52,000ft (15,850m) tactical radius with 16 750lb bombs (D) 230 miles (370km); ferry range with maximum fuel (typical) 2,390 miles (3,846km).

Armament: One 20mm M-61 gun with 1,029 rounds in left side of fuse-lage internal bay for ordnace load of up to 8,000lb (3,629kg), and five externa pylons for additional load of 6,000lb (2,722kg).

History: First flight (YF-105A) 22 October 1955; (production B) 26 May 1956; (D) 9 June 1959; (F) 11 June 1963; final delivery 1965.

Development: The AP-63 project was a private venture by Republic Aviation to follow the F-84. Its primary mission was delivery of nuclear or conventional weapons in all-weathers, with very high speed and long range Though it had only the stop-gap J57 engine the first Thunderchief exceeded the speed of sound on its first flight, and the B model was soon in production for Tactical Air Command of the USAF. Apart from being the biggest single seat, single-engine combat aircraft in history, the 105 was notable for its large bomb bay and unique swept-forward engine inlets in the wing roots Only 75 B were delivered by 600 of the advanced D were built, with Nasarr monopulse radar and doppler navigation. Production was completed with

Above: Three-view of F-105D with three tanks.

Above: Two-seat F-105G Wild Weasel pictured when serving with the 35th TFW at George AFB, California; note Standard ARM missile.

Below: High level bombing by an F-105F doing double duty in the anti-radar role with a white AGM-45A Shrike anti-radiation missile.

▶143 tandem-seat F with full operational equipment and dual controls. The greatest of single-engined combat jets bore a huge burden throughout the Vietnam war. About 350 D were rebuilt during that conflict with the Thunderstrick (T-stick) all-weather blind attack system--a few also being updated to T-stick II--with a large saddleback fairing from cockpit to fin. About 30 F were converted to ECM (electronic countermeasures) attackers, with pilot and observer and Wild Weasel and other radar homing, warning and jamming systems. Westinghouse jammers and Goodyear chaff pods were carried externally. Prolonged harsh use over 20-odd years had by 1982

Below: Already bearing insignia and badges of their new units, these F-105Ds are making a peel-off over March AFB on 11 July 1980 on ceremonial transfer from the 35th TFW to various AFRES and ANG units, in this case mainly to the 108th TFW. Others were in the distance out of the picture. Note differences in centreline payloads.

degraded flight performance of these tough and well-liked aircraft, whose nicknames of Thud, Ultra Hog (the F-84 having been the original Hog and the F-84F the Super Hog) and Lead Sled in no way reflected pilot dissatisfaction with what had been in its day the nearest thing to a one-type air force. By 1982 all had gone from the regular units and survivors were grouped in three Afres squadrons for a short period; 457th and 465th TFSs converted to F-4s in 1982-83 and the last F-105 unit, 466th TFS, carried out the final operational flight on February 25 1984. A few aircraft remain operational, the last of the remarkable Republic fighters.

Below and bottom: Two F-105G Thunderchiefs operating in the dedicated Wild Weasel mode on electronic defence suppression. Missiles are AGM-45 Shrike outboard and AGM-78 Standard ARM inboard. A Westinghouse QRC-380 conformal ECM pod is snug against the fuselage; tanks and dispensers complete the load.

Rockwell B-1

B-1A, B

Origin: Rockwell International, North American Aerospace Operations, El Segundo, California.

Type: Strategic bomber and missile platform.

Powerplant: Four General F101-GE-102 augmented turbofans each rated at 29,900lb (13 563kg) with full afterburner.

Dimensions: (B-1A) Span (fully spread) 136ft 8½in (41.67m), (fully swept, to 67° 30ft) 78ft. 2½in (23.84m); length (including probe) 150ft 2½in (45.78m); wing area (spread, gross) 1,950sq ft (181.2m²).

Weights: Empty (B-1A) about 145,000lb (65,772kg), (B) over 160,000lb (72,576kg); maximum loaded (A) 395,000lb (179,172kg), (B) 477,000lb (216,367kg).

Performance: Maximum speed (B, over 36,000ft/11km) about 1,000mph (1,600km/h, Mach 1.5), (B, 500ft/152m) 750mph (1,205km/h, Mach 0.99); typical high-altitude cruising speed, 620mph (1,000km/h); range with maximum internal fuel, over 7,000 miles (11,265km); field length, less than 4,500ft (1,372m).

Armament: Eight ALCM internal plus 14 external; 24 SRAM internal plus 14 external; 12 B28 or B43 internal plus 8/14 external; 24 B61 or B83 internal plus 14 external; 84 Mk 82 internal plus 44 external (80,000lb, 36,288kg).

History: Original (AMSA) study 1962; contracts for engine and airframe 5 June 1970; first flight 23 December 1974; decision against production June 1977; termination of flight-test programme 30 April 1981; announcement of intention to produce for inventory, September 1981; planned IOC, 1 July 1987.

Development: Subject of a programme whose length in years far outstrips the genesis of any other aircraft, the B-1 was the final outcome of more than

The fourth B-1A (76-0174) represented a standard close to that for the originally planned production aircraft, with inclined fixed inlets, full defensive and offensive electronics (resulting in a blunt tail to the fuselage) and conventional ejection seats.

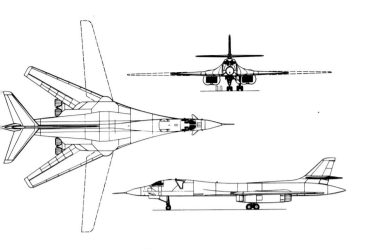

Above: Three-view of early B-1 prototypes.

ten years of study to find a successor to the cancelled B-70 and RS-70 and subsonic in-service B-52. Originally planned as an extremely capable swing-wing aircraft with dash performance over Mach 2, the four prototypes were built with maximum wing sweep of 67° 30ft and were planned to have variable engine inlets and ejectable crew capsules of extremely advanced design. The latter feature was abandoned to save costs, and though the second aircraft reached Mach 2.22 in October 1978 this end of the speed spectrum steadily became of small importance. By 1978 the emphasis was totally on low-level penetration at subsonic speeds with protection deriving ▶

▶ entirely from defensive electronics and so-called 'stealth' characteristics. Not very much could be done to reduce radar cross-section, but actual radar signature could be substantially modified, and the effort applied to research and development of bomber defensive electronic systems did not diminish.

The original B-1A featured a blended wing/body shape with the four engines in paired nacelles under the fixed inboard wing immediately outboard of the bogie main gears. Though designed more than ten years ago, the aerodynamics and structure of the B-1 remain highly competitive, and the extremely large and comprehensive defensive electronics systems (managed by AIL Division of Cutler-Hammer under the overall avionics integration of Boeing Aerospace) far surpassed those designed into any other known aircraft, and could not reasonably have been added as post-flight modifications. During prototype construction it was decided to save further costs by dropping the variable engine inlets, which were redesigned to be optimized at the high-subsonic cruise regime. Another problem, as with the B-52, was the increased length of the chosen ALCM, which meant that the original SRAM-size rotary launcher was no longer compatible. The original B-1 was designed with three tandem weapon bays, each able to house many free-fall bombs or one eight-round launcher. Provision was also originally made for external loads. A particular feature was the LARC (Low-

Below: This is believed to be the third prototype, photographed near Edwards AFB in early 1980 soon after application of camouflage.

Altitude Ride Control), an active-control modification which by sensing vertical accelerations due to atmospheric gusts at low level and countering these by deflecting small foreplanes and the bottom rudder section greatly reduced fatigue of crew and airframe during low-level penetration. All four prototypes flew initially from Palmdale and exceeded planned qualities. The third was fitted with the ECM system and DBS (doppler beam-sharpening) ▶

Above: The fourth prototype, escorted by a chase F-111A on one of its last missions in April 1981. Soviet 'Ram-P' is very similar.

Above: Rockwell ground personnel still plugged in to the nose gear as No 4, with camouflaged radome, prepares to leave on one of its last missions in 1981.

▶of the main radar, while the fourth had complete offensive and defensive electronics and was almost a production B-1A. The Carter administration decided not to build the B-1 for the inventory, and the four aircraft were stored in flyable condition after completing 1,985.2h in 247 missions.

After further prolonged evaluation against stretched FB-111 proposals the Reagan administration decided in favour of a derived B-1B, and announced in September 1981 the intention to put 100 into the SAC inventory from 1986, with IOC the following year. The B-1B dispenses with further high-altitude dash features, the wing sweep being reduced to about 59° 30ft. As well as refined engines the B-1B can carry much more fuel; a detailed weight-reduction programme reduces empty weight, while gross weight is raised by over 37 tonnes. Main gears are stronger, wing gloves and engine inlets totally redesigned, many parts (ride-control fins, flaps and bomb doors, for example) made of composite material, pneumatic starters with cross-bleed fitted, offensive avionics completely updated (main radar is Westinghouse's APG-66), the ALQ-161 defensive avionics subsystem fitted, RAM (radar-absorbent material) fitted at some 85 locations throughout the airframe, and the whole aircraft nuclear-hardened and given Multiplex wiring. Radar cross-section will be less than one-hundredth that of a B52. Deploying this LRCA (Long-Range Combat Aircraft) is intended to bridge the gap until the next generation 'stealth' aircraft is fielded in a programme so shrouded in secrecy that no IOC date has yet been announced.

Above: Aerial refuelling, here of the third B-1A, extended the duration of test sorties.

Below: Inflight refuelling of one of the early white-painted prototypes in 1977.

Rockwell OV-10 Bronco

OV-10A

Origin: Rockwell International, designed and built at Columbus, Ohio, Division of North American Aircraft Operations (now Columbus plant of NAA Division).

Type: Forward air control.

Powerplant: Two 715ehp Garrett T76-416/417 turboprops.

Dimensions: Span 40ft 0in (12.19m); length 41ft 7in (12.67m); wing area 291sq ft (27.03m²).

Weights: Empty 6,893lb (3,127kg); loaded 9,908lb (4,494kg), overload 14,444lb (6,552kg).

Performance: Maximum speed (sea level, clean) 281mph (452km/h); initial climb (normal weight), 2,600ft (790m)/min; service ceiling, 24,000ft (7,315m); takeoff run (normal weight), 740ft (226m); landing run, same; combat radius (max weapon load, low level, no loiter), 228 miles (367km); ferry range, 1,382 miles (2,224km).

Armament: Carried on five external attachments, one on centreline rated at 1,200lb (544kg) and four rated at 600lb (272kg) on short body sponsons which also house four 7.62mm M60 machine guns with 500 rounds each. ▶

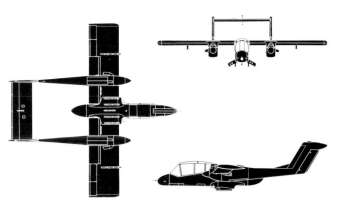

Above: Three-view of standard OV-10A in clean configuration.

Below: An OV-10A, with centreline tank, from the 51st Composite Wing, based at Osan AB, South Korea, part of Pacific Air Forces.

▶**History:** First flight 16 July 1965, (production oV-10A) 6 August 1967; USAF combat duty, June 1968.

Development: This unique warplane was the chief tangible outcome of prolonged DoD studies in 1959-65 of Co-In (Counter-Insurgency) aircraft tailored to the unanticipated needs of so-called brushfire wars using limited weapons in rough terrain. The Marines issued a LARA (Light Armed Recon Aircraft) specification, which was won by NAA's NA-300 in August 1964. Features included superb all-round view for the pilot and observer seated in tandem ejection seats, STOL rough-strip performance and a rear cargo compartment usable by five paratroops or two casualties plus attendant. Of the initial batch of 271 the Air Force took 157 for use in the FAC role, deploying them immediately in Vietnam. Their ability to respond immediately with light fire against surface targets proved very valuable, and the OV-10 was always popular and a delight to fly. In 1970 LTV Electrosystems modified 11 for night-FAC duty with sensors for detecting surface targets and directing accompanying attack aircraft, but most OV-10s now in use are of the original model. Units include TAC's 1st SOW at Hurlburt Field, Florida; the 602nd TACW, Bergstrom AFB, Texas; the 601st TCW, Sembach AB, Germany; Pacaf's 51st CW, Osan, Korea; and certain specialized schools.

Rockwell T-39 Sabreliner

T-39A, B and F

Origin: North American Aviation (later Rockwell International Sabreliner Division), El Segundo, California.
Type: (A) pilot proficiency/support, (B) radar trainer, (F) EW trainer.
Powerplant: Two 3,000lb (1,361kg) thrust Pratt & Whitney J60-3 turbojets.
Dimensions: Span 44ft 5in (13.53m); length (original A) 43ft 9in (13.33m); wing area 342.05sq ft (31.79m^2).
Weights: Empty (A) 9,300lb (4,218kg); loaded 17,760lb (8,056kg).
Performance: Maximum speed (A) 595mph (958km/h) at 36,000ft (11km); typical cruising speed, 460mph (740km/h, Mach 0.7) at 40,000ft (12.2km); maximum range (A), 1,950 miles (3,138km).
Armament: None.
History: First flight (NA-246 prototype) 16 September 1958, (T-39A) 30 June 1960; service delivery, October 1960.

Development: The Air Force's UTX requirement issued in August 1956 was the first in the world for an executive-jet type aircraft, though at that time the main mission was expected to be training and utility transport. The winning design from NAA, which had only the faintest kinship to the Sabre, was planned with wing-root engines but these were moved to the novel rear-fuselage position before construction began. The wing was swept and slatted, and stressed to fighter-type g loads. Rather cramped, the main cabin had two rounded-triangle windows each side and a door forward on the left immediately behind the comfortable flight deck. The prototype was put through Phase II at Edwards only six weeks after first flight, and so captivated Air Force pilots that seven T-39s were ordered in January 1959. Ultimately the Air Force bought 149, the majority serving as pilot-proficiency trainers, utility transports and, in a few cases, as VIP aircraft. Some spent their lives on research and special trials, the 6th to 9th were delivered with Nasarr radar to train F-105D pilots (designation T-39B), and at least three As were substantially modified as T-39F electronic-warfare trainers, originally for crews of the F-105G Wild Weasel aircraft. Though usually absent from published lists, almost all the T-39 force remain at work, many being assigned to combat wings (eg, the 86th TFW at Ramstein, Germany).

Above: The OV-10A has the capability of carrying almost all light tactical stores, these S. Korean-based examples having rocket pods.

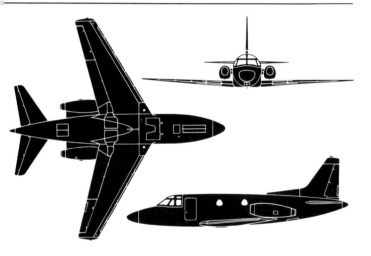

Above: Three-view of the original T-39A utility trainer.

Below: A T-39A in white-top garb; some T-39s are camouflaged.

Vought A-7 Corsair II

A-7D, K

Origin: Vought Corporation, Dallas, Texas.
Type: (D) attack, (K) combat trainer.
Powerplant: One 14,250lb (6,465kg) thrust Allison TF41-1 turbofan.
Dimensions: Span 38ft 9in (11.8m); length (D) 46ft 1½in (14.06m), (K) 48ft 11½in (14.92m); wing area 375sq ft (34.83m).
Weights: Empty (D) 19,781lb (8,972kg); loaded (D) 42,000lb (19,050kg).
Performance: Maximum speed (D, clean, SL), 690mph (1,110km/h), (5,000ft/1,525m, with 12 Mk 82 bombs) 646mph (1,040km/h); tactical radius (with unspecified weapon load at unspecified height), 715 miles (1,151km); ferry range (internal fuel) 2,281 miles (3,671km), (max with external tanks) 2,861 miles (4,604km).
Armament: One 20mm M61A-1 gun with 1,000 rounds, and up to 15,000lb (6,804kg) of all tactical weapons on eight hardpoints (two on fuselage each rated 500lb/227kg, two inboard wing pylons each 2,500lb/1,134kg, four outboard wing pylons each 3,500lb/1,587kg).
History: First flight (Navy A-7A) 27 September 1965, (D) 26 September 1968, (K) January 1981.

Development: The Corsair II was originally derived from the supersonic F-8 Crusader fighter to meet a Navy need for a subsonic tactical attack aircraft with a much heavier bomb load and greater fuel capacity than the A-4. So effective did the A-7 prove that in 1966 it was selected to equip a substantial proportion of TAC wings, and ultimately 457 were acquired. Compared with the Navy aircraft the A-7D introduced a more powerful engine (derived from the Rolls-Royce Spey) with gas-turbine self-starting, a multi-barrel gun, and above all a totally revised avionic system for continuous solution of navigation problems and precision placement of free-fall weapons in all weather. The folding wings and arrester hook were retained, and other features included a strike camera, boom receptacle instead of a probe, boron carbide armour over cockpit and engine, and a McDonnell Douglas Escapac seat. Avionics have been further improved over the years, but the

Below: The prototype A-7K was a rebuilt A-7D, seen here after delivery to the Air National Guard in December 1980.

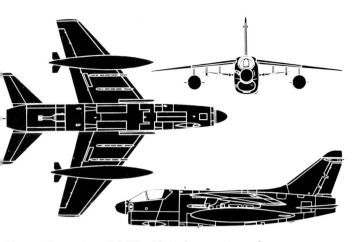

Above: Three-view of A-7D with tanks on outer pylons.

Above: A-7Ds of an unidentified USAF squadron taxiing out on a mission with free-fall bombs. The 20mm M61 guns will be loaded.

▶APQ-126 radar had been retained, programmable to ten operating models together with British HUD, inertial system, doppler radar, direct-view storage tube for radar or Walleye guidance, and central ASN-91 digital computer. For laser-guided weapons the Pave Penny installation is hung externally in a pod, but the ALR-46(V) digital radar warning system is internal. There is no internal jamming capability, however, and the usual ECM payload is an ALQ-101 or -119 hung in place of part of the bombload.

Below: By 1982 almost all surviving A-7Ds had been passed to the Air National Guard; these are in Colorado (140th TFW, Buckley Field).

Foot of page: Takeoff by a pair of A-7Ds of an Air National Guard unit, with tanks inboard but no bombs. Small and compact, these aircraft can each carry an external weapon load in excess of 15,000lb.

Immediately below: KC-135 boomer's view of an A-7D. The latter appears to carry the mountain lion emblem of the ANG 120th TFS, and thus comes from the same 140th TFW as those on the left. In its day the A-7D set a new high standard of precision bombing accuracy, but in recent years this has been consistently surpassed by the newer-technology F-16.

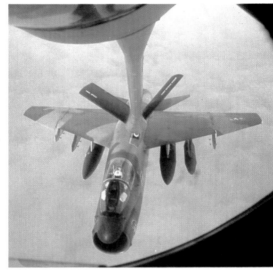

► Production of the A-7D has long been completed, but Vought has recently also completed delivery of 31 dual-control A-7K Corsair IIs which retain a full weapons capability. 16 of these have been assigned to the ANG's 162nd TFTG at Tucson and a pair to each of the 11 ANG's 13 operational units equipped with the A-7D. These units are the 112th TFG, Pittsburgh,

Pennsylvania; 114th TFG, Sioux Falls, Iowa; 121st TFW, Rickenbacker AFB, Ohio; 127th TFW, Selfridge AFB, Michigan; 132nd TFW, Des Moines, Iowa; 138th TFG, Tulsa, Oklahoma; 140th TFW, Buckley, Colorado; 150th TFG, Kirtland AFB, New Mexico; 156th TFG, San Juan, Puerto Rico; 162nd TFG (TFTG), Tucson; 169th TFG, McEntire Field, S Carolina; 178th TFG, Springfield, Ohio; and the 185th TFG, Sioux City, Iowa. In the 1981 Gunsmoke tactical gunnery meet at Nellis the 140th, from Colorado, shot their way to the top team title with an exceptional 8,800 out of 10,000 points (the team chief, Lt-Col Wayne Schultz, winning the Top Gun individual award). The meet involves not only gunnery but bombing and maintenance/loading contests. The chief of the judges said: 'Some of the scores are phenomenal--pilots are so accurate they don't need high explosive to destroy a target, they are hitting within 1½ to 2 metres, with ordinary free-fall bombs.' Few tactical aircraft are as good at attack on surface targets.

Left: Four of the first definitive A-7Ds (with boom receptacle instead of a probe as on the first 15 aircraft) were assigned to the 57th Fighter Weapons Wing at Nellis AFB.

Below: Snakeye retarded bombs drop from an A-7D of the 23rd Tactical Fighter Wing (England AFB, Louisiana) and slow down violently as their drag-brakes snap open.

Air Weapons

Since its formation in 1948 the USAF has been a world leader in aircraft armament. This section outlines the chief aircraft guns, bombs and missiles at present in use. To these hardware items must be added the electronic software necessary for their delivery, and the ECM and decoys for survival.

Guns

The most important gun used by the Air Force is the General Electric M61A-1, T-171 and related six-barrel rotary cannon in 20mm calibre. This family of guns can be self-powered (GAU-4) but most are driven hydraulically or electrically, with firing rates usually in the region of 4,000 or 6,000 shots/min. Ammunition of various types is drawn from a tank and in all current installation the feed system is linkless (a few link belts are still on charge for F-104s and some contemporary aircraft), and a typical muzzle velocity is 3,400ft (1,036m)/s.

There are many related guns, including the GAU-12/U with five barrels in 25mm calibre which may be adopted in future USAF aircraft. Largest of all guns in this family, and most powerful gun known in any aircraft, the GAU-8/A Avenger has a calibre of 30mm but fires ammunition with more than double the energy of other 30mm guns (except for the Swiss KCA and Russian NR-30, which have about 75% as much kinetic energy per round). This monster gun weighs 3,800lb (1,723kg) and fires from seven barrels in sequence at rates of 2,100 or 4,200 shots/min. It has a hydraulic drive rated at 77hp, and in its sole application, the Fairchild Republic A-10A, is fed by a linkless conveyor from a drum of 1,350 rounds, each roughly the size of a milk bottle. At the opposite end of the scale is the rifle (7.62mm) calibre M134 Minigun, firing at various rates to 6,000spm and used (now only in much-reduced numbers) in fixed, manually aimed and pod installations.

Small numbers of less sophisticated guns are in use. The famed 0.5-calibre (12.7mm) Browning is no longer in service, but the 20mm M-39 with

Above: The most important guns in the Air Force are the 'Gatling' weapons of 20-mm size, such as the M61A-1 under the nose of this F-4E.

Above: By far the hardest-hitting gun in any air force is the GAU-8 of the A-10A; here ammo is loaded at the 354th TFW.

revolving chamber feed survives in a few early F-5s and even in the F-5E (two guns) and F-5F (one). A small number of aircraft, including the OV-10, use the Army M60 7.62mm machine gun. For the future the Air Force has a number of possible guns including the CHAG (Compact High-Performance Aerial Gun) of 30mm calibre, for which competing prototypes are on test by Ford Aerospace (two barrels, 260lb/118kg, 2,000spm) and GE (three barrels, 280lb/127kg, 2,500spm). Various guns using careless ammunition have been tested (one was designed for the F-15 but not selected) and there are high hopes for guns using liquid propellants instead of regular cartridges.

Bombs

There are many hundreds of free-fall ordnance packages either in Air Force service or available. Though large numbers of earlier M-numbered bombs are still on charge, virtually all held at TAC and similar units are of the low-drag type, the most numerous being the Mk 82 of nominal 500lb but actually having a mass around 580lb (262kg). Mk 82 Mod 1 is the same bomb with the Snakeye high-drag tail retarder. The equivalent 250lb (113kg) stores are Mk 81 and Mk 81 Mod 1, while the 2,000-pounder (907kg) is the Mk 83. The commonest 3,000lb (1,361kg) bomb is the older-series M118E2. Nuclear free-fall bombs include the B28 (tactical and strategic versions); the widely used B43, with at least five different yields and carried by such differing aircraft as the B-52 (four), A-7 (four), F-16 (two) and FB-111 (six); the B57 and B61 tactical bombs, and the TX-61. In place of the ▶

▶cancelled B77 the newest nuclear bomb in advanced development is an updated B43 designated B43Y-1 which has the FuFo (full-fuzing option) and free-fall or retarded aerodynamics together with a lifting-aerofoil parachute and setting for airburst or groundburst. The first FAE (fuel/air explosive) bomb was the BLU-76, to which other types such as HSF-1 and -2 are being added. Cluster bombs are very numerous, dispensing HE, fragmentation, incendiary, gas, anti-armour and other kinds of bomblet; designators include prefixes CBU for cluster bomb unit, BLU for bomb live unit and SUU for suspended underwing unit. (Some SUU loads are gun pods, notably SUU-16A and -23A housing M61-type cannon.)

Above: Powered hoist at the 354th TFW loads a Mk 83 (bomb, low-drag, 1,000-lb) on to an A-10A, which lacks precision aiming for it.

Left: One of the most capable military aircraft ever built, the Strike Eagle (here toting cluster bombs) has been ordered as the F-15E.

Below: Hold the page diagonally to see the angle of this attack by an F-4E with free-fall Mk 83s (a Paveway nose is also visible).

Air/surface missiles

▶There is no clear distinction between an air-to-surface missile and a guided or 'smart' bomb. Oldest missile in this category, AGM-12 Bullpup, is seldom seen in front-line units. A radio-command missile, it comes in two sizes (250 and 1,000lb warhead, 113 or 454kg) with packaged liquid rocket propulsion. Another mature weapon is AGM-62A Walleye I, a free-fall bomb with wings (but no motor) with an 850lb (385kg) warhead and guidance by radio command, but having the crucial difference that, instead of the operator in the aircraft having to keep tracking flares lined up with the target, he watches a screen giving a TV picture of the target as seen by a vidicon camera in the nose of the missile. In theory this gives near-perfect guidance, the accuracy increasing as the target is approached, instead of falling off with increasing range. Walleye II is larger, with a 1,565lb (709kg) warhead but is rare in the Air Force. Numerically the top Air Force ASM, Maverick is a smaller tactical missile developed by Hughes Aircraft and initially issued in AGM-65A form with a solid motor, 130lb (59kg) warhead and self-homing TV guidance. The missile camera can be locked on the target before launch, so this missile can be launched by single-seat aircraft which can leave the scene immediately the missile has fired. The Air Force had 19,000 of these handy rounds, followed by 7,000 AGM-65B Scene-Magnification models in which the missile could be locked-on to a target scene as a clear and much-enlarged image in the cockpit, even if invisible to the pilot. AGM-65C has laser homing, with individual coding so that each missile responds to just one friendly laser designator (in the air or aimed at the target by friendly troops). AGM-65D, which entered full service in 1983, has IIR (imaging infra-red) guidance and can be slaved to a laser pod, FLIR or the APR-38 radar warning set carried in the F-4G. It is hoped the IIR Maverick will be worth its high cost because—especially in rainy and misty weather conditions prevalent in Central Europe—it can be locked-on at more than double the range of previous versions or other tactical missiles. Even AGM-65A can in theory be

Right top: Most numerous precision-guided air/surface missile is the Hughes AGM-65A Maverick, here seen on an A-7D.

Right: This A-7 (of the Navy) carries AGM-88A Harm (high-speed anti-radar missile) inboard and AGM-45 Shrike (same mission) outboard.

Below: This F-111 is one of the first to carry the Pave Tack target designator; the missile is a GBU-15 of CWW type.

Below: Dive attack with one of the Paveway series (on Mk 84
bomb) of LGB (laser-guided bomb) missiles, dropped from an F-15.

▶effective without the aircraft coming closer to its target than 14 miles (22.5km)

Dedicated anti-radar missiles include Shrike, Standard ARM and Harm Shrike was the first such missile in use, and it was derived from the AIM-Sparrow AAM. With a range of around 18 miles (29km) it could be tuned t known hostile emissions and left to home automatically on the source. Earl Shrikes in Vietnam suffered from many problems and were largel ineffective, but those still in use are vastly superior. Standard ARM (AGM-78B) is a much bigger weapon based on the ship-to-air Standar missile and having a launch weight of some 1,400lb (635kg), and range c up to 35 miles (56km) to a powerful emitter. The Mod 1 missile is compatib with the F-4G's APR-38 system; the much-delayed AGM-78C, D and D-2 (a with significant improvements) were not funded, and development has con centrated instead on the AGM-88A. The AGM-88A Harm (High-speed ant radiation missile) looks like a larger edition of Shrike, this being partly t house a motor of tremendous power which is hoped to accelerate the missil to such a speed that it will strike home before the target radar can b switched off. Launch weight is about 809lb (367kg), but Harm is no expected to be used at ranges greater than 12 miles (19km).

Smart weapons in the recent past have included a wide variety of Pavewa and Hobos (Homing Bomb System) missiles, all comprising regula conventional bombs fitted with a homing head and flight controls. In the A Force the Paveway laser-homing seeker has been adapted to steer the M 82 and 84 bombs, the M117 (750lb/340kg) and M118 (3,000lb/1,361kg and Mk 20 Mod 2 Rockeye family of cluster bombs. Hobos has been use most commonly with the Mk 84 or M118 bombs and has flown guided by E(seekers or, less often, TV or IR. This series of smart bombs led to the GBU-1! and -15(V) series with greater stand-off performance gained through the

Above: Though called a Short-Range Attack Missile the AGM-69A (here carried by FB-111A) can fly ranges up to some 100 miles (160km)

Below: This artist's impression shows an ASALM (Advanced Strategie Air-Launched Missile) fired by a B-1. This project is slipping.

Above: A Mk 84-based Hobos (homing bomb system) with electro-optical guidance. Launch weight is 2,240lb (1,016kg).

use of large wings, either of the planar (variable-sweep) type or as a cruciform of four wings. The two families were thus called PWW and CWW for planar-wing weapon and cruciform-wing weapon. PWWs have demonstrated impressive ranges from B-52 and other aircraft, but since 1980 the CWW has been seen far more often, and can be carried by most Air Force tactical bomber and attack aircraft. The usual size has a 2,000lb (907kg) payload and weighs about 2,617lb (1,187kg).

There are also two strategic missiles carried by aircraft of SAC. AGM-69A SRAM (Short-Range Attack Missile) is a neat wingless dart-like round weighing 2,230lb (1,012kg) and able to carry a W-69 (200-kT) warhead at highly supersonic speed at treetop height or over any other pre-programmed flight path, if necessary making feints and violent changes in course or height, before striking a target up to 105 miles (169km) from the point of release. It is used by the B-52G and H as a defence-suppression missile, and about 1,200 ageing SRAMs remain available. The improved AGM-69B was fully developed but cancelled in 1976. A very different and much slower weapon, ALCM (Air-Launched Cruise Missile) is fractionally larger but in the B-52G and B-1B can be carried in similar numbers (20 in the old bomber, 30 in the future one). Made by Boeing as the AGM-86B, the ALCM is dropped up to 1,550 miles (2,495km) from its target, immediately spreading its swept wings and lighting up its small turbojet engine. This missile entered production in 1981 and achieved IOC with B-52G squadrons in late 1982. The Air Force is procuring 1,739 ALCMs for air launch and production is currently scheduled to end in FY 1987.　　　　　　　　　　　▶

Below: Launch of a production AGM-86B ALCM from a B-52G of SAC.

Above: Sparrows being prepared for loading on Phantoms. First Sparrow flight was almost 35 years ago.

Air-to-air missiles

▶The Falcon and Genie missiles have been withdrawn from service and the Air Force now has only two AAMs in the inventory, both old in conception (and originally developed by the Navy) but kept up to date by a long series of improvements. AIM-9 Sidewinder is a short-range missile; AIM-7 Sparrow is classed as medium-range. All versions of Sidewinder in use have IR homing guidance effected by a small seeker head driving four control fins near the front of the 5in (127mm) diameter tubular body. Though large numbers of earlier versions remain in use, most front-line USAF aircraft today carry the greatly improved AIM-9J family, with part-solid-state electronics and detachable double-delta control fins, or the much better still AIM-9L with control fins of greater span and pointed tips, a totally new guidance system

Below: This gives a good idea of the size of a sidewinder. It is a J/N or P series, rebuild of an AIM-9B or 9E.

Above: Back in 1977 a prototype F-16 fired AIM-7F Sparrow
missiles, which are not normally carried by these aircraft.

Above: Distinguished by its blunt double-delta control surfaces,
the AIM-9J Sidewinder was replaced in production by the AIM-9L.

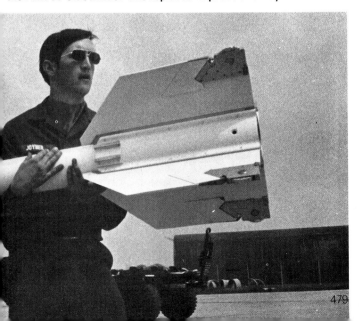

Above: Sequence showing F-16A launching an AIM-120 AMRAAM test missile. This is a launch-and-leave, all-aspect, look-down, shoot-down weapon, smaller than Sparrow but with tremendous advantages. Wingtip missile is an AIM-9J.

and an annular blast/frag warhead triggered by an annular proximity fuze with a ring of eight miniature lasers. The range of early AIM-9s was little more than 2 miles (3.2km), but AIM-9L can be used effectively over ranges up to 11 miles (18km). This approaches the range of early models of AIM-7 Sparrow, which is much larger and has semi-active radar homing guidance. Signals from the CW (continuous-wave) fighter radar illuminate the target aircraft, and the missile aerial inside its nose radome senses the reflections from the target and steers the missile towards their source by means of four large hydraulically driven delta wings at mid-length along the body. Again, though many older versions are in use, the current production model is a much-improved missile, designated AIM-7F. Solid-stage guidance is so compact in the 7F that the warhead has been moved ahead of the wings, making room for a much longer motor which increases the maximum effective range from 25/28 miles to 62 miles (100km). Not many Air Force aircraft can carry AIM-7, the main fighters being the F-15 and F-4, though Sparrow has been fired from the F-16A and it would not be a major task to make the two fully compatible. Despite the British Sky Flash, a very much improved AIM-7 serving with the RAF and Sweden and with performance of a wholly new order in severe clutter or jamming conditions, or against low-level targets, this missile has not been adopted by the Air Force which instead has ordered the Hughes AIM-120A AMRAAM (Advanced Medium-Range AAM) to be deployed later in the decade. Planned procurement (for both the Air Force and the US Navy) is expected to be 24,474 missiles.